Faithful Ministry

Faithful Ministry

*An Ecclesial Festschrift in Honor of
the Rev. Dr. Robert S. Rayburn*

EDITED BY
Max Rogland

FOREWORD BY
Eric Irwin

WIPF & STOCK · Eugene, Oregon

FAITHFUL MINISTRY
An Ecclesial Festschrift in Honor of the Rev. Dr. Robert S. Rayburn

Copyright © 2019 Wipf and Stock Publishers. All rights reserved. Except for brief quotations in critical publications or reviews, no part of this book may be reproduced in any manner without prior written permission from the publisher. Write: Permissions, Wipf and Stock Publishers, 199 W. 8th Ave., Suite 3, Eugene, OR 97401.

Wipf & Stock
An Imprint of Wipf and Stock Publishers
199 W. 8th Ave., Suite 3
Eugene, OR 97401

www.wipfandstock.com

PAPERBACK ISBN: 978-1-5326-5805-1
HARDCOVER ISBN: 978-1-5326-5806-8
EBOOK ISBN: 978-1-5326-5807-5

Excerpt from "Sunday Morning with the Sensational Nightingales" from *The Art of Drowning*, by Billy Collins, © 1995. Reprinted by permission of the University of Pittsburgh Press.

Scripture quotations are from the ESV® Bible (The Holy Bible, English Standard Version®), copyright © 2001 by Crossway, a publishing ministry of Good News Publishers. Used by permission. All rights reserved.

Manufactured in the U.S.A.

Contents

List of Illustrations | vii

List of Contributors | ix

Foreword: Faith Presbyterian Church in the Late 1980s | xi
   —Eric Irwin

Preface: An "Ecclesial Festschrift" | xix
   —Max Rogland

Acknowledgements | xxiii

List of Abbreviations | xxiv

Introduction: A Survey of the Theological Contribution of the Rev. Dr. Robert S. Rayburn | 1
   —C. John Collins and Robert G. Rayburn II

Publication List for the Rev. Dr. Robert S. Rayburn | 7

Chapter 1: Reflections on Church History from a Recent Reading of Jonathan Edwards's *A History of the Work of Redemption* | 9
   —William Barker

Chapter 2: A Tension-Filled Assignment: Reflections on the "Poles" of the Christian Worldview | 23
   —Joel Belz

Chapter 3: Parents as Covenant Mediators in Deuteronomy | 31
   —Ron Bergey

Chapter 4: Ministry After Christ: The Long-Term Pastorate | 38
—John Birkett

Chapter 5: Insights from the Westminster Standards for Today's Preaching and Preachers | 51
—Bryan Chapell

Chapter 6: The New Covenant and Redemptive History | 67
—Jack Collins

Chapter 7: The Catholicity of John Calvin | 92
—Ian Hamilton

Chapter 8: Gospel Harmony: American Popular Sacred Music, 1871–1969 | 101
—David Jones

Chapter 9: A New Participation in an Old Identity: 1 Peter and the Church's Inclusion into Israel | 117
—Joshua Moon

Chapter 10: The Body is for the Lord: Physicality in Worship | 134
—George Robertson

Chapter 11: "And So I Will Go Unto the King": Prayer and the Book of Esther | 153
—Max Rogland

Chapter 12: That Your Generations May Know: Epistemology and Covenant Succession | 168
—Kevin Skogen and Jacob Skogen

Chapter 13: Goudimel's Simple Setting of the Genevan Psalter | 180
—John Wykoff

Bibliography | 193

Illustrations

Figure 1: Psalm 68 "God Shall Arise"—Goudimel's Harmony with the Tune in the Tenor | 182

Figure 2: Goudimel, *Rendez à Dieu* | 183

Figure 3: Two Settings of Psalm 1 | 187

Figure 4: Beginning of Psalm 42 Reconstructed | 190

Figure 5: Claudin de Sermisy, *Tant que vivray* | 191

Contributors

Eric Irwin (MDiv, Covenant Theological Seminary), Senior Minister, Covenant Presbyterian Church, Issaquah, WA

Max Rogland (PhD, Leiden), Associate Professor of Old Testament, Erskine Theological Seminary, and Senior Minister, Rose Hill Presbyterian Church, Columbia, SC

Robert G. Rayburn II (ThD, Ludwig-Maximilians University, Munich)

William Barker (PhD, Vanderbilt), President and Professor Emeritus of Church History, Covenant Theological Seminary, Saint Louis, MO, and Professor Emeritus of Church History, Westminster Theological Seminary, Glenside, PA

Joel Belz (MA, University of Iowa), founder of *World* magazine and God's World Publications, Inc.

Ron Bergey (PhD, Dropsie), Professor Emeritus of Hebrew and Old Testament, Faculté Jean Calvin, Aix-en-Provence

John Birkett (MDiv, Covenant Theological Seminary), Minister, Christ Presbyterian Church, Owensboro, KY

Bryan Chapell (PhD, Southern Illinois University), Senior Minister, Grace Presbyterian Church, Peoria, IL; former President, Chancellor, and Professor of Homiletics at Covenant Theological Seminary, Saint Louis, MO

Jack Collins (PhD, Liverpool), Professor of Old Testament, Covenant Theological Seminary, Saint Louis, MO

Ian Hamilton (MA, Edinburgh), Pastor Emeritus of Cambridge Presbyterian Church; Instructor at Edinburgh Theological Seminary and Greenville Presbyterian Theological Seminary, Greenville, SC

David Jones (ThD, Concordia), late Professor of Systematic Theology and Ethics, Covenant Theological Seminary, Saint Louis, MO

Joshua Moon (PhD, Saint Andrews)

George Robertson (PhD, Westminster Theological Seminary), Senior Minister, Second Presbyterian Church, Memphis, TN

Max Rogland (PhD, Leiden), Associate Professor of Old Testament, Erskine Theological Seminary, and Senior Minister, Rose Hill Presbyterian Church, Columbia, SC

Kevin Skogen (MDiv, Covenant Theological Seminary), Senior Minister, Sandhills Presbyterian Church, Southern Pines, NC

Jacob Skogen (ThM, Duke), Associate Minister, Sandhills Presbyterian Church, Southern Pines, NC

John Wykoff (PhD, City University of New York), Associate Professor of Theory and Composition, Lee University, Cleveland, TN

Foreword

Faith Presbyterian Church in the Late 1980s

WE ARRIVED AT FPC in the fall of 1985, having never attended a liturgical reformed church. To listen to Rob in those years, on the heels of the west coast evangelical revivals of the 1970s, was an awakening of its own. Often his sermons evoked a particular Anglo, old-world godliness that was unfamiliar to most of us, as were the Scottish churchmen and dissenting Englishmen whose lives he used as illustrations. His best sermons, which were many, created a deep longing for a lost reverence and piety. I remember a particularly powerful Sunday worship service and sermon in the late 1980s. This was a Communion Sunday before the switch to weekly observance. I had become a deacon after a handful of years at FPC and, along with other officers, had helped distribute the elements. At the close of the service, we were standing together at the front of the room, each of us alone in his thoughts, when the elder next to me turned and said, "Sometimes God opens the curtain and lets us see inside." That was one of the many gifts Rob gave to us: he let us see inside.

It's difficult to say what qualities of personality and preaching make moments like that possible. The Spirit does as he chooses. Yet it has always seemed to me the Spirit powerfully used two aspects of Rob's ministry.

The first of these was the people he chose to set before us as examples of reformed piety. Whether it was Rutherford or Whyte or Boston or Owen, they were invariably, in J. I. Packer's words, people whose knowledge *of* God surpassed their knowledge *about* God; people concerned with "how they pray and what goes on in their hearts." As Packer writes,

> I am sure that many of us have never really grasped this. We find in ourselves a deep interest in theology (which is, of course, a most fascinating and intriguing subject—in the seventeenth century it was every gentleman's hobby). We read books of

theological exposition and apologetics. We dip into Christian history, and study the Christian creed.... Others appreciate our interest in these things, and we find ourselves asked to give our opinion in public on this or that Christian question.... Our friends tell us how much they value our contribution, and this spurs us to further explorations of God's truth, so that we may be equal to the demands made upon us.... [Y]et interest in theology, and knowledge *about* God, and the capacity to think clearly and talk well on Christian themes, is not at all the same thing as knowing him. We may know as much about God as Calvin knew—indeed, if we study his works diligently, sooner or later we shall—and yet all the time (unlike Calvin I may say) we hardly know God at all.[1]

Rob not only understood Packer's distinction, but he had a habit, a gift almost, of setting before us in sermons and conversations people whose intellectual lives were remarkable, yet not as remarkable as the beauty and vitality of their lives hidden in Christ.

We all knew where Rob got his material. He read relentlessly and was the embodiment of Samuel Davies's cutting truth: "the venerable dead are waiting in my library to relieve me from the nonsense of surviving mortals." For our part, it was almost impossible to listen to him and not become readers ourselves. Somewhere in our early years at FPC, inspired by quotes in sermons, I bought a copy of William Law's *A Serious Call to a Devout and Holy Life*. Law was Church of England in the day of John Bunyan, but *Serious Call* was a stake through the heart of formal religion and a self-congratulatory orthodoxy. While I was reading Law, I'm sure I still had a vinyl copy of *No Compromise* by Keith Greene, the pop-rock prophetic voice of under-thirty California evangelicals. Yet here was Law in a higher orbit entirely, radiating an intellectually rigorous, uncompromising pursuit of Christ:

> Do not therefore please yourself with thinking, how piously you would act and submit to God in a *plague*, a *famine*, or a *persecution*, but be intent upon the perfection of the present day; and be assur'd that the best way of shewing a *true zeal*, is to make *little things* the occasions of *great piety*. Begin therefore in the smallest matters, and most ordinary occasions, and accustom your mind to the daily exercise of this pious temper, in the lowest occurrences of life. And when a *contempt*, an *affront*, a little *injury*, *loss*, or *disappointment*, or the smallest event of every day raises your mind to God proper resignation, then you may justly

---

1. Packer, *Knowing God*, 26.

hope that you shall be numbered amongst those that are resign'd and thankful to God in the greatest trials and afflictions.[2]

I did not know at the time that Rob had (presumably) come to Law through his hero, nineteenth-century Scottish Free Church minister Alexander Whyte, who often quoted Law and had edited a volume devoted to his life and writings. Law was "chief of the English mystics," as Whyte called him, a title that would have kept most people in the reformed world at a safe distance.[3] The usual problem with mystics is they blur the line between the divine and the human. Law certainly presented problems to reformed orthodoxy, chief among them his insistence on God's unmediated communication with his children through his Spirit. But unlike other mystics, he was far less taken by his own experience of God than by the majesty and glory of God himself. This characteristic—the intimacy of being on one's face before God—gave his writing what Boston would have called "tincture" and we would call ethos or tone. As Owen wrote, "The difference between believers and unbelievers as to knowledge is not so much in the *matter of their knowledge* as in the *manner* . . . [T]hat what he doth apprehend, which perhaps may be very little, he sees it in the light of the Spirit of God."[4] Law's manner of knowing was informed by and filled with the Holy Spirit. He wrote with a kind of violence, a passion for God in his essence and majesty resonant of Calvin in the early chapters of the *Institutes*. And while Rob never quoted people like Law in anything like the measure with which he quoted Rutherford or Whyte, he nevertheless illustrates something important in Rob's ministry. To show us what it meant to love God himself, with all that that entailed, he was willing to risk exposing us to thinkers and followers of Christ who were not on the reformed reading list. So we found ourselves exposed not only to Law, but to John of the Cross, Bernard of Clairvaux, Jerome, Origen and so on. He assumed a certain maturity on our part, and it worked in us a desire to educate ourselves and rise to the occasion. I suspect the influence of Whyte played a large part in this, but that doesn't account for the courage it took to stand firmly in the reformed tradition while simultaneously challenging its narrowness. In this and so many other things, Rob chose for us the better portion of the reformed tradition or, rather, was teaching us from a deeper, richer vein of that tradition.

It's important to say that things might have been otherwise. What exactly it means to be reformed has always been open to interpretation, often bad interpretation. Another minister with Rob's doctrinal commitments

---

2. Law, *Serious Call*, 458 (emphasis original).
3. Whyte, *Characters and Characteristics*, xxxvii.
4. Owen, *Works*, 6.69.

and discernment might have gone down that other road with roots in Scotch Presbyterianism. That other road is touched on, vaguely but tellingly, in C. S. Lewis's anthology of George Macdonald's writings.

> George MacDonald's family . . . were of course Calvinists. On the intellectual side his history is largely a history of escape from the theology in which he had been brought up. Stories of such emancipation are common in the nineteenth century; but George MacDonald's story belongs to this familiar pattern only with a difference. In most such stories the emancipated person, not content with repudiating the doctrines, comes also to hate the persons, of his forebears, and even the whole culture and way of life with which they are associated.[5]

The Calvinistic reformed tradition is certainly capable of producing the sort of theology and churches from which people seek emancipation. Wherein exactly the poison lies is difficult to say—one man's defense of "the faith once delivered to the saints" is another man's reincarnation of the circumcision party. The gravitas, rational coherence, and defensibility of the Calvinist system can attract a certain type of person who identifies more strongly with ideas than with other persons, including the person of Christ. For this type, there is an inability to embrace, in Owen's words, the *matter* of doctrine in a *manner* characterized by the fruit of the Spirit. Without that spiritual sense, which is akin to emotional intelligence, all words become fighting words, all hills become hills to die on. This is the notorious side of the reformed world.

How Rob managed to lead us with intellectual rigor and doctrinal integrity, without turning us into people given to "quarreling about words," is not entirely clear to me. It certainly helped that, through his father, he had watched as reformed thought grew in influence in the middle and latter-half of the twentieth century. He was an old soul from the beginning and would have understood the consequences of personalities and ideas in the formation of institutions and traditions. Along with this, or perhaps because of it, he chose his mentors well, most of them English, Scottish, and long dead. Whatever the character trait exactly, his unfailing ability to combine it with guiding us time and again to the most winsome personalities in Christian history was more than powerful. It changed our lives.

The second influential aspect of Rob's ministry is a much harder sell. I would imagine I'm the only person to ever say this in public, but it's a statement I can defend: Rob is a romantic.

---

5. Lewis, "Preface," xxiv–xxv.

"Romance" is itself a word open to broad interpretation, so let me give shape to it by borrowing from Robert Louis Stevenson. Although Stevenson came into public consciousness with the publication of *Dr. Jekyll and Mr. Hyde*, he was also an essayist, poet, playwright, and correspondent. Most of his essays were written when he was obscure, but the quality of thought and expression is consistently high. In *A Gossip on Romance*, he writes,

> In anything fit to be called by the name of reading, the process itself should be absorbing and voluptuous; we should gloat over a book, be rapt clean out of ourselves, and rise from the perusal, our mind filled with the busiest, kaleidoscopic dance of images, incapable of sleep or of continuous thought. The words, if the book be eloquent, should run thenceforward in our ears like the noise of breakers, and the story, if it be a story, repeat itself in a thousand colored pictures to the eye.[6]

Replace "reading" with "listening" and "book" with "sermon" and you get the idea. We live in a day in which so much of biblical preaching is artless. Our day fits T. S. Eliot's lament that wisdom has been lost in knowledge, and knowledge lost in information. Rob's sermons left us gloriously ill-at-ease and, once every few months, "incapable of sleep or continuous thought." He preached sermons that opened the soul and filled it with a yearning that troubled the sleeping or self-satisfied conscience. Certainly he believed in the power of eloquence and frequently made the case for it. He also explained his own preaching, or his intention in preaching, as putting "mind" back in the command to love God with "heart, soul, mind, and strength." He agreed with Mark Noll's assessment that the scandal of evangelicalism, at least in the latter twentieth century, was its intellectual anemia. So, these two things—a commitment to eloquence and the full force of the greatest commandment—may account for some of the force of Rob's preaching. But not all of it. There was something else. And without at all dismissing the working of the Holy Spirit, the name I would give to that something else is "romance." Alongside his care with the text and depth of theology, Rob's illustrations were filled with romance.

Stevenson may be following Wordsworth's notion of the child being father to the man when he writes that the romance of reading is rightly formed in us when we are young and unaware that we are in pursuit of certain moments, incidents, and settings that place us under a spell.

> It was for this last pleasure that we... loved our books so dearly, in the bright, troubled period of boyhood. Eloquence and thought,

---

6. Stevenson, *Essays*, 224.

> character and conversation, were but obstacles to brush aside as we dug blithely after a certain sort of incident. . . . For my part, I liked a story to begin with an old wayside inn where, "toward the close of the year 17—," several gentlemen in three-cocked hats were playing bowls. . . . Give me a highwayman and I was full to the brim; a Jacobite would do, but the highwayman was my favorite dish. . . . [E]ach with his particular fancy, we read story-books in childhood, not for eloquence or character or thought, but for some quality of the brute incident. . . . [for] drama is the poetry of conduct, romance the poetry of circumstance.[7]

What Rob knew from the beginning is that the history of the church is filled to overflowing with the poetry of conduct and circumstance. In his own reading, which, again, was relentless and usually done (at least when he was younger) at night when everyone else in the house had gone to bed, he made notes on index cards, filing them by topic. It was a practice grounded in a comment made by Whyte, who himself had taken to heart the admonition of Proverbs 12:27: "whoever is slothful will not roast his game." His notecards were, as he used to say, "roasting what he hunted." But there was far more to his anecdotes, vignettes, and stories than hunting and roasting. There was art. As Stevenson says, "His stories may be nourished with the realities of life, but their true mark is to satisfy the nameless longings of the reader."[8] All stories tell, but not all evoke and awaken.

> The right kind of thing should fall out in the right kind of place . . . [so that] all the circumstances in the tale answer one to another like notes in music. The threads of a story come from time to time together and make a picture in the web . . . which stamps the story home like an illustration. Crusoe recoiling from the footprint, Achilles shouting over against the Trojans, Ulysses bending the great bow, Christian running with his fingers in his ears, these are each culminating moments in the legend, and each has been printed on the mind's eye forever.[9]

So, yes, Rob did a great deal of reading, but his gift was the artful distillation of all that labor. I remember his retelling of the execution of the two Margarets, both Scottish Covenanters, in the rising tide of Solway Firth. I had read the account in Jock Purves's *Fair Sunshine*, but it was Rob's retelling, fitted to the moment and ideas of the sermon, that gave it legs and a beating heart. I was similarly moved by his usage of John Paton's account of

---

7. Stevenson, *Essays*, 220–21.
8. Stevenson, *Essays*, 224.
9. Stevenson, *Essays*, 224–25.

parting with his father. That account is powerful and stands on its own, but accounts of such force must be carefully matched to the subject matter or the effect is nothing more than emotional manipulation.

In honesty, though, I remember fewer moments than I thought I would when I began writing this essay. What's more, I asked my wife about her own memories, and hers were few as well. I was troubled by this until I happened to re-read a passage in Stevenson's essay.

> We may forget the words, although they are beautiful; we may forget the author's comment, although perhaps it was ingenious and true; but these epoch-making scenes, which put the last mark of truth upon a story and fill up, at one blow, our capacity for sympathetic pleasure, we so adopt into the very bosom of our mind that neither time nor tide can efface or weaken the impression.[10]

Then, some time later, I was listening to an address to preachers at one of those huge conferences so common to North American evangelicalism. Tim Keller, a far wider and deeper reader than most of his admirers (and none of his detractors) appreciate, was commenting on a thought he had come across in reading Jonathan Edwards: "preaching does not change you through supplying information, but by an impression made on the listener during the sermon. Christ becoming vividly real, touching the affections."[11] There is no denial of the importance of truth in this. Rather, in addition to the plain Scriptural truthfulness of it, a good sermon shapes us in the manner Paul suggests in his prayer for the Ephesians regarding the love of Christ: it must ultimately be a kind of knowing that surpasses knowledge. It is the place where diligence with the text, doctrinal clarity, and the Holy Spirit come together and "fill up, at one blow, our capacity for sympathetic pleasure." In such moments, with such sermons, we are forced to think, but the manner of our thinking is changed; we are compelled to act, but our manner of acting is changed. In the end, it is our being that is changed as we are "conformed to the image of his son."

Granting all these things—winsome saints, the romance of preaching, and the art of answering human longing—what exactly was the catalyst in all that? If there was an "impression . . . touching the affections" that changed us, what was that? And what does that even mean? Was it just a desire to imitate good examples and to be moved by good stories? I suspect the majority of those who sat under the teaching of the Rev. Dr. Robert S. Rayburn will remember him as someone who rearranged the architecture

---

10. Stevenson, *Essays*, 225.
11. Keller, "Preaching to the Heart," 16:38.

of their minds. Most people will praise him on the grounds of his intellectual gifts, so well developed through discipline and industry. While this is certainly true, for my part, what I saw at work in the early years of Rob's ministry was the anointing of the Holy Spirit, "that gracious work of his in the spiritual, saving illumination of our minds, teaching us to know the truth, and to adhere firmly unto it in love and obedience." Though powerful, the working of the Spirit is often elusive because "we have no way to know the nature of it except by its effects,"[12] and those reveal themselves only with time. I join with others in praying that the effect of the work of the Spirit in our lives, through Rob's diligence as a secondary cause, would redound to the praise of the glorious grace of God.

---

12. Owen, *Works*, 4.394.

Preface

An "Ecclesial *Festschrift*"

IN ACADEMIA, THE SCHOLARLY *Festschrift* or "celebratory writing" represents an honored tradition: upon a major occasion in the life of a distinguished senior scholar—most often a retirement or a significant birthday—a collection of learned essays is produced by other eminent scholars, colleagues, former students, and the like. Such collections celebrate the achievements and distinctive contributions of their dedicatees, typically demonstrating the influence of their work on their particular fields of academic specialization. As such, the *Festschrift* is a fitting vehicle for expressing the esteem in which a scholar is held.

The general lack of *Festschriften* produced for notable senior clergy stands in marked contrast. Some such volumes exist,[1] but they are few and far between, and given the current relationship between the church and the academy this is not terribly surprising. To be sure, there have been devoted churchmen who have also earned reputations as productive and influential scholars; in recent times one thinks of the distinguished New Testament specialist N. T. Wright, who also served the Church of England as the Bishop of Durham. Most clergy, however, have neither the prominence of a bishopric nor the publication record of a Bishop Wright (very few New Testament academicians have the latter, for that matter). Moreover, few pastors can claim to have "made a contribution to their field" in the way that a specialist in a scholarly discipline can. Even to speak in such terms of a particular pastor sounds almost nonsensical, for the ministry is not a field in which advances in knowledge are continually being made. Progress in ministry is notoriously difficult to define, let alone to measure in any objectively meaningful way. The diligent scholar can point to a corpus of monographs and journal articles, and the number of times these are cited by other scholars, as evidence of influence on his or her chosen field of specialization,

---

1. E.g., Storms and Taylor, *For the Fame of God's Name* (for John Piper), and Ryken et al., *Give Praise to God* (for James Montgomery Boice).

but a minister's "publication record" consists chiefly of people's lives, which obviously defies measurement.

Nevertheless, compared to academicians, clergy arguably exert a much more profound and lasting influence on a wider range of people, as they shepherd their parishioners through a broader scope of life situations. True, doctoral advisors guide and support their students through the grueling experience of earning a PhD. At the same time, it surprises no one that, in moments of crisis, most people turn to their pastors, not to their thesis supervisors. While it may be objectively harder to measure the impact of someone's ministry than to determine the number of times a book is cited in academic journals, experience testifies that the effects of faithful pastoral service are profound indeed.

What is more, the contributions of parish ministers to "academic" theological conversations should not be overlooked. It must be borne in mind that the current divide between the church and the academy with respect to biblical and theological scholarship is a relatively recent development when considered against the entire history of the church. Jaroslav Pelikan observes that the church's theologians have been university professors roughly since 1500, but for the first five to six centuries of her history most of them were bishops or, in the medieval era, monks.[2] The assumption that a theologian of significance would hold an academic post appears to have gained ascendency starting around the time of the Reformation, and one is not surprised therefore to see significant discussion in Calvin and other Reformed writers of the "doctor" as a distinct ecclesiastical office, though the line between it and the pastoral office was often an ambiguous and fluid one.[3] Such debates notwithstanding, one can find references to *doctores presbyteri* or *doctores ecclesiae* in early Christian sources.[4] While the latter term was eventually adopted into a more formal declarative act of the church,[5] clearly, many clergy have been recognized as such without the need for an academic appointment.

This serves as a helpful reminder that, for much of the church's history, most of the church's "doctors" fulfilled their callings not as university or seminary professors but chiefly as ministers. This is obvious with regard to pre-eminent doctors recognized by the church in the West (Ambrose, Augustine, Jerome, Gregory the Great) and in the East (Chrysostom, Basil,

---

2. Pelikan, *Christian Tradition*, 5.
3. Henderson, *Teaching Office*.
4. E.g., Cyprian uses the former phrase; see also Bavinck, *Het Doctorenambt*, 19n.
5. The first of such appears to have been by Pope Boniface VIII in 1298; see Henderson, *Teaching Office*, 20.

Gregory Nazianzus). Yet even considering such influential Protestant theologians as Luther and Calvin, both of whom lectured in academic settings, one must be impressed by the fact that they were pastors first and foremost, and many of their doctrinal writings were produced out of the varied ecclesiastical contexts of pastoral ministry.[6] The same could also be said of what many would nowadays consider more narrowly technical aspects of biblical study. For example, it is remarkable to learn that Thomas Boston—best known as one of the "Marrow Men" who sought to preserve the preaching of the free offer of the gospel in eighteenth-century Scotland—also produced a detailed study of the accents of biblical Hebrew while dutifully serving as a parish pastor.[7]

But should an achievement such as Boston's really seem as unusual as it undoubtedly does nowadays? Should it really surprise us that parish clergy, who study the Scriptures and who seek to communicate and apply those Scriptures weekly to the lives of actual people in their congregations, might have important contributions to make to the conversations of the contemporary theological guild? Shouldn't the Christian church want her exegesis and theology to be "road tested" in the parish as it is formulated, refined, and passed down from generation to generation? A doctrine or a biblical interpretation that cannot stand up under the real-life trials of pastoral ministry at best needs further refinement or at worst is simply not worth maintaining at all.

In recent years, the ecclesiastical and ministerial context of Christian dogmatic reflection has begun to be more openly acknowledged,[8] and we seem to be witnessing a welcome return to earlier, more holistic understandings of the theological enterprise. The church will continue to need the labors of academic specialists, certainly. It may even be in the best interests of the Protestant church to renew her unfinished discussions of the doctoral ministry as a distinct ecclesiastical office. Nevertheless, perhaps we are at a point where we can begin to appreciate once again that some *doctores ecclesiae* are to be found behind pulpits rather than lecterns.

This brings us to the reason for the current volume: a celebration of the forty-year ministry of the Rev. Dr. Robert S. Rayburn at Faith Presbyterian Church in Tacoma, Washington. The rarity of such a long-term pastorate nowadays in itself deserves special notice, and it seems fitting to celebrate this important milestone with what we might call an "ecclesial *Festschrift*"—a

---

6. On Calvin, see McNeil, "John Calvin," 10.

7. Boston, *Tractatus Stigmologicus*.

8. See, for example, the work of the Center for Pastor-Theologians: https://www.pastortheologians.com/.

celebratory collection of biblical, historical, and theological essays with a churchly and pastoral bent. The significance of Dr. Rayburn's forty-year ministry lies in more than its longevity, however. It seems unlikely that he will ever receive an *expressa ecclesiae declaratio* naming him officially a "doctor of the church," but we would suggest that Rob (as we must call him) has truly embodied their spirit by being a dedicated student of the Scriptures, a deeply reflective thinker with an appreciation for the catholicity of the Christian theological tradition, and a devoted churchman. Although he was well qualified for an academic post and produced some significant works of theological scholarship, Rob's conviction was to remain "faithful"—pun obviously intended—to his call to pastoral ministry. Indeed, it was precisely his pastoral work that provided the context for his distinctive contributions to "the Great Conversation" of the Christian theological tradition.

A brief sketch of these contributions is provided by Jack Collins and Robert G. Rayburn II, which will serve to introduce the essays in this *Festschrift*. Written by friends, colleagues, "disciples," and even a couple of his former teachers, this book was produced because we "esteem him very highly in love because of his work" (see 1 Thess 5:13), and it is affectionately dedicated to him with gratitude to God. Forty years of faithful ministry—a biblical "generation"—is a testimony above all to the faithfulness of God, and it is something worth celebrating.

Max Rogland
May 2018

Acknowledgements

SEVERAL PEOPLE DESERVE SPECIAL mention for the important role they played in helping to bring this volume to light. Dr. Andrew Milton, Mike Pfefferle, and the Session of Faith Presbyterian Church of Tacoma, Washington, were the driving force in getting this project off the ground. Dr. C. John ("Jack") Collins was a helpful sounding board for me at key moments as it developed. Lionel Jauvert deserves many thanks for making an English translation of Ron Bergey's essay, which originally appeared in French. I am grateful to Erskine Seminary's librarians Fred Guyette and Heath Milford for their valuable assistance in innumerable ways.

Dr. David Jones passed away before this volume was completed—may his memory be for a blessing! I am grateful to his widow, Sue Jones, and to Will Barker and Brady Shuman, for their editorial help in preparing his essay for publication.

Above all, I wish to thank my father, Dr. Robert Rogland (an emeritus elder at Faith Presbyterian Church), for devoting much time and effort to the present volume in matters of both substance and style. Many aspects of this book have been greatly improved by his diligent labors.

Abbreviations

BDB	Brown, Francis, et al. *A Hebrew and English Lexicon of the Old Testament*. Oxford: Clarendon, 1907.
Directory	*Westminster Directory for the Publick Worship of God*
ESV	*English Standard Version*
HB	Hebrew Bible
Institutes	Calvin, John. *Institutes of the Christian Religion*. Translated by Ford Lewis Battles and edited by John T. McNeil. Library of Christian Classics 21. Philadelphia: Westminster, 1960.
LXX	Septuagint
NA[27]	Aland, Kurt, et al. *Novum Testamentum Graece*. 27th ed. Stuttgart: German Bible Society, 1993.
NPNF[1]	Schaff, Philip, ed. *The Nicene and Post-Nicene Fathers, Series 1*. 14 vols. Reprint, Peabody: Hendrickson, 1994.
NPNF[2]	Schaff, Philip, ed. *The Nicene and Post-Nicene Fathers, Series 2*. 14 vols. Reprint, Peabody: Hendrickson, 1994.
NT	New Testament
OT	Old Testament
WCF	*Westminster Confession of Faith*
WLC	*Westminster Larger Catechism*
WSC	*Westminster Shorter Catechism*

Introduction

A Survey of the Theological Contribution of the Rev. Dr. Robert S. Rayburn

Robert S. Rayburn's intellectual journey embodies this maxim: *reformata, semper reformanda* ("reformed, always to be reformed"). His commitment to the Reformed tradition is clear and unequivocal; and, as an expression of that commitment, he has shown time after time his willingness to rethink aspects of his own beliefs, with a view of making the Reformed tradition even more biblical.

Many people serve in Reformed and Presbyterian churches and schools, and legitimately call themselves loyal to the Reformed heritage. We know of no one else who, in the introduction to a PhD thesis in New Testament studies at a British university, would begin the discussion by declaring, "The stimulus for this study is a personal interest in reformed theology's historic difficulty in—" and then go on to cite such figures as Heinrich Heppe, early federal theologians, Ernest Kevan, Robert Dabney, and J. Oliver Buswell. These figures are all *theologians*, not exegetical scholars, and (to someone unfamiliar with the landscape) might seem parochial in the extreme.[1]

The Reformed commitment is readily visible in other ways as well: he took his family to Amsterdam in 1984 to read Reformed scholastic theologians (in Latin and Dutch). His writings and sermons are full of references to exemplars of Reformed learning and piety; "the authorities of Reformed theology" is a representative phrase in both.[2]

---

1. See his 1978 PhD thesis, "Contrast Between the Old and New," vii–xiv.

2. We have included a list of Rayburn's writings at the end of this essay. Further, anyone can visit the webpage of Faith Presbyterian Church in Tacoma (www.faithtacoma.org) to see sermon manuscripts and various other essays.

But this loyalty to the Reformed tradition shows itself in a hearty embrace of the primacy of scripture, which has the right to call into question even cherished positions of the "Reformed authorities"; the goal is to attain greater consistency in theology and practice. This loyalty to scripture comes out, for example, at the very beginning, in his PhD thesis, "The Contrast between the Old and New Covenants in the New Testament" (University of Aberdeen, 1978). His advisor was I. Howard Marshall, a highly-regarded scholar of the New Testament, and an evangelical Methodist, and his outside reader was another prominent New Testament scholar, F. F. Bruce (also evangelical). Some thoughts from one of his seminary professors, Wilber Wallis, provided the impetus for this work. It began with a simple question: If the "old covenant" refers to the first thirty-seven books of the Bible, the Old Testament, or the system of religion found there, then how are we to reconcile the harsh words spoken about the old covenant in the New Testament (in Galatians, 2 Corinthians, and Hebrews)? If the old covenant was God's work and expressed God's will and plan of salvation, how is its passing away to be considered a ministry of judgment or condemnation, as the book of Hebrews asserts (Heb 8:13)? These questions and many others led Rayburn to a reconsideration of the biblical understanding of the old and new covenants, ultimately concluding that the distinction refers not to redemptive-historical epochs, but rather to a subjective condition of unbelief vs. faith.[3] While his thesis remained unpublished, it has been picked up and expanded upon by others who have found its argument compelling (see footnote 4). Rayburn himself would later explore the implications of his research for the ministry, worship, sacraments, ethics, and communal life of God's people.[4]

For example, Rayburn contributed to a debate within Presbyterianism on the number and natures of the offices in the Christian church. In contending for a difference between the pastoral office and the lay elder (called "teaching elder" and "ruling elder" in Rayburn's Presbyterian Church in America), he opened the door to seeing a greater continuity between the Levitical priesthood and the Christian ministry, and a correspondingly higher

---

3. For further discussion, see Jack Collins's essay, "The New Covenant and Redemptive History," in this volume.

4. For reflections on this point, see Joshua Moon, "A New Participation in an Old Identity: 1 Peter and the Church's Inclusion into Israel," included in this volume. Also included here are fitting tributes to his interest in music as an important element of Christian worship; see David C. Jones, "Gospel Harmony: American Popular Sacred Music, 1871–1969," and John Wykoff, "Goudimel's Simple Setting of the Genevan Psalter."

regard for leadership in liturgy and sacraments.[5] Rayburn's own developments in worship leadership and practices reflect this perspective—things such as weekly communion, raising of hands, provision for kneeling, and the congregation moving forward to participate instead of sitting passively in the pews. (This last change came together in his mind, after much study, when he saw marathon runners stopping at a table, running in place, to take a drink and continue their race. "That is what the Supper is for a Christian," he said—a moment to be refreshed for the continuing race.[6])

This spiritual continuity within the epochs of God's plan of salvation led Rayburn to perceive a further liturgical continuity, and he became an advocate for "paedocommunion" (the including of very young baptized children at the Lord's Table). The inclusion of all family members in the Passover meals provided a strong argument. He was made a member of the denominational study committee on the subject, for which he provided the minority report favoring the practice. There is no reason to doubt that the view of paedocommunion is so markedly a minority position in evangelicalism, and that therefore the majority did not feel much of a burden of proof; and still, Rayburn's careful research and argumentation over twelve pages contrasts strikingly with the brief six-page majority report. Though his minority report was not adopted, its influence continues, as evidenced by the increasing openness to the subject in Reformed circles. Rayburn himself contributed to an academic forum on the subject, as well as to a more popular one.[7]

The question of paedocommunion ties in to the larger issue of how Christian parents, and their churches, are to view their children, which has a corresponding impact on how parenting is to be carried out. In a nutshell, is Christian parenting to be seen under the rubric of *evangelism* (assuming the children are not yet believers) or of *discipling* (seeing them as believers who must be taught the way of following Jesus)? Rayburn has become noteworthy for his advocacy of what is called "covenant succession," a vigorous form of the latter perspective.[8] He published an article

---

5. Rayburn's essay entitled "Three Offices: Minister, Elder, Deacon," was a response to George W. Knight III's article, "Two Offices (Elders/Bishops and Deacons) and Two Orders of Elders (Preaching/Teaching Elders and Ruling Elders): A New Testament Study"; Rayburn took special notice of Knight's subtitle ("A *New Testament* Study").

6. As a testimony to Rayburn's influence in such matters, see the essay in this volume by George Robertson, "The Body is for the Lord: Physicality in Worship." See also Rayburn's address, "The Liturgical Authority of the Old Testament," delivered to the symposium, "Church Music at a Crossroads" (July 20, 1999).

7. "A Defense of Paedocommunion" (2005) and "Historic Practice is Invisible in the Bible: the Paedocommunion Debate" (2013).

8. This perspective is logically at home with paedocommunion views, though

on the subject, in the Covenant Seminary journal, which produced quite a stir. The editor of the journal took the unusual step of adding a series of questions as an appendix to the essay. Some may count this as undercutting Rayburn's strong argument in his paper; but the editor, with Rayburn's agreement, offered these questions in order to advance the conversation. Some of the concerns expressed involved issues of contingency and covenant conditions, many of which were later addressed explicitly in his 2005 essay, "Parental Conditions and the Promise of Grace to the Children of Believers."[9] Rayburn has continued his reflections on the subject, and a more recent article, jointly written with his assistant Steven Nicoletti, addresses carefully, as it must, a matter that this doctrinal position raises: "An Elder Must Have Believing Children: Titus 1:6 and a Neglected Case of Conscience." The conclusion of this article, in which they call for the exercise of judgment calls, should not be seen as backing away from the earlier one; it is rather adding some helpful nuance.

In keeping with his convictions, Rayburn, who loves to describe Christian preaching as "the gospel of Christ mediated through personality," has developed a style of preaching that is a unique blend of elements ancient and modern. He counted it a momentous discovery to realize that scripture often speaks to dozens of important topics, both theological and practical, from two opposite and seemingly opposed perspectives. He described this as "the Bible's dialectic," and he therefore advocates what he calls "preaching the poles."[10] Polarity, as he sees it, pervades scripture's teaching in many spheres. It moves from the sovereignty of God to the responsibility of humanity. We see God's promises of blessing and read of a Christian's responses when God seems completely absent. It teaches Christian sinfulness and culpability and the blamelessness of God's people, the necessity of modesty and the wonder of erotic love; and so on (Rayburn's own list includes some fifty examples).[11]

His preaching style displays other effects of his appreciation of the spiritual continuity of the Old and New Testaments. For example, he lays a heavy

---

not inextricably tied to them. For example, Rayburn's pastor in Aberdeen, William Still, ardently held a kind of covenant succession position, but never embraced paedocommunion.

9. For exposition of this theme, see Ron Bergey's contribution to this volume, "Parents as Covenant Mediators in Deuteronomy."

10. See https://www.covenantseminary.edu/resources/preaching-lectures-1996/ for Rayburn's 1996 lectures on the subject at Covenant Seminary.

11. For an example of this approach to reading the Bible, see the essay by Joel Belz in this volume, "A Tension-Filled Assignment: Reflections on the 'Poles' of the Christian Worldview."

stress on the importance of obedience for Christian people.[12] Listening to a Rayburn sermon is an education. One hears a scholar's reflections on the meaning of a text; one hears quotations from all manner of people, from a wide spectrum of Christian denominations and time periods; one hears anecdotes from church history and Christian biography.[13] There is no question that Rayburn has read widely and voraciously: Augustine, Saint Patrick of Ireland, and Ratramnus (a ninth-century monk who developed an understanding of the Lord's Supper that most reformed scholars would appreciate), along with Alexander Whyte, poems from Christina Rossetti and Anna Cousins, John Bunyan's *Pilgrim's Progress*, Thomas Boston's *Memoirs*, and Andrew Bonar's biography of Robert Murray M'Cheyne.[14] Those whom he has influenced share his catholicity and his healthy interdisciplinarity.

In the philosophy of science, one of the tests for a good theory is its fruitfulness—that is, its ability to unlock other areas of understanding. Rayburn's ministry has borne fruit in a distinct way: young men from Faith Presbyterian Church have gone on to finish PhDs, especially in the Old Testament disciplines: Jack Collins (University of Liverpool, 1989); Max Rogland (University of Leiden, 2001);[15] and Christopher Bechtel (University of Edinburgh, 2011). Further, his PhD work enabled him to produce a short commentary on Hebrews (1989), and also inspired two more PhD theses: Joshua Moon (University of St Andrews, 2007) and Robert G. Rayburn II (Ludwig-Maximilians-Universität München, 2018), both of which have been or will be published. All of these, besides their specific topics, have taken many of Rayburn's theological and practical emphases, and added their own twists to them.

A further aspect of fruitfulness is the way that many of his emphases can work together on fresh subjects. For example, Jack Collins, influenced by Rayburn's stress on Old and New Testament spiritual continuity, the Eucharist, the priestly antecedents to the Christian ministry, children's participation in the liturgical life of the church, and respect for tradition, produced a study in 2004 on the Old Testament background of the Lord's Supper as

---

12. For a fitting tribute to Rayburn's preaching gifts, see the contribution to this volume by Bryan Chapell, one of the deans of contemporary homiletics, "Insights from the Westminster Standards for Today's Preaching and Preachers."

13. As a tribute to this aspect of Rayburn's personality, see Will Barker's essay in this volume, "Reflections on Church History from a Recent Reading of Jonathan Edwards's *A History of the Work of Redemption*."

14. For an appreciation of this aspect of Rayburn's perspective, see Ian Hamilton, "The Catholicity of John Calvin," in this volume.

15. Rogland's dissertation was published in 2003 as *Alleged Non-past Uses of Qatal in Classical Hebrew*.

seen through the eyes of the early Christians.[16] In 2015, Steven Nicoletti, profiting from many of these ideas (some mediated through others), offered a careful study on the ways in which baptism would have been understood in the first century of Christianity.[17]

Finally, we will offer some thoughts about where we go from here. We are grateful for Rob's influence on the academic, ecclesiastical, and personal planes.[18] We do not advocate being uncritical, but we do urge those with critiques to be sure of their ground, and to be sure that their arguments will stand the test of time. One thing Rayburn has never been is trendy! We might suggest that Rayburn's insights can be developed to take a greater account of the overarching story in the Bible. Although an interest in story sounds very current now, it is in fact the case that many of the theological ancestors whom Rayburn cherishes have seen the narrative shape of the Bible clearly—the storyline of creation, fall, redemption, and ultimate consummation. One way in which the interest on children's participation can be broadened is in exploring the place among the people of God of those who for one reason or another cannot supply the visible expression of faith.[19] This would be applicable, of course, to the church's stance toward people with handicaps, but also toward people who, through pain or depression, experience dullness, and need their fellow believers' faith to carry them along. An underexplored aspect of this has to do with what Bible scholars sometimes call "solidarity"—the common participation in the life of a corporate entity. It would also be worthwhile to examine the early Christians' use of priestly categories in describing the Christian ministry, to see whether that sheds light on that subject. And, in addition to his emphasis on the "Bible's dialectic," we might suggest ways in which the stark presentations might need more filling out when preached to Christian congregations.

The tool that is Rayburn's theology and piety was forged in strong academic preparation, continued reading and study, and the needs of an active and faithful pastorate. Many of the essays you will find here seek to appropriate Rayburn's insights, though not every contributor agrees with him in all of these points. But the church is richer for his work, and we pray that she will indeed lay hold of these gifts.

16. Collins, "Eucharist as Christian Sacrifice."

17. Nicoletti, "Infant Baptism in the First-Century Presupposition Pool." When this was published, Nicoletti was the assistant pastor at Faith Presbyterian in Tacoma. He had been working on it for quite some time before then, however.

18. For an appreciation of Rob's enduring commitment to the pastoral ministry, see John Birkett's essay in this volume, "Ministry After Christ: The Long-Term Pastorate."

19. For reflections relevant to this theme, see Kevin and Jacob Skogen, "That Your Generations May Know: Epistemology and Covenant Succession," in this volume.

Publication List for the Rev. Dr. Robert S. Rayburn

Academic:

"The Contrast between the Old and New Covenants in the New Testament." PhD diss., University of Aberdeen, 1978.

"A Defense of Paedocommunion." In *The Covenant: God's Voluntary Condescension*, edited by Joseph A. Pipa and C. N. Willborn, 147–62. Taylors, SC: Southern Presbyterian Press, 2005. Reprinted as "A Presbyterian Defense of Paedocommunion" in *The Case for Covenant Communion*, edited by Gregg Strawbridge, 3–18. Monroe, LA: Athanasius, 2006.

"An Elder Must Have Believing Children: Titus 1:6 and a Neglected Case of Conscience" (with Steven A. Nicoletti). *Presbyterion* 43 (2017) 69–80.

"Hebrews." In *Evangelical Commentary on the Bible*, edited by Walter A. Elwell, 1124–49. Baker Reference Library. Grand Rapids: Baker, 1989.

"Historic Practice is Invisible in the Bible: the Paedocommunion Debate." *ByFaith*, January 16, 2013. http://byfaithonline.com/our-historic-practice-is-invisible-in-the-bible/.

"Parental Conditions and the Promise of Grace to the Children of Believers." In *To You and Your Children: Examining the Biblical Doctrine of Covenant Succession*, edited by Benjamin K. Wikner, 3–27. Moscow, ID: Canon, 2005.

"The Presbyterian Doctrines of Covenant Children, Covenant Nurture and Covenant Succession." *Presbyterion: Covenant Seminary Review* 22 (1996) 76–112. Reprinted in *The Case for Covenant Communion*, edited by Gregg Strawbridge, 167–202. Monroe, LA: Athanasius, 2006.

"Report of the Ad-Interim Committee on Divorce and Remarriage to the Twentieth General Assembly" (contributing author). In *PCA Digest Position Papers 1973–1993 Part V*, edited by Paul R. Gilchrist, 182–293. Atlanta: Presbyterian Church in America, 1993.

"Report of the Ad-Interim Committee to Study the Question of Paedocommunion." In *PCA Digest Position Papers 1973–1993 Part V*, edited by Paul R. Gilchrist, 498–519. Atlanta: Presbyterian Church in America, 1993.

"Three Offices: Minister, Elder, Deacon." *Presbyterion: Covenant Seminary Review* 12 (1986) 105–14. Reprinted as "Ministers, Elders, and Deacons" in *Order in the Offices*, edited by Mark R. Brown, 219–33. Duncansville, PA: Classic Presbyterian Government Resources, 1993.

Published Sermons, Addresses, and Short Articles:

"Charge to Oliver Claassen." *Presbyterion: Covenant Seminary Review* 6 (1980) 67–70.

"The Christian's Greatest Means of Grace." *Presbyterion: Covenant Seminary Review* 16 (1990) 1–7.

"The Counsel of the Elders: A Sermon Preached on the Occasion of the Ordination and Installation of Elders." *New Horizons*, May 2002. http://www.opc.org/new_horizons/NH02/05f.html.

"Hope that Heals the Hurting Heart." In *The Hardest Sermons You Will Ever Have to Preach*, edited by Bryan Chapell, 139–44. Grand Rapids: Zondervan, 2011.

"Nothing Like the Church." *Tabletalk Magazine*, October 2011.
"Pride and Humility." *Tabletalk Magazine*, May 2008.
"A Refuge for the Weary Soul." *Tabletalk Magazine*, June 2006.
"Seeing the Triumph in the Tragedy." In *The Hardest Sermons You Will Ever Have to Preach*, edited by Bryan Chapell, 191–96. Grand Rapids: Zondervan, 2011.

1

Reflections on Church History from a Recent Reading of Jonathan Edwards's *A History of the Work of Redemption*

Introduction

IN MORE THAN ONE place, Jonathan Edwards pronounced God's work of providence as greater than the work of creation: "if it be inquired which of the two works, the work of creation or the work of providence, is greatest, it must be answered 'the work of providence.' But the Work of Redemption is the greatest of the works of providence."[1] This is a remarkable statement in view of Edwards's notable appreciation of natural creation, including his acceptance of the scientific discoveries of Isaac Newton and other recent Enlightenment figures.

The intellectual prowess of Jonathan Edwards (1703–58) has increasingly been recognized in modern scholarship. Not only has the Yale University Press been publishing a multi-volume new edition of his works, but *The Jonathan Edwards Encyclopedia* was also published in 2017 under the auspices of Yale University and Eerdmans Publishing Company. Among all his works, there is evidence he considered what became *A History of the Work of Redemption* as potentially his magnum opus. Originally a series of

---

1. Edwards, *History*, 286; see also 336 and 512–13. In the summer of 2015, while recuperating from a broken right femur, I read Edwards's *History* from a revised and slightly abridged nineteenth-century edition published in New York by the American Tract Society (no date, but after 1808), which I obtained from Rev. Jay E. Adams, probably in 1960–1961, when I had just graduated from Covenant Theological Seminary and had become pastor of the Hazelwood (Missouri) Presbyterian Church, where the young teenager Rob Rayburn worshiped with his family. Citations from the work are from the critical edition published by Yale University Press and edited by John F. Wilson.

thirty sermons that he preached in Northampton, Massachusetts between March and August 1739, the work was still being developed when he was approached in 1757 by the trustees in Princeton to become president of the College of New Jersey:

> "I have had on my mind and heart," he wrote, "(which I long ago began, not with any view to publication) a great work, which I call *A History of the Work of Redemption,* a body of divinity in an entire new method, being thrown into the form of an history, considering the affair of Christian theology, as the whole of it, in each part, stands in reference to the great work of redemption by Jesus Christ; which I suppose to be the grand design of all God's designs, and the *summum* and *ultimum* of all the divine operations and decrees; particularly considering all parts in the grand scheme of their historical order."[2]

Edwards was to die in 1758, leaving the work in notebooks to be edited and published by others.

Having possessed a copy of this significant work for more than fifty years, but giving it only cursory reviews during more than thirty years of teaching church history, I now have given it a recent thorough reading that has stimulated me to share some reflections on church history. Knowing of Rob Rayburn's interest and expertise in historical theology, I believe it is appropriate to share these reflections in this volume.[3]

I. Providence Greater Than Creation

Edwards's conviction that God's work of providence is greater than his work of creation is based on his view that the history of the world, from creation to culmination, is the unfolding of God's work of redemption. Church history is most basically an account of the conflict between God and Satan. All of God's word is meant to reveal and proclaim the gospel:

> Christ and his redemption are the great subject of the whole Bible. Concerning the New Testament the matter is plain, but by what has been said on this subject hitherto it appears to be so also with the Old Testament. Christ and his redemption is

---

2. Edwards, letter of October 19, 1757 to the Trustees of the College of New Jersey, quoted in Marsden, *Jonathan Edwards*, 482. See also Edwards, *History*, 544.

3. I recall that Rob Rayburn took my course on church history at Covenant College, and then when we had both moved to Covenant Seminary in 1972, I required that he take my expanded church history course there. I trust that these further reflections are not an inflicting of further punishment on this excellent student of the subject!

the great subject of the prophecies of the Old Testament, as has been shown. It has also been shown that he is the great subject of the songs of the Old Testament, and the moral rules and precepts of it are all given in subordination to him. And Christ and his redemption is also the great subject of the history of the Old Testament, from the beginning all along, and even the history of the creation is brought as introduction to the history of redemption that immediately follows it. The whole book, both Old Testament and New, is filled up with gospel.[4]

In light of this understanding of history, Edwards goes on to describe the greatness of the incarnation of Christ:

> But Christ's incarnation was a greater thing than had ever come to pass before. The creation of the world was a very great thing, but not so great a thing as the incarnation of Christ. It was a great thing for God to make the creature, but not so great as for the Creator himself to become a creature. We have spoken of many great things that were accomplished from one age to another in the ages between the fall of man and the incarnation of Christ, but God's becoming man was a greater thing than they all. When Christ was born, the greatest person was born that ever was or ever will be born.[5]

Even greater than the incarnation is the atoning sacrifice of Christ: "So the greatest thing that Christ did in the execution of his office, and the greatest thing that ever he did, and the greatest thing that ever was done, was the offering up [himself a sacrifice to God]."[6] With the death of Christ, Edwards continues, "thus was finished the greatest and most wonderful thing. . . . And then was finished that great work, the purchase of our redemption, that such great preparation had been made for from the beginning of the world."[7]

Subsequent to the resurrection of Christ, what we usually view as "church history," Edwards claims to be the Father's granting to the Son his reward for the purchase of redemption: "And all the dispensations of God's providence henceforward, even to the final consummation of all things, is to give Christ his reward, and fulfill his end in what he did and suffered upon earth, and to fulfill the joy that was set before him."[8] With his post-millennial

---

4. Edwards, *History*, 289–90.
5. Edwards, *History*, 299.
6. Edwards, *History*, 318.
7. Edwards, *History*, 331.
8. Edwards, *History*, 346.

eschatology, Edwards sees church history to its culmination as fulfillment of the covenant of redemption between the Father and the Son:

> This Work of Redemption is so much the greatest of all the works of God, that all other works are to be looked upon either as part of it, or appendages to it, or are some way reducible to it. And so all the decrees of God do some way or other belong to that eternal covenant of redemption that was between the Father and the Son before the foundation of the world; every decree of God is some way or other reducible to that covenant.[9]

Thus, for Edwards, church history is essentially the redemptive victories of Christ over Satan and his minions.

Reflection: This understanding of church history, extending from creation through all of biblical history to the consummation of all things, might challenge the current organization of most seminaries' curriculum. The teaching of OT history and church history might profitably be combined. At least such subjects might be team-taught for the sake of the mutual stimulus that might arise from seeing the overall patterns of redemptive history.

II. Turning Points in the History of Redemption

Generally speaking, Edwards sees history, both in the Bible and in subsequent church history, as occurring in a series of spiritual awakenings by which God revives his people and advances the course of redemption. Such awakenings are usually preceded by low points of darkness.[10] Discussing the time of Ezra, he says:

> 'Tis observable that it has been God's manner in every remarkable new establishment of the state of his visible church, to give a remarkable outpouring of his Spirit; so it was on the first establishment of the church, the Jews at their first coming into Canaan under Joshua, as has been observed. And so it was now in the second settlement of his church in the same land in the time of Ezra. And so it was in the first establishment of the Christian church after Christ's resurrection, God wisely and graciously laying the foundation of those establishments in a work of his holy Spirit for the lasting benefit of the state of his church thenceforward continued in those establishments. And this pouring out of the Spirit was a final cure of that nation of

---

9. Edwards, *History*, 513; see also 509.
10. See, for example, Edwards, *History*, 457–58.

that particular sin which just before they had especially, viz. intermarrying with the Gentiles; for however inclined they were to it before, they ever after showed an aversion to it.[11]

So with each subsequent awakening there is a progress of the kingdom.

With regard to the advance of Christ's kingdom after his ascension, Edwards sees this as happening in four stages:

> The first is Christ's appearing in those wonderful dispensations of providence in the apostles' days in setting up the kingdom of Christ and destroying the enemies of his kingdom, which ended in the destruction of Jerusalem.... The second is that which was accomplished in Constantine's time in the destruction of the heathen Roman empire.... The third is that which is to be accomplished at the destruction of Antichrist [understood by Edwards to be manifested in the Church of Rome].... The fourth and last is his coming to the last judgment, which is the event principally signified in Scripture by Christ's coming in his kingdom.[12]

What is especially remarkable in this understanding of church history is the emphasis given to the conversion of Constantine: "the great revolution that was in the world in Constantine's [time], which was in many respects like Christ's appearing in the clouds of heaven to save his people and judge the world."[13] As a result,

> The Christian church was thereby wholly delivered from persecution.... God now appeared to execute terrible judgments on their enemies.... Heathenism now was in a great measure abolished throughout the Roman empire.... The Christian church was brought into a state of great peace and prosperity.... This revolution was the greatest revolution and change in the face of things on the face of the earth that ever came to pass in the world since the flood.[14]

Also notable is Edwards's emphasis upon the return of the Jews from Babylonian captivity: "The return of the Jews out of the Babylonish captivity is, next to the redemption out of Egypt, the most remarkable of all the Old Testament redemptions, and most insisted on in Scripture as a type of the

---

11. Edwards, *History*, 266.
12. Edwards, *History*, 351.
13. Edwards, *History*, 394.
14. Edwards, *History*, 395–96.

great redemption of Jesus Christ."[15] Since the recent liberation theology has tended to emphasize the Exodus from Egypt, it is interesting to see Edwards's emphasis on the return from the Babylonian exile as comparable.

Not surprisingly, Edwards sees a major turning point in the era of the Protestant Reformation, preceded by a period of darkness: "And this is the darkest and most dismal day that ever the Christian church saw, and probably the darkest that ever it will see."[16]

> The two great works of the devil that he in this space of time wrought against the kingdom of Christ are his erecting his Antichristian and Mohammedan kingdoms, which have been and still are two kingdoms of great extent and strength, both together swallowing up the ancient Roman empire; the kingdom of Antichrist swallowing up the western empire, and Satan's Mohammedan kingdom the eastern empire.[17]

Edwards sees resistance to Roman papal dominion in a great part "of the churches in England and Scotland and France, who retained the ancient purity of doctrine and worship much longer than many others that were much nearer the chief seat of Antichrist."[18] Following the revival brought by the Reformation, there ensued persecutions: "Such a persecution was it that occasioned our forefathers to fly that country 'to come and settle in this land.'"[19] Down to the Glorious Revolution of 1688, only a half-century before his preaching of these sermons, Edwards sees the providential hand of God in his contemporary history:

> And at last God wonderfully revived his church in the time of the Reformation, and made it to stand, as it were, up on its feet in the sight of its enemies, and carried it out of their reach. And so since when the popish powers have plotted the overthrow of the Reformed church, and have seemed just to bring their matters to a conclusion, and to have finished their design, then God wonderfully appeared for the deliverance of his church, as it was in the time of the revolution by King William.[20]

---

15. Edwards, *History*, 263.
16. Edwards, *History*, 409.
17. Edwards, *History*, 410.
18. Edwards, *History*, 418.
19. Edwards, *History*, 429.
20. Edwards, *History*, 449.

Edwards continued to watch for signs of God's providence and the fulfillment of biblical prophecies in his own time.[21]

Reflection: Modern historical scholarship tends to deplore the idea of "providential history." The evangelical Christian historian, however, should not decry the effort to see God's hand in history. One must humbly admit that there are many mysteries in God's providence. Even those who believe in God's providence may differ in their interpretations of specific historical events. Our knowledge is always partial as we "see through a glass darkly" in this life. But that is not to say that Bible believers cannot recognize the main directions of both God and Satan in the world. Otherwise, how could we meaningfully have days of prayer or thanksgiving?

III. The Importance of Scripture

As Edwards charts the history of redemption from the creation and fall on through the OT and NT, at each stage he makes a significant point of the development of the canon of Scripture. Describing the time of Moses, he says:

> About this time was given to God's church the first written word of God that ever was enjoyed by God's people. This was another great thing done towards the affair of redemption, a new and glorious advancement of the building. Not far from this time was the beginning of that great standing written rule that God has given 'em for the regulation of the faith, worship, and practice of his church in all ages henceforward to the end of the world, which rule grew and was added to from that time for many ages till it was finished and the canon of Scripture completed by the apostle John.[22]

Edwards concludes this section: "The written word of God is this main instrument Christ has made use of to carry on his Work of Redemption in all ages since it was given. There was a necessity now of the word of God's being committed to writing for a steady rule to God's church." He continues, "God having now separated a nation to be his peculiar people partly for that end to be the keepers of the oracles of God, God saw it to be a needful and convenient time now to commit his word to writing to remain henceforward for a steady rule throughout all ages."[23]

---

21. See, e.g., Edwards, *Apocalyptic Writings*, 253–84 and 285–97.
22. Edwards, *History*, 182.
23. Edwards, *History*, 182–83.

He likewise emphasizes the establishment of a school of prophets in the time of Samuel, producing a line of prophets to extend the canon of Scripture.[24] Samuel himself would add to the canon,[25] and then Nathan and Gad in the era of David,[26] and again in the time of Solomon by Nathan, Ahijah, Shemaiah, and Iddo.[27] It is significant that Edwards records these names of writers of Scripture alongside the more prominent actors in Israel's history such as kings and military leaders. Then great emphasis is given to the period of the writers of prophetic books (such as Hosea and Isaiah down through Micah and Nahum) all pointing to Christ and his redemption.[28] The canon of the OT was then settled in the time of Ezra, with copies of the Law multiplied and appointed for reading in all cities and synagogues.[29] "After this the canon of the Old Testament was completed and sealed by Malachi.... Soon after this, the spirit of prophecy ceased among that people till the time of the New Testament."[30]

Then, in the NT era, the Holy Spirit bestowed extraordinary gifts upon the apostles and others: "by means of these extraordinary gifts of the Holy Ghost, the apostles and others were enabled to write the New Testament to be an infallible rule of faith and works and manners to the church to the end of the world."[31] All the books of the NT were written before the destruction of Jerusalem, with the exception of the writings of the apostle John. Among these is Revelation, the one prophetical book

> which takes place after the end of the history of the whole Bible, and gives an account of the great events that were to come to pass, by which the Work of Redemption was to be carried on to the end of the world.... So that now the canon of the Scriptures, that great and standing written rule, that was begun about Moses' time, is completed and settled and a curse denounced against him that adds anything to it or diminishes from it.[32]

Thus Edwards gives prominence to the role of Scripture in the unfolding work of the history of redemption.

---

24. Edwards, *History*, 199–203.
25. Edwards, *History*, 208–9.
26. Edwards, *History*, 220–21.
27. Edwards, *History*, 232.
28. Edwards, *History*, 237–40.
29. Edwards, *History*, 266–68.
30. Edwards, *History*, 269.
31. Edwards, *History*, 365.
32. Edwards, *History*, 369–70.

This prominent role of Scripture is manifested also in Edwards's account of the church's history following the NT era. The various spiritual awakenings, through the Reformation era and down to his own time in the 1730s, are accompanied by the spread, discovery, or rediscovery of the Bible. One fascinating example is the advance of the gospel in Russia during the reign of Peter the Great (1682–1725):

> The most considerable success of the gospel that has been of late of this kind [i.e., reformation in doctrine and worship in countries that are called Christian] has been in the empire of Muscovy, which is a country of vast extent. The people of this country, so many of them as call themselves Christians, professed to be of the Greek church, but were barbarously ignorant and very superstitious till of late years their last emperor, Peter Alexander [the Great], who reigned till within these twenty years, set himself to reform the people of his dominion and took great pains to bring 'em out of their darkness and to have 'em instructed in religion. And to that end he set up schools of learning, and ordered the Bible to be printed in the language of the country, and made it a law that every family should keep the holy Scriptures in their houses, and that every person should be able to read the same, and that no persons should be allowed to marry till they were able to read the Scriptures. And he also reformed the churches of his country of many of their superstitions—whereby the religion professed and practiced as in Muscovy is much nearer that of the Protestants than formerly it used to be. This emperor gave great encouragement to the exercise of the Protestant religion in his dominions. And since that Muscovy is become a land of light in comparison of what it used to be before; wonderful alterations have been brought about in the face of religion for the better within this fifty years past.[33]

The increase of availability of the Bible in Russia as a result of Peter the Great's reforms, just a generation or two before Edwards's sermons on the work of redemption, had a profound effect on Russian culture, and some have traced this influence down to such nineteenth-century Christian writers as Fyodor Dostoyevsky and Leo Tolstoy.[34]

---

33. Edwards, *History*, 433.

34. See, for example, Kuchumov, "Eldership in Russia," 38–65, esp. 47 and 58–59. Edwards clearly had some knowledge of developments in Russia (see, e.g., Edwards, *Apocalyptic Writings*, 294 and 304), though one may wonder how he came by it on the Massachusetts frontier. Possibly he had access to such works as *The State of Russia under the Present Czar*, by Captain John Perry, *The Present State and Regulations of the Church of Russia*, by Thomas Consett, and *The History of the Propagation of Christianity*

Reflection: Historical scholarship has duly recognized Edwards's acceptance of such figures as Isaac Newton and John Locke and the Enlightenment's epistemological combination of rationalism and empiricism. Even more basic to his knowledge, however, is the authority of God's word. Key to the spiritual awakenings he sees as the outworking of the history of redemption is the role of Scripture. He indeed put an emphasis on prayer for the sake of revival, as the title of his 1747 work indicates: *An Humble Attempt to Promote Explicit Agreement and Visible Union of God's People in Extraordinary Prayer for the Revival of Religion and the Advancement of Christ's Kingdom on Earth, Pursuant to Scripture-Promises and Prophecies Concerning the Last Time.*[35] Even more basic than such "concerts of prayer" and God producing spiritual awakenings in Edwards's *A History of the Work of Redemption* is the translating, reading, preaching, and hearing of the Scriptures. The teacher of church history will rightly emphasize this matter.

IV. Further Reflections

The combination of Edwards's brilliant mind and his broad knowledge of the Bible led to his production of some uncommon insights in his *History of the Work of Redemption*. For example, he comments on the older and younger generations of Israelites coming out of Egypt in the Exodus:

> Another thing by which God carried on this work at this time was a remarkable pouring out of his spirit on the younger generation in the wilderness. The generation that was grown up when they came out of Egypt from twenty years old and upward was a very froward and perverse generation. They were tainted with the idolatry and wickedness of Egypt and were never weaned from it. . . . This generation God was exceeding angry with and swore in his wrath that they should not enter into his rest. But the younger generation were not so, the generation that were under twenty years old when they came out of Egypt and those that were born in the wilderness. . . . This generation God was pleased to make a generation to his praise, and they were eminent for piety, as appears by many things said in the Scriptures about them. . . . Those terrible judgments that were executed in the congregation after their turning back from Kadesh Barnea

---

and the Overthrow of Paganism, Vol. 2, by Robert Millar, all of which give some description of affairs in Russia. I am grateful to my daughter, Anne K. Barker, Head of Research Services at the University of Missouri's Ellis Library in Columbia, for providing me with these references.

35. Edwards, *Apocalyptic Writings*, 308.

in the matter of Korah and the matter of Peor, were chiefly of the old generation whom God consumed in the wilderness. For those rebellions were chiefly in the elders of the congregation which were of the older generation that God had given up to their heart's lust; and they walked in their own counsels and God was grieved with their manners forty years in the wilderness.

But that this younger congregation were eminent for piety appears by all their history. The former generation were wicked and followed with curses, but this was holy, and wonderful blessings followed them. God did great things for them. He fought for them and gave them the possession of Canaan, and as 'tis God's manner when he has very great blessings to bestow on a visible people first to fit them for them and then to bestow them upon 'em, so it was here. . . .

The men of the former wicked generation being dead and God having sanctified this younger generation to himself, he solemnly renewed his covenant with them as we have a particular account in the twenty-ninth chapter of Deuteronomy. We find that such solemn renovations of the covenant commonly accompanied any remarkable pouring out of the Spirit, causing a general reformation. So we find it was in Hezekiah's and Josiah's time. 'Tis questionable whether there ever was a time of so great a flourishing of religion in the Israelitish church as in that generation. And whether, as it was in the Christian church, religion was in its most flourishing circumstances in the day of its espousals—first setting up that church in the days of the apostles. So it was with the Jewish church in the days of its first establishment in Moses' and Joshua's times. Thus God at this time did gloriously advance the Work of Redemption both by his word and by his Spirit.[36]

Reflection: As one born into the era of the fundamentalist/modernist controversy, and then teaching college and seminary students from the 1950s into the 2000s, I can testify to the differences between generations. It was difficult for the students to have the same sense of cause concerning such things as the doctrinal purity of the visible church. One perceives a difference of experience and perception in one's children who are of the "baby boomer" generation and one's grandchildren who are of the "millennial" generation. Those of us who grew up in the era of World War II certainly have a different sense of America and her role in the world than do those who grew up in the era of the Vietnam War. It behooves those of us who preach and teach to be aware of where we and the generations to follow appear to be in the

---

36. Edwards, *History*, 189–92.

providential scheme of God. As Psalm 78 and other passages of Scripture indicate, one of our most important roles is to tell the next generation the glorious deeds of the Lord and the wonders that he has done.

Another uncommon insight in Edwards's *History of the Work of Redemption* is his answer to the question of "why the setting up of Christ's kingdom after his humiliation should be so gradual, by so many steps that are so long in accomplishment, when God could easily have finished it at once."[37] He answers this inquiry in two ways:

> 1. In this way the glory of God's wisdom in the manner of doing this is more visible to the creature's observation. . . . For if all that glory that appears in all these events should be manifested at once, it would be too much for us and more than we at once could take notice of; it would dazzle our eyes and be too much for our sight.

> 2. Satan is the more gloriously triumphed over. God could easily by an act of almighty power at once have crushed Satan. But by giving him time to use his utmost subtilty to hinder the success of what Christ had done and suffered, he is not defeated merely by surprise but has large opportunity to ply his utmost power and subtilty again and again, to strengthen his own interest all that he can by the work of many ages. Thus God destroys and confounds him, and sets up Christ's kingdom time after time, in spite of all his subtile machinations and great works, and by every step to advance it still higher and higher, till at length it is fully set up and Satan perfectly and eternally vanquished in the end of all things.[38]

Reflection: Contemplation of God's providence in the history of the church and the world requires great patience and a long view. Scientists take great pains to understand the natural creation. If, as Edwards claims, God's work of redemption in providence is greater than his work of creation, then we should be even more diligent, with all humility, in seeking to plumb the depths of his providence. Edwards's optimism with regard to the church's victory over Satan is a matter of his faith in God's promises, to the praise of the glory of his grace.

Edwards's main Scriptural source for his understanding of his own times and the future was the book of Revelation. His eschatology is post-millennial, and his interpretation of Revelation is historicist—that is, he takes the seven seals, the seven trumpets, and the seven vials of wrath to refer to

---

37. Edwards, *History*, 355.
38. Edwards, *History*, 355–56.

events during the history of the church. Of particular interest is his comment concerning the seven vials in Revelation 16: "how many are already poured out, and how many yet remain to be poured out; though a very late expositor that I have before mentioned to you seems to make it very plain and evident that all are already poured out but two, viz. the sixth on the river Euphrates and the seventh into the air."[39] This recent contemporary expositor was an English nonconformist minister, Moses Lowman (1680–1752), whose *Paraphrase and Notes on the Revelation* was published in London in 1737 and obtained by Edwards by mid-1738.[40] Edwards's interpretation of Revelation was much influenced by his reading of Lowman; however, he disagreed with him on various details. One of these was Lowman's view that the 1,260 years of the antichrist's reign began with the investment of the papacy with temporal dominion by the Frankish king Pepin in 756, whereas Edwards would place this some three centuries earlier.[41] Whether the fifth or the sixth vial had already been poured out, the result for Edwards's historicist and postmillennial reading of Revelation is a certain immediacy of expectation for the fulfillment of prophecy in the current events of history.

Reflection: One of the startling discoveries in perusing Moses Lowman's *Paraphrase and Notes* was to see that his prediction for the end of the reign of the antichrist was in 2016, the year that this essay was written![42] However one may interpret prophecies concerning the end times, it is important to be aware of Scripture's promises, to be cognizant of current events, and to be watchful for the return of our Lord.

Conclusion

Jonathan Edwards concludes his *History of the Work of Redemption* with another glorification of God's work of providence:

> This shows us how much greater the Work of Redemption is than the work of creation, for I have several times observed before that the work of providence is greater than the work of

---

39. Edwards, *History*, 457; see also 422n3.

40. On Moses Lowman, see Stein, "Introduction," 55–59, and also Zakai, *Edwards's Philosophy of History*, 211 and 266. (The copy of Lowman's *Paraphrase and Notes* in Covenant Seminary's J. Oliver Buswell Jr. Library evidently once was in the library of Southern Presbyterian pastor and theologian John L. Girardeau.)

41. On Edwards's differences with Lowman, see Stein, "Introduction," 57–59, and Edwards, *History*, 394–412.

42. See Lowman, *Paraphrase and Notes*, xxxi and xxxiii; see also Stein, "Introduction," 58.

creation because 'tis the end of it, as the use of a house is the end of the building of an house. But this, as I have just said, is the sum of God's works of providence; all are subordinate to it. So the work of the new creation is more excellent than the old. So it ever is, then when one thing is removed by God to make way for another, the new one excels the old: tabernacle and temple; so new covenant, new dispensation: throne of Saul and David, priesthood of Aaron and priesthood of Christ, old Jerusalem and new; so old creation and new. God has used the creation that he has made to no other purpose but to subserve to the design of this affair. To this he has disposed mankind, to this angels, to this earth, to this highest heaven. God created the world to provide a spouse and kingdom for his Son. And the setting up of the kingdom of Christ, and the spiritual marriage of the spouse to him, is what the whole creation labors and travails in pain to bring to pass.[43]

May this be what preachers and teachers of church history faithfully proclaim!

---

43. Edwards, *History*, 513.

2

A Tension-Filled Assignment

Reflections on the "Poles" of the
Christian Worldview[1]

As Rob Rayburn has often spoken of the apparent contradictions Scripture presents for the believer's life, it seems fitting here for me to address what I've found to be the absolutely most perplexing part of a Christian's walk before God. Wherever you are in your Christian experience—whether you're still getting your education, whether you're already putting your education to work, or perhaps you are already in your "golden years"—this, I say, is the hard part.

My guess is also that this is something that really ought to have been more perplexing to you. The more serious you are about your role as a disciple of Jesus, the more you'll be perplexed with this issue. My own experience is that the perplexity gets worse with age.

I say this as a layman in the church. And my calling to the laity also enhances the perplexity of which I speak.

That perplexity grows, you see, because of the very nature of that thing to which I have devoted my own life—this thing we call a Christian worldview, a biblical perspective on life. It is a perspective almost unique to our Reformed view of things, popularized in our own lifetime by Francis Schaeffer, who devoted so much of his life to demolishing the pietistic view of things that says there's a secular downstairs to life and a sacred upstairs. Before Schaeffer, of course, was Gresham Machen, who wrote in 1912 that "Christianity must pervade not only all nations, but also all of human thought. The Christian, therefore, cannot be indifferent to any branch of earnest Christian endeavor. . . . The church must seek to conquer not merely

---

1. This essay is an edited version of a commencement address given at Reformed Theological Seminary in Charlotte, NC, on May 20, 2000.

every man for Christ, but also the whole of man."[2] But before Machen was Abraham Kuyper, who said once that God looks out over all his vast creation, sizing things up as an artist does when he checks his perspective, and says, "There's not a thumb's width of it that doesn't belong to me!" I love that enough that I actually carry a picture of Kuyper in my wallet!

But well before Kuyper was the apostle Paul, who reminded us in Colossians 1 that Jesus wants "in all things" to have the preeminence (Col 1:18). That, of course, is the theme verse at Covenant College—where Rob's father and mine invested so much of their energy and resources during the school's early years,[3] and where Rob himself has served on the Board of Trustees. And that concept—that God insists on lordship not just of the so-called religious issues, but also of absolutely every reality you encounter—that concept has been drummed into me since my boyhood. Everything has to be rooted in the wisdom of Christ; in him, Paul says, everything consists and holds together (Col 1:17).

Now, in one sense, this wonderful idea of rooting all reality in Christ is gaining ascendancy. Among evangelical Christians, the early half of the last century was characterized by pietism—the sense that the answer to every problem was ultimately a spiritual answer. During the second half of the century, evangelical Christians flocked to Schaeffer's keen insights, and to those of people like Charles Colson since Schaeffer's death.

But my goal here is not to argue that point. We will rather just assume it. Worldview thinking is in. But what I want to stress here is how difficult it is to live out that assertion in everyday life. I want to assert to you that just because biblical worldview thinking is growing as an intellectual concept doesn't mean that it's meshing gears with people's lives—including, maybe,

---

2. Machen, "Christianity and Culture," 6. This was a published version of his address, "The Scientific Preparation of a Minister," delivered on a couple of occasions in 1912.

3. Rob's father (Robert G. Rayburn) and mine (Max V. Belz) were more than fellow churchmen; they were personal friends. I remember the two of them herding some of us boys on a camping trip from Pasadena to Colorado Springs in 1952, just following the annual Synod of the Bible Presbyterian Church. The two men talked denominational politics much of the way—but they also managed somehow to keep me in the conversation. I loved it. And it was a thrill to me to have this Army chaplain show me some of the fine points of pitching a tent.

Both men doggedly worked themselves to early graves. As a member of the founding board of trustees of Covenant College and Covenant Theological Seminary, my father saw himself as the loyally persistent defender against the darts and criticisms typically hurled at any front man. When a small minority of the Covenant board the mid-sixties called for a Rayburn resignation from the presidency, an infuriated Belz rallied others on the board to bid farewell instead to the "traitors." I remember a grateful Rayburn driving from St. Louis to Iowa to thank my father for his support in the matter.

your life and mine. Just because this idea is sound doesn't mean it's easy. In fact, it's very hard to deliberately set about the task of being faithful in exploring every single facet of life as though Jesus Christ really matters and really rules in every detail. Yet you are called upon to do this yourself—and it is perhaps even more difficult to help the people who in the future may come under your influence.

What does it specifically mean to live a day under the realization that this person we know as Christ intends to illuminate (and even dominate) our understanding of history; our appreciation of literature and art; our love of music; our amazement at the discoveries we make in biology, chemistry, and physics; our excitement over a basketball game; our awe when we reach the top of a backpacking trail; and our rapture about being in love or having our first—or even fifth—baby? By the word of his power, Christ created all these aspects of life. Now he challenges us to pursue the discovery of how he means to be at the center of all his works of creation and providence.

But if this distinctive of our Reformed understanding includes the regular reminder that every facet of life is to be lived under King Jesus, and if you really want to take this concept seriously and pass this on in the years ahead to those whom you will influence, which I earnestly hope you will, then first I am obliged to remind you of what happened embarrassingly soon to the society Abraham Kuyper helped create. If you want to see the disjunction between having things right in your head and having them right in your heart and your life, go look today at the Netherlands. Get off the train in downtown Amsterdam and begin to view the degradation that has occurred in the very place where these great people of God had everything together—and rightly so—only a little more than a century ago.

The point is that, fairly soon, those of us who hold to this thing we call a Christian worldview ought to start running into a very practical question. It goes something like this: Just how often during any average day am I supposed to be talking about this issue of Christ's preeminence over all things? How frequently am I supposed to be mentioning him? If he means to dominate all of life, how long dare I go through any day's conversations, activities, or assignments without somehow turning the direction of what's going on to a—well, you know—sort of spiritual sounding tone? At what point am I being unfaithful if I fail to start weaving a little Scripture into the discussion?

Some years ago, one of our editors at God's World Publications was reviewing an item submitted by one of our writers. "This is fine as far as it goes," he responded. "But there's absolutely nothing uniquely Christian in what you've written." "Oh," she exclaimed with very real embarrassment, "I forgot the God thing again, didn't I?" And both her omission and her clumsiness in talking about it were symbolic, I believe, of similar failure by us all.

So may I suggest a frankly evasive answer to the question? It is simply that we all tend to be guilty on both sides of the issue.

On the one hand, we already talk far too soon and too much in such terms. Yet on the other hand, we are far too silent and too reticent to mention Christ in what we do.

Let me explain—and I do so with much embarrassment, because, you see, I'm writing here quite specifically about what I consider to be my own personal failure. Nor is it a failure just in some marginal part of my life. It is, as I stressed at the beginning of this essay, a failure right at the core of what I say and believe is the most important part of my existence.

On the one hand, I say, we talk too glibly about a Christian perspective on life, about a biblical framework for living. It's as if we have cornered the market on those handy-dandy bracelets that say "What Would Jesus Do?" and we let them serve as devices where you punch in a question about reality and guidance in life and out comes the answer. At its worst, we develop mechanistic formulas for knowing which movies are good and which ones are bad. We can look at charts and see whom we ought to vote for and whom we should campaign against. We know exactly which economic system is most in keeping with biblical norms, and we don't even furrow our brow when asked which forms of music are fit for worship and which ones aren't. We know with finality what approaches to counseling God would approve of and which ones he would abhor. We're not troubled, you see, because we know all this in advance, and we don't even have to ask or to beg a little time to study the matter. It's all part of a neat formula. So it's in that sense that I think we're a little too ready to talk. We might do well to slow down a bit and make sure we know what we're talking about before we spout off about everything we know is true.

But if on the one hand we're overly confident that we have our worldview together, and maybe a little cocky in expressing things we think we know but really ought to study a bit more, maybe on the other hand we don't talk nearly enough about whatever it is that constitutes a Christian view of things. Maybe we're too cautious in exploring with each other how vastly different a God-centered view of life is from those worldviews with which we are bombarded every day. Yes, I believe in common grace, and there's no question that unredeemed people have been strangely blessed with many insights that are still seen only dimly by many who are redeemed. But if Paul was right in Colossians 1, that it is in Jesus that all things consist, then we have a huge assignment yet before us to discover all that is meant by that cryptic comment.

I should say that, especially in academic circles, there tends to arise a spirit of cautious skepticism, a reluctance to commit ourselves to anything. We love to keep an open mind. But let me say this, with Christian academics more than welcome to listen in: It's not an arrogant kind of presumption to suppose that we should, sooner or later, begin to affirm a significant number of things as absolutely true. After all, we're just launching the third millennium since the time of Christ. Oughtn't we to have gotten a few things figured out about this world we live in? Aren't there at least a few things about this world that we as Christians can say with a good bit of unanimity and certainty?

At Covenant College, I like to encourage prospective students and their families to visit the campus for a day, and on that visit not simply to sit in several classes, but also to ask these questions of the professors: "Hey, you folks are always talking about a Christian perspective on life; could you give me a specific example of what you mean by that? Can you explain why we find thoughtful Christians this year supporting half a dozen different candidates for president? Can you explain why Christians after hundreds of years can't agree on capital punishment and on welfare and on free trade?" What would your response be?

After all, we've been around for a while now. Isn't it fair to claim we ought to be accumulating some body of truth on which we are agreed, and that we should be able to say with a little gusto—and even with some unanimity—"Yes, here are some important ideas that we are agreed constitute a biblical way of thinking about a few different facets of life"?

I know academia likes to keep questioning, keep weighing, keep analyzing. But, just as certainly, part of being a Christian academic institution means that we are not shy about asserting some things to be immediately and eternally true. And that list of things that we assert ought to be growing. Every believer's personal list of things he or she can assert ought also to be growing.

I'm saying that, first of all, just with our own experience of seeing and knowing things, we have a tendency as Christian thinkers to err in both directions at the same time. We tend to act on the one hand as if we knew things we don't, and we tend to act on the other hand as if we don't know things we should. We need to pray for God's Spirit to correct us in both modes.

But now secondly, may I propose that exactly the same disjunction can easily exist with reference to how we speak of our faith to others. When I refer to "speaking of our faith," I don't mean just the simple truths of the gospel, but all these other attendant truths we've been considering as part of the "all things" character of biblical truth.

I've been illustrating this tension or this disjunction to myself this way. When I sit down on an airplane, I have a choice. I can extend my hand, greet my seatmate, and say, "Hi! I'm Joel Belz, and I'm a born-again Christian." I hurry to tell you, of course, that I don't do that. Maybe I should. I've got friends who do that. Actually, maybe I should call them acquaintances, because they tend to embarrass me greatly. But that's my point. Should they embarrass me? For the other end of that continuum, you see, always forces me to ask myself, "OK, coward, when *are* you going to say you're a believer in Christ? After five minutes? After twenty-five minutes? After two hours? What if it's a one-hour flight?" What does God expect?

So the second half of my perplexity is this: even after we've worked through the first issue of how frequently and how explicitly we are to bring Christ himself into our view of all our studies and all our realities, then we still have to struggle with a related follow-up question: How frequently and how explicitly are we to bring Christ himself into our contacts and discussions with those who don't know him yet as we do?

My cautious answer here is pretty much the same as with the first. In talking with others, I think we need to be more cautious and more circumspect than we have a tendency to be—and still also be bolder, more explicit, and more audacious.

In my own task of publishing, for example, I find a weekly challenge of the same sort I experience when I sit down on an airplane. At what point in my editorial construction of each issue am I obligated, as a journalist trying to do his work faithfully before God, to state my allegiance explicitly or to explain out loud, if you will, what is going on? On the front cover? By page five? By page twenty-five?

After forty years in different aspects of both journalism and education, I've accumulated a few regrets about hurrying too much to get too explicit on the cover, or even on the early pages. One of those regrets has to do with the fact that we really do turn off a lot of people who might otherwise listen for a while if we kept them guessing about our identity. But the other regret has to do with the fact that too often we've announced our Christian identity up front and then gone on to do a shoddy job of whatever it is we are about. It isn't just in journalism, but also in music and art and criticism and science and even philosophy. We call it Christian, we slap a cross or a dove or a fish on it, and call it good when maybe we should be ashamed of what we've created.

But if I have regrets about sometimes announcing my allegiance too soon, I also have regrets about far too many occasions when I never announced my allegiance at all. Here is a sneaky danger that grows right out of the essence of a Reformed perspective on life. If it's true that you can bring glory to God as faithfully by being an attorney or an oncologist as by being a missionary nurse or a pastor or a Christian school teacher—and that is indeed absolutely true—and if it's true that a big part of that faithfulness is in being an absolutely excellent attorney or oncologist, and not simply one who uses his or her profession as a platform for witness—and that is also absolutely true—then we still have to watch out that we not fall into the tricky trap of assuming that our life work, all by itself, is an adequate expression of what we believe.

None of us is good enough at doing what we set out to do in life that the mere quality of our performance, all by itself, will give adequate testimony or explanation of this very personal (and incidentally jealous) God whom we serve. I cannot do a good enough job of reporting, or put out a sufficiently polished magazine, so that such a performance, all by itself, leads people to the Christ who commands such standards. Nor will you be able to do that in any other walk of life.

So, just as we discover a mystical relationship, even a union, between word and deed, and between deed and word, so there is a parallel mystery in the relationship of our task of both living and explaining the word and the deed of the gospel. Neither of them comes alone, nor does either come dominatingly first or with a presumed priority. Even Jesus, the incarnate Word, presented himself both ways and sometimes with perplexing obscurity about just exactly what he was saying and doing.

I had a great friend almost fifty years ago, John M. L. Young, a missionary to Japan, who frequently reminded me that our deeds are necessary to validate the words we say, but our words are essential to explain the deeds we do. Such an understanding may help us through this conundrum.

My own pastor has helped me much as well, and I hope that, by pointing out the difference between the face-to-face relationship of two people who are married and the side-by-side relationship which also fills much of their lives, this might help you too. Wonderful and necessary though the intimacy of being face-to-face might be, it also just might be too intense to live our whole lives that way. So we go away from those face-to-face experiences, where we use words to voice our deepest intimacies, and we head off to do our work, side by side. And the work we find to be good in and of itself, and we don't have to fill the time of our work chattering incessantly about the marvel of what it was like to be face-to-face. We are, of course, still awed by the wonder of the face-to-face, and we anticipate the experience of that wonder again sometime soon, but we're happy nonetheless in the fulfillment that we also get from being side by side. The side by side interaction is not therefore somehow second best;

nor is the face-to-face that which we wish we could have all the time. We come instead to glory in the appropriateness of each.

So it is between us and our God, who deliberately calls us part of the time to a sort of rapture over his love for us and our explicit response to him for all he has done. But then he also calls us for portions of our time to glory in his works of creation and providence just for the wonder of them, and with no special need to fill the air with artificial God-words.

May we all be filled, of course, with wonderful face-to-face experiences with our great God. But may that filling also include the glory he allows us as we labor side by side with him as coworkers in his kingdom. And I hope and pray as well that we will not be daunted and frustrated by the tension he has deliberately established between these two kinds of activity. May we all be found faithful as we walk that wonderful tightwire—both in living out this delicate balance and in telling others about it as well.

3

Parents as Covenant Mediators in Deuteronomy[1]

IN THE CONTEXT OF God's covenant, what is the specific role of parents concerning their children?[2] How does this role qualify itself as a covenant? In this regard, the marital union between a man and a woman is called a "covenant" (Prov 2:7; Mal 2:14).[3] Specifically, what connection exists between this parental role and the covenant of grace? Scripture affirms: "I will establish my covenant between me and you, and to your offspring after you" (Gen 17:7) and "For the promise is for you and for your children" (Acts 2:39; cf. Acts 13:32–33). If it is through a covenant promise that God reaches out to the children then how, on a practical level, can parents help their children to enter it?

The covenant has been established by God, on a horizontal level, to administer and conduct the life of his people. Regulating the relationship

---

1. Both as friend and minister, Rob has had a great impact on my life. His encouragement and counsel led to my ordination in the Presbytery of the Pacific Northwest given the seminary teaching ministry I was already engaged in. Later, his generous hand in raising support led, through the organization Mission to the World, to France and, following a two-year internship with a French pastor, to Aix-en-Provence as Professeur d'Hébreu et d'Ancien Testament at the Faculté Jean Calvin. I trust that, through my ministry, Rob's blessing to me will extend to God's people in France and elsewhere in the French-speaking world.

2. This essay is a translation, with minor changes, of a seminar paper later published under the title "Les parents comme médiateurs de l'alliance dans le Deutéronome," in *La Revue réformée* 63.4 (2012) 1–8. That essay developed an earlier paper read for a public conference, Carrefour Théologique, held at La Faculté Jean Calvin, in Aix-en-Provence, in the spring of 2002 on the theme of "Covenant and Family," subsequently published as "L'alliance et la famille au travers de l'Ancien Testament," *La Revue réformée* 53.5 (2002) 1–12. Thanks are due to Lionel Jauvert for his initial translation of the article.

3. These texts read together show that the covenant is bilateral, with commitments taken by both parties.

between the members of the covenantal communities requires mediators, because living together, as shown by the story of God's people, is not always easy. This is also true, vertically viewed, of their relationship with him! Therefore, God raised between himself and his people mediators, anointed ones, prophets, priests, and kings. Life within the family is not without problems, itself a reason why the ministry of mediator is needed within the household.

The mediator's role is to maintain the relationships between the members of a community. In a society organized with several levels of paternity—family, clan, and tribe—God initially entrusted this mediating mission to parents, particularly the fathers. Mediation works first within the family; it is not limited to this aspect, but the family is the first link in God's chain of mediation between him and his people. Since God has raised other mediators of the covenant, what is the nature of the role entrusted to parents?

There is a striking resemblance to priestly mediation. It is clear, however, that there is a fundamental difference between this priesthood, which can be described as parental, and the mediation of classical priesthood. For the latter, mediation takes place mainly within the framework of worship. Priests have a religious mission that is accomplished within ceremonial institutions. The word of God, essential to worship, is institutionally bound. Thus, priests exercise their ministries of mediation at a specific time and in a localized way, particularly at sacred celebrations of pilgrimage to the sanctuary (Deut 31:9–13; Neh 8).

So how is the gap bridged between home and sanctuary, and between daily life and sacred celebrations punctuating the year, if not by the parents who extend this role of mediation in the home every day. The specific role of parents in the family is parallel with the priestly ministries of mediation.

1. Mediation Through Teaching

The primary ministry of priestly mediation is the teaching of the Word. This didactic service was entrusted to priests: "They shall teach [Hebrew *yrh*] Jacob your rules, and Israel your law [Hebrew *torah* < *yrh*].[4] They shall put incense before you, and whole burnt sacrifice on your altar" (Deut 33:10; see also Deut 17:11; 2 Chr 15:3; 17.9; Ezra 7:6, 10; Neh 8). Now, this service

---

4. This verb (Hebrew *yrh*) also means "pointing the finger" at the path, the direction; the latter is the very meaning of *torah* (BDB, 435b). When he arrived in Egypt with his family, Jacob sent Judah to Joseph so that he could show them where they were going to settle in Egypt and direct them there (Hebrew *yrh*; Gen 46:28). This verb also means "to investigate" a judicial record against someone (Deut 17:10–11; 24:8), then to "instruct" the law.

is at work in the family, as the father and mother also exercise it: "These words . . . you shall teach to your children" (Deut 11:18–19; cf. Exod 13:8–9; Deut 4:9–10; 6:6–7; 8:5; Prov 1:8; 6:20; 31:1). The emphasis, in this passage and in others, is put on the ordinary, daily task: "You shall teach [these words] diligently to your children, and you shall talk of them when you sit in your house . . . when you lie down, and when you rise" (Deut 6:6–7; 11:19).[5] It is ongoing, *in situ* instruction which was not possible for priests.

Deuteronomy and Proverbs, entrust the role of mediation equally to the father and the mother, a matter which is not unrelated to the marriage covenant mentioned above. Their equal parental authority summarized in the fifth commandment (Deut 5:16): "Honor your father and your mother"—with the corresponding penalty in the event of infringement—"cursed be anyone one who dishonors his father or his mother" (Deut 27:16; cf. 22:15; 27:26; 33:9). Regarding the children, this role equality concerning their instruction is expressed in the book of Proverbs as follows: "My son, keep your father's commandment [Hebrew *mitsvah*], and forsake not your mother's teaching [Hebrew *torah*]" (Prov 6:20). Martin Luther perceives and summarizes this idea very well when he writes, "But the greatest good in married life . . . is that God grants offspring and commands that they be brought up to worship and serve him. . . . Most certainly *father* and *mother* are apostles, bishops, and priests to their children, for it is they who make them acquainted with the gospel."[6]

The father to whom his son asks (Deut 6:20) "What is the meaning . . . of the rules that the Lord has commanded you?" will have a twofold answer to give him: First (vv. 21–23), "The Lord brought us out of Egypt," and second (v. 24), "the Lord commanded us to do all these statutes . . . for our good always, that he might preserve us alive, as we are this day." The father's words do not seem to answer the son's question. They stress the grace of deliverance and the benevolence of the Lord toward those who obey him. In the end, the law itself is a grace for those who make the Lord their God, for the practice of the law delivers from evil: it is the source of happiness and life. This is the profound meaning of the instructions highlighted by the father's answer. The pedagogy of the father is well suited to

---

5. Cf. Deut 4:9–10: "Only take care, and keep your soul diligently, lest you forget the things that your eyes have seen, and lest they depart from your heart all the days of your life. Make them known [hiphil of Hebrew *yd'*] to your children and your children's children—how on the day that you stood before the LORD your God at Horeb, the LORD said to me, 'Gather the people to me, that I may let them hear my words, so that they may learn to fear me all the days they live on the earth, and that they may teach [piel of Hebrew *lmd*] their children so.'"

6. Luther, *Christian in Society*, 46 (emphasis added).

the youth who often reacts negatively to the idea of having to follow rules. This father does not insist here on the implementation of the law, but on the object of the Torah, which shows the path of life.[7]

2. Sacramental Mediation

The second priestly ministry of mediation is sacramental. Sacraments illustrate divine actions. The priests preside over rites and liturgies at festivals, and at the sacrifices (Deut 33:10; 1 Chr 23:31). Like the priest, the father also exercises a sacramental ministry. Some rites, such as circumcision (Gen 17:26; 21:4; Exod 4:25—in which Zipporah, Moses' wife, circumcised their son!), Passover (Exod 12:3) and the redemption of the firstborn (Exod 12:11-16) were practiced within the family. The father has the task of answering, at home, questions asked by children about the meaning of things ritually symbolized: "And when your children say to you, 'What do you mean by this service?' you shall say" (Exod 12:26-27; 13:14; Deut 6:20-24; Josh 4:6-7, 21-23). The father presides over these rites that highlight the divine work. He leads all his family to the pilgrimage (1 Sam 1:3-7). He offers sacrifices for his children (Job 1:5).

The offering of prayers is among the priestly responsibilities. According to 2 Chronicles, "Hezekiah appointed the divisions of the priests and of the Levites, division by division . . . for burnt offerings . . . to give thanks and praise" (2 Chr 31:2; cf. Ps 50:14, 23). The writer of Hebrews exhorts his audience (Heb 13:15): "Through him then let us continually offer up a sacrifice of praise to God, that is, the fruit of lips that acknowledge his name." Parents have the great responsibility to intercede for their children. The prayer of intercession can be defined as follows: to apply God's attributes and promises to the matter calling for prayer. Following the incident of the golden calf, the Lord threatened to destroy his people (Exodus 32). As a mediator,

---

7. One point that deserves to be developed is the trans-generational responsibility of education. Some verses are pointing to the transmission of the faith to three generations: "teach them *to your children and the children of your children*" (Deut 4:9, emphasis added). The responsibility to learn also falls to the children: "Remember the days of old, consider the years of many generations; ask *your father*, and he will show you, *your elders*, and they will tell you" (Deut 32:7, emphasis added; cf. Ps. 71:18). Culturally, these exhortations view the nuclear family as multigenerational. This same injunction applies to the new covenant prophesied by Isaiah (59:21): "And as for me, this is my covenant with them, says the LORD: My Spirit that is upon you, and my words that I have put in your mouth, shall not depart out of your mouth, or out of the mouth of your offspring, or out of the mouth of your children's offspring, says the LORD, from this time forth and forevermore." We also note here the inseparable link between the Spirit of God and the word.

Moses brought to bear God's gracious saving character and promises made to Abraham and his descendants upon the grave situation of the people (vv. 11–13). The Lord thereupon overturned the decreed judgment on the people (v. 14) because, by doing so, he acted in accordance with his gracious character and his promise, and remained faithful to his covenant. Psalm 106:23 relates this incident:

> Therefore, he said he would destroy them—
> Had not Moses, his chosen one,
> stood in the breach before him,
> to turn away his wrath from destroying them.

The key promise concerning children is recalled when the law was given: "Showing steadfast love to thousands of those who love me and keep my commandments" (Exod 20:6; Deut 5:10). Yet this promise goes back to the covenant established with Abraham:

> He remembers his covenant forever,
> the word that he commanded, for a thousand generations,
> the covenant that he made with Abraham,
> his sworn promise to Isaac. (Ps 105:8–9; cf. 1 Chr 16:6–17).

Parents, in their prayers of intercession, are assured of the merciful character of God and his covenant promises to their children. This promise invites parents to pray not only for their children but also for the spiritual blessing of future generations.

3. Mediation Through Discipline

The role of priests is included in a collection of laws relating to civil and religious authorities (Deut 16:18—18:22). Sacerdotal mediation includes as its third element the prerogative to pronounce judgments: "Then the priest, the sons of Levi, shall come forward, for the LORD your God has chosen them to minister . . . by their word every dispute and every assault shall be settled" (Deut 21:5; cf. 17:8–13; 21:5; Ezek 44:23–24). In the family, parents are invested with this same authority. It is summarized in the fifth commandment. This requirement is central to all laws relating to the respect due to mediating authorities, which extends the scope of the fifth commandment. Daily respect for parents extends to all authorities, civil authorities, judges, and kings, or religious authorities, priests, and prophets.

Parents not only have the right to apply correction, but also judgment (Deut 21:18-21). Severe sanctions reinforce the respect due to parents. Juvenile rebellion is punishable by capital punishment (v. 21). Parents who were in the tragic situation of not being able to control their child, though they had tried to correct him, had to decide his unhappy fate and bring it to the place of judgment.[8] The same sanction against the rebellious son applies to the one who refuses to act in accordance with the judgment of the priest (Deut 17:13). The collateral and corroborating roles of priests and parents is evident in this matter, since one party could not act independently of the other.

4. Mediation of the Blessing

Fourthly, the priestly mediation is crowned with the duty of blessing. God, the author of the covenant, blessed his work of creation. He blessed the couple, male and female, by granting fertility and power to steward the created world. The ultimate object of priestly mediation is the divine blessing. As mediators, the priests pronounce the blessing on the people to cause the divine grace sown by their services to grow: "Then the priests, the sons of Levi, shall come forward, for the Lord your God has chosen them to bless in the name of the Lord" (Deut 21:5; cf. Num 6:32-37).

To raise his children in the knowledge of the Lord, fathers (like Abraham, Isaac, and Jacob) pronounce the divine blessing upon them (Gen 27:48-49; 28:1, 3-4; 48:15; 49:1). Jacob even blessed his grandchildren (Gen 48:9-20). The blessing crowns all other parental ministries. Transmitted to the child who honors his father and mother, the benediction according to the Decalogue leads to a long and happy life (Exod 20:12; Deut 5:16). The same blessing of longevity is promised to parents who transmit such a faith (Deut 11:21). As the promise at the heart of the Abrahamic covenant shows, the blessed family is a source of physical and spiritual blessing for all the clans (Hebrew *mishpahot*) of the earth (Gen 12:2-3). This blessing, transmitted from generation to generation, extends to all levels from kinship to families, to clans and tribes, and to the nation thus composed. It is the blessing, through the mediation between God and Israel, that allows the people of the covenant to enjoy a fullness of life onto eternal life (Ps 133:3; Acts 3:25; Gal 3:8-9, 13-14).

---

8. Deut 21:18-19: "If a man has a stubborn and rebellious son who will not obey the voice of his father or the voice of his mother, and, though they discipline him, will not listen to them, then his father and his mother shall take hold of him and bring him out to the elders of his city at the gate of the place where he lives."

By way of conclusion, we may affirm that parents, by the instrumentality of these ministries of sacerdotal order—word, sacrament, authority, and blessing—function as covenant mediators within the family, a great service among the people of God. Far from circumventing or competing with the mediation of priests under the old covenant, God raised up, in a complementary way, the mediation of parents. This remains a sacred mission, vital to the growth of the church. Parents who endeavor to fill this role firmly build their homes on the unshakable foundations of God's covenant. Thus, the knowledge of the covenant, with its responsibilities and privileges, is transmitted from one generation to another.

4

Ministry After Christ

The Long-Term Pastorate

THE BEST WAY TO improve[1] the example of a faithful minister is by imitation. And while it would be grossly oversimple to describe decades of committed ministry in Tacoma as one shepherd's mere mimicry of his own pastor,[2] Scotland's footprints can certainly be traced in America's Pacific Northwest today.[3]

William Still had been the pastor of Gilcomston South Church of Scotland since VE Day in 1945 when the Rayburns arrived in Aberdeen to worship, work and study in the mid-1970s. He was minister of that single congregation for over fifty years until shortly before his death in 1997. "The

---

1. In the old sense of the word, e.g., *WLC* 167: How is our baptism to be improved by us?

2. Dr. Rayburn (or "Rob," as I must call him) still speaks fondly of "my pastor in Aberdeen, Scotland, William Still" (e.g., Rayburn, "Miscellany," para. 1). He says, "I got great help from my pastor and preacher, William Still, during those three years in Scotland in the mid-70s" (Rayburn, "Studies in the Book of Kings," para. 35). He is not, however, entirely uncritical of his mentor's ministry: "One of the features of the late William Still's ministry in Aberdeen, Scotland . . . was a purposefully Spartan church program. They had services twice on Sunday, a Bible study Wednesday night, and a three-hour prayer meeting on Saturday night. They had little else in the way of church meetings. They didn't have a women's group or a men's group, a young people's group, or even what we would think of as a Sunday School. Mr. Still was against these things and efforts on the part of well-meaning church members to start them were quietly squelched. Now, I'm not saying that I agree with that or that the church didn't even suffer for the want of some of those ministries. But it is noteworthy that Mr. Still had a very definite philosophy of Christian ministry to which he appealed in justifying this very simple approach to church life" (Rayburn, "Retirement," para. 4).

3. "As many of you know, our Wednesday evening prayer meeting was modeled after the prayer meeting Florence and I encountered at Gilcomston South Church of Scotland in Aberdeen between 1975 and 1978" (Rayburn, "Colossians," para. 6).

central task of his life, to which he devoted both his love and his energy, was pastoring his congregation."[4]

Members of Mr. Still's congregation have not been the only beneficiaries of his ministry: "Many ministers owe much to his counsel and example. Many 'lay' people received their grounding in the faith through him, and many world-wide retain their links with 'Gilc.' established during their time in Aberdeen."[5] What caused Mr. Still's ministry to go both deep and wide for the sake of God's kingdom? Certainly, as one observes, "he followed in the footsteps of the Good Shepherd who knew his sheep and cared for them."[6] But another might wish to argue that it was his long-term commitment to a single parish that rendered his ministry so effective. Upon closer observation, however, these two amount to a distinction without a difference.

It was precisely through persevering in the footsteps of the Good Shepherd, wielding the shepherd's rod and staff on the same familiar wind-blown pasture, that Mr. Still both knew and cared for the sheep divinely assigned to his flock. His intimate knowledge of the sheep rose from long bearing them as lambs in his bosom. His pastoral care was the paint that splashed with vivid depth and color the pastoral landscape. This landscape filled a single seamless canvas requiring a frame five decades wide to exhibit its beauty, displayed on the cobbled streets of a city otherwise known for its uniformly grey granite architecture. Who could have anticipated while the Artist was halfway through his strokes in Aberdeen that from his brush a drop would be launched across an ocean and a continent to a place nicknamed "The City of Destiny," on Washington State's Puget Sound, to grow into another grand work, similar in breadth, depth and length?

But Still's long pastorate was no novelty to Scotland or to the Reformed Church in general. In the mid- and late-nineteenth century, Alexander Moody Stuart was for forty-four years the pastor of Free St. Luke's Church of Scotland in Edinburgh, and Alexander Whyte,[7] after a short associate pastorate

---

4. Ferguson, "Foreword," 7.

5. Lyall, "Introduction," 13. Ferguson ("Foreword," 8) adds that "through his influence on many students for the ministry, his frequent speaking to student groups, and perhaps especially through the way he quietly trained his people by example and encouragement to pray for the work of pastors through the world, William Still also became a *pastor pastorum*, a pastor of other pastors." In this, too, Rob Rayburn has followed in the footsteps of his own pastor, being called by one of the elders of Faith Presbyterian Church in Tacoma "a pastor to pastors" because of the number of ministers who regularly seek his personal counsel and benefit from his sermons.

6. Ferguson, "Foreword," 7.

7. Whyte, the Scottish Presbyterian pastor who died in 1921, is often heralded in his sermons and addresses as one of Rob's heroes. See, e.g., Rayburn, "Ministry by the

in Glasgow, became the minister of Free St. George's, Edinburgh, where he remained for the next forty-five years. "Whyte as a young divinity student was what we would call nowadays an intern under Moody Stuart."[8]

These men's names are linked to the places they served as Samuel Rutherford's will ever be to Anwoth (his only pastorate), Richard Baxter's to Kidderminster, Thomas Boston's to Ettrick, and John Bunyan's to Bedford. Robert Murray McCheyne died a young man while serving his St. Peter's, Dundee congregation, to which his name is forever fixed, but even in his relatively short pastorate he demonstrated an unwavering commitment to that congregation's spiritual welfare, too deep to be broken by enticements to leave them in order to pursue more impressive charges. "He died their minister and, no doubt, would have died their minister had he lived fifty more years."[9] Long-term ministries like these, not limited to Scottish Presbyterianism,[10] are rightly held before a rising generation of pastors as faithful ministries to be improved by imitation.[11]

Alas, the lesson seems to be falling flat in our generation, or at least failing to make a wide mark on modern ministry. Lengthy pastorates are now the exception, while the norm has become a series of short, serial pastorates lasting often just a few years each. Men move from pulpit to pulpit, only ever laying shallow roots that are easily plucked and transplanted several times over the course of a pastor's life as he jumps, family in tow, from one pasture to another and from one flock to another.

Rather than steadfast shepherds, transient ranch hands may be a more accurate, if tragic, metaphor to describe the majority of modern American ministers. Congregants are correspondingly prodded through the chutes of programs that abruptly change direction according to the latest pastor's unique vision, rather than finding green pastures and still waters under the gentle and consistent leadership of a shepherd who is well acquainted with their tender souls.

Generation," delivered at Covenant Theological Seminary in 1996 as part of the Joseph Ruggles Wilson Preaching Lectures.

8. Rayburn, "Mystery," para. 18.

9. Rayburn, "Ministry by the Generation," 13:19.

10. One thinks of ministries like that of evangelical Anglican Charles Simeon, who occupied the pulpit of Holy Trinity Church in Cambridge for fifty-four years, or Baptists Alexander MacLaren, who in 1905 finished a forty-five year ministry at Union Chapel in Manchester, and Charles Spurgeon, pastor of New Park Street Church (later named the Metropolitan Tabernacle) for thirty-eight years until his death in 1892 at the age of fifty-seven.

11. This is not to imply that men are never called by the Lord to shorter ministries, nor that such ministries are somehow unfaithful or untrue because of their relative brevity.

As a consequence, instability and a proneness to division often mar the lives of churches whose pastors continually pass through revolving doors. The pattern perpetuates itself as the expectation of ministers begins to align with the congregations' understanding that they hold the right to retain or reject ministers the way that Pharisees divorced their marriage partners "for any reason" (Matt 19:3). Previously disappointed congregations become jaded, keeping their pastors at arm's length from their hearts lest they suffer the sting of yet another shepherd's pious departure for greener, larger, pastures in order to "expand his usefulness to the Church."[12] Meanwhile, energy that might be given to the work of advancing the kingdom is expended instead on the seemingly perpetual displacing and replacing of ministers.

Forgetful of history, we fail to appreciate the vast difference between our current practice and not-so-distant past experience, particularly of churches that identify themselves with the Reformation. David Wells observes that

> the most remarkable thing about pastoral life in the eighteenth century was the extent to which pastors and their communities were bonded together. For example, of the 221 graduates of Yale College between 1745 and 1775 who went into the ministry, 71% remained in the church to which they were first called until their deaths. Only 4 percent held four or more pastorates. By contrast, today the average pastoral stint is as low as two years in some areas and denominations and seldom more than three years. Lying between the eighteenth century and our own is a cluster of steadily declining graph lines indicating shorter and shorter tenures, growing pastoral impermanence, and increasingly shallow bonds between pastors and their churches.[13]

To be sure, there are many factors that contributed to this major shift and to the current state of affairs. Wells goes on to note, for example, that

> Impermanence has become one of the defining characteristics of the twentieth century. It is a thread that is impossible to remove from the fabric of modern life. It runs through our relationships to place, through vocation, through the manufactured goods

---

12. One hates to admit such things publicly, but temptation, being common to men (1 Cor 10:13), renders ministers susceptible to the siren call of careerism in which churches all too easily and often may become stepping stones to "success." Eugene Peterson laments, "Somehow we American pastors, without really noticing what was happening, got our vocations redefined in the terms of American careerism. We quit thinking of the parish as a location for pastoral spirituality and started thinking of it as an opportunity for advancement" (*Under the Unpredictable Plant*, 20).

13. Wells, *No Place for Truth*, 228.

we use, through our families. One of the most deeply ingrained features of modern experience is the belief that nothing lasts, so most people find it quite natural that churches and their ministers should constantly be seeking different partners.[14]

But, of course, the church and her ministers must march to the beat of a higher drum, working not under the bondage of culture—particularly as that culture rebels against God and reaps the bitter fruit that it sows—but rather transforming the culture through the gospel of Christ by the power of the Holy Spirit. Transformation, not conformation, is the clarion call of Scripture to all Christians, clergy and laity alike, who would more and more think Christ's thoughts after him and, taking their thoughts captive to Christ, live as followers of Christ (Rom 12:2; 2 Cor 10:5; Prov 23:7).

Happily, recognition of the deficiencies of our current state and need for reformation in the matter of pastoral tenures is beginning to awaken. One pastor concludes his doctoral dissertation by asserting that "the *long-term* pastorate is consistent with the Scriptural view of the pastorate itself."[15] Popular scholars are giving voice to the view that "in a day when fewer and fewer Christians commit themselves to *long-term pastorates*, career missions, lifetime service as elders or deacons, or other multi-year ministries, we need people who will make such commitments to Christ and to a particular local body of believers."[16] Even Methodist bishops are beginning to keep ministers in their pulpits for noticeably longer periods of time rather than moving them every couple of years, as had been the prevailing practice, having come to recognize the stabilizing factor of longer pastoral terms for both pulpit and pew.[17]

Some careful thought about the role of the Christian minister as the chief local representative and instrument of the servant-Savior after whom he is named will surely help us recognize the fitting nature and usefulness

---

14. Wells, *No Place for Truth*, 249.

15. Welden, "Long-Term Pastorate," 107.

16. Blomberg, *1 Corinthians*, 189 (emphasis added). Eugene Peterson adds, "But the *norm* for pastoral work is stability. Twenty-, thirty-, and forty-year-long pastorates should be typical among us (as they once were) and not exceptional. Far too many pastors change parishes out of adolescent boredom, not as a consequence of mature wisdom. When this happens, neither pastors nor congregations have access to the conditions that are hospitable to maturity in the faith" (*Under the Unpredictable Plant*, 29).

17. Para. 429 of the 2012 *Book of Discipline of the United Methodist Church* states with regard to pastoral appointments that "Appointments are made with the expectation that the length of pastorates shall respond to the long-term pastoral needs of charges, communities, and pastors. *The bishop and cabinet should work toward longer tenure in local church appointments to facilitate a more effective ministry*" (emphasis added).

of long-term pastorates. Ministry after Christ, that is, not only after the fashion, but as the hands-and-feet of Christ, will faithfully reflect and resemble, in every way possible, the Chief Shepherd's own ministry. Should not the hands and feet operate in concordance with the Head? Should not the undershepherd's ministry match that of the Chief Shepherd's, not only in matter but in manner (viz., for the long-term)?

Here one might anticipate the objection that Christ's ministry lasted only three years, and therein the short-term pastorate finds a divine imprimatur, but that would be a misunderstanding. His incarnate ministry is but the tip of the iceberg that stretches, beneath the surface of time, all the way back to the Garden of Eden and forward to the New Jerusalem. Christ's is the ultimate long-term pastorate. The Word through whom all things were made in the beginning is also the Lord God who planted Eden and formed and placed our first father there. He is the "I Am" who met with Moses in a flaming bush at Horeb. It was Jesus, writes Jude,[18] who saved a people out of the land of Egypt and who, according to Paul, accompanied them through the wilderness (1 Cor 10:4). Christ has been steadfastly shepherding his flock from time immemorial and continues to do so until the day he personally escorts his sheep into the next life.[19] Undershepherds who would minister after Christ do well to improve his example by persevering in their charges.

While there are several offices which Christ is pleased to exercise mediatorially through his church officers that contain an element of permanence,[20] it is to the metaphor of shepherd that Scripture appeals most widely and often with regard to ministers. It is worthy of note that this metaphor is applied to both Christ[21] and his representatives[22] before, during, and after the incarnation.

What qualities of a true shepherd commend to us a lengthy, rather than shorter pastorate? Among others, certainly a fundamental confidence, contentment and commitment are basic to faithful ministry after Christ.

---

18. Some translations retain "the Lord" in Jude 5, but Metzger points out that "Critical principles seem to require the adoption of *Iēsous*, which admittedly is the best attested reading among Greek and versional witnesses" (*Commentary*, 657). Cf. Green, *Jude & 2 Peter*, 64–65, 77–78.

19. John 1:1–3; Gen 2:7–8; Exod 3:14; cf. John 8:58; 1 Cor 10:4; Matt 25:31–46; 28:20.

20. Christ as priest, prophet, king, father, brother, etc., are all worthy of further study as informing pastoral tenure, as are metaphors employed for Christ such as rock, fortress, husband, etc.

21. Ps 23; John 10:11–30; Heb 13:20; Isa 40:11; Jer 31:10; Rev 7:17.

22. Isa 63:11; Jer 3:15; 23:1–4; Ezek 34; John 21:15–17; Eph 4:11; 1 Pet 5:1–4.

CONFIDENCE

There are divers and sundry reasons why a minister's confidence might be shaken while laboring in the particular pasture in which he finds himself. Difficult circumstances, difficult sheep, and even personal problems may cause a shepherd to question his placement in the kingdom.[23] On occasion, his eye may stray to greener-looking meadows and sleeker flocks. Here a robust confidence in the precision of God's providence in the placement of his shepherds according to his determined plan (Acts 17:26) will greatly aid a shepherd to persevere in tending the flock (1 Pet 5:1–2).

Although there was a time when the congregation in Ettrick so treasured their pastor, the famed seventeenth-century Thomas Boston, that they actually called a congregational fast to pray against a call that had come to him from another, more influential church,[24] it had not always been so. In the early years of that charge, it was likely the bare conviction that God had called him to Ettrick that carried Boston through the resentment and resistance with which he met in that country parish. Eight years into his Ettrick pastorate he confessed to his wife that "his heart was alienated from his people because of their stubborn refusal to heed the Word of God from his lips."[25]

Scottish minister and theologian John Brown of Haddington, out of concern for what he quaintly called the "transportation of ministers," commended "earnest prayer for the Lord's special direction in the choice of pastors" in a sermon he preached in 1782 because "it encourageth both minister and people to hope for the Lord's presence and blessing on their connection. Notwithstanding their respective shares of the afflictions of the gospel, *the minister's heart quietly trusts that God sent him to the place*; and the people look on him as the messenger of the Lord of hosts to them."[26]

Trusting that the Chief Shepherd makes no mistakes in the assignment of his shepherds to their fields, a minister may confidently obey the Lord right where he has been placed, leaving the results to God. In this way, the

---

23. Of course, a minister must provide for his family's needs, which may present him with the necessity of considering a move in order to fulfill this fundamental duty (1 Tim 5:8) if no reasonable arrangements can be secured in a particular situation.

24. Boston, for his part, actually fought against the courts of the church from Presbytery to General Assembly to resist that call.

25. Rayburn, "Ministry by the Generation," 4:17.

26. Brown, *Necessity and Advantage of Earnest Prayer*, 18 (emphasis added).

faithful shepherd is also an example to the flock (1 Pet 5:3). And examples are, by nature, best observed over long periods of time.[27]

Congregational flocks benefit greatly by watching the example of their pastor in his youth, middle age, and autumn years and, if married, in the way he loves his wife, children, and grandchildren through all the changing scenes of life. He is divinely summoned to lead his congregation by both the confident proclamation of the word and the confidence of his life of faith and obedience under the various trials and triumphs that he will doubtlessly meet. By *persisting* in these, Paul says to young pastor Timothy, he saves both himself and his hearers (1 Tim 4:16).

CONTENTMENT

Remote from towns he ran his godly race,
Nor e'er had changed, nor wished to change his place.

The quote above is Oliver Goldsmith's description of the faithful and contented rural pastor in his poem *The Deserted Village*.[28] It may be of little coincidence that the line "there is great gain in godliness *with contentment*" was first addressed to a minister (1 Tim 6:6–8)! This is the discipline that all shepherds after Christ must learn. Many otherwise faithful pastorates have been dismantled by discontentment, and many regretful "transportations" have hinged on it. But a faithful minister must deny himself, take up his cross daily, and follow Christ, learning in whatever situation he is to be content (Luke 9:23; Phil 4:11).

The Chief Shepherd in the days of his incarnation was content to make for his parish the obscure dusty roads of jerkwater villages on the outskirts of the Roman Empire. At one point in his earthly ministry, a great portion of his followers abandoned him over a single sermon, and in the end he was abandoned by all (John 6:66; Mark 14:50). Yet he remained content to do the Father's will (John 4:34; 6:38). Ministry after Christ requires the same filial contentment.

27. Cf. Welden, "Long-Term Pastorate," 101; see also Rayburn: "Churches need to be able to watch their ministers grow up into spiritual manhood and maturity, to ripen and sweeten before their eyes. They need to learn from them how to avoid the deep ruts of spiritual mediocrity, how to detect when the fire is cooling and how to stoke it hot again. They need fully formed graces to admire" ("Ministry by the Generation," 22:37).

28. Curiously, a controversy (rather a tempest in a teapot) developed between a certain "evangelical" publication and *The Orthodox Churchman's Magazine* (January–June, 1802) over whether Goldsmith was referring in his poem to a Methodist dissenting preacher or a parish priest, the argument turning on the supposed long-term commitment of the latter versus the former.

It will help the local pastor to remember that it is not fame but faithfulness, not earthly treasures but heavenly, that weigh on the scales of eternity. All else is but dust and dung. In the end, the words "well done, good and faithful servant" will swell and flood the heart of the pastor who was content in this life to serve the Lord in the place and under the circumstances that divine wisdom dictated.[29]

Such a one is William Gouge, who is best known as a celebrated member of the Westminster Assembly. He pastored his congregation at St. Ann, Blackfriars in London for forty-six years until his death in 1653. He is buried in the church. Unsurprisingly, his star was given many opportunities and invitations to shine from more prominent places within the Puritan galaxy. "His usual saying was that it was his highest ambition to go 'from Blackfriars to Heaven.'"[30]

> *Content to fill a little space,*
> *If Thou be glorified.*

In this, too, a minister is an example to the flock he serves. How may the sheep be expected to practice contentment in their respective stations if their shepherd will not be content in his own?[31]

COMMITMENT

A third mark of true ministry after Christ is commitment to the flock. Mixing metaphors a bit, Lynn Anderson, preaching minister at Highland Church of Christ in Abilene from 1971 to 1990, explained his longevity with a single church in an article entitled "Why I've Stayed": "Ministry, like marriage, finds its fulfillment in faithfulness. Marriage vows are intended to last until death brings separation; a ministerial covenant does not imply such

---

29. Brown points out that "Messrs Wm. Guthrie of Finwick (sic.) and T. Boston of Etterick, notwithstanding their obscure settlements, have been more useful in the church of Christ, than multitudes who have been fixed in far more large and conspicuous charges" (*Necessity and Advantage of Earnest Prayer*, 6).

30. White, *Churches and Chapels*, 33.

31. In his commentary on Psalm 131:1, Calvin says: "In this he teaches us a very useful lesson, and one by which we should be ruled in life—to be contented with the lot which God has marked out for us, to consider what he calls us to, and not to aim at fashioning our own lot—to be moderate in our desires, to avoid entering upon rash undertakings, and to confine ourselves cheerfully within our own sphere" (*Commentary on the Psalms*, 3.138).

sacred permanence. Nevertheless, when a shepherd is called to a covenant with a flock, that union is not to be terminated lightly."[32]

Would that the majority of modern shepherds held the same conviction! Ministers typically enter their office with vows to be zealous and faithful to their charge whatever persecution or opposition may arise, promising to discharge the duties of a pastor.[33] Such vows cannot be lightly dismissed; though, alas, pastors too often do just that. And, far too often, they are allowed to act more like hirelings (John 10:12–13) than shepherds by their passive fellow presbyters, bishops, or congregations who should instead encourage and assist the local pastor to remain steadfast in service at his post, plotting the coordinates of his course by the map of Scripture and navigating by Christ as the North Star. This is not to say, of course, that all ministers must remain in the first church they serve in order to be faithful, but who can doubt the benefits that would derive from long, fully committed pastorates becoming the majority? Ministers and congregations who live long together are forced to mature mutually by the arrangement, going deep in the things of God over time. Preaching in such situations must cover much more of the counsel of God to the benefit of both pulpit and pew.[34]

---

32. Anderson, "Why I've Stayed," 77.

33. See, for example, the 2016 *Book of Church Order of the Presbyterian Church in America*, section 21-5. "When barbarians were overrunning North Africa and preparing to lay siege to Hippo, the city where Augustine served as bishop and pastor, many were fleeing the city. It is reputed that Augustine said, 'It is not right for the shepherd to flee when the flock is left; the priest of God must stay at his post.'" So Welden, "Long-Term Pastorate," 29–30, citing Horne, *Forty Years*, 25.

34. Stuart remarks: "There must for a lengthened ministry be spiritual growth, and therefore spiritual variety. If there is the same man in the pulpit, with the same people in the pews for many years, there is a great risk of his rehearsing the same thought to unimpressed listeners. Now, while reading and study and other means are necessary to variety, and largely conducive to it, there is nothing so helpful as personal spiritual growth, because there is no such sameness as the sameness of death. Life is variety, death is sameness. A minister should also seek indefatigably to be an example to his people and ought therefore to aim at being the holiest man in his congregation; the meekest, the lowliest, the kindest, the most joyful, most watchful, most prayerful, the strongest in faith, the liveliest in hope, the highest above self, the nearest to God and to heaven, the purest or the least spotted image of our Lord Jesus Christ" (*Alexander Moody Stuart*, 271). The late Dr. James Montgomery Boice, pastor of the historic Tenth Presbyterian Church of Philadelphia for thirty-two years until his death at sixty-one years of age in 2000, revealed a struggle common to ministers who persevere in the same church: "Over the years, it has been my privilege as a pastor preaching at the normal worship services of a local church to come repeatedly to the Christmas season and explore the Christmas story in a variety of ways. I confess that at times I have approached this task reluctantly, particularly in later years. I have wondered, having preached so many sermons on Luke 2, Matthew 2, and related "Christmas" passages, if I was going to be able to find anything new or even interesting for a congregation

Two things develop between shepherds who minister after Christ by staying with their flocks and the sheep under their care. One is intimacy. The sheep come to know and trust their shepherds, and the shepherds, having become deeply acquainted with each individual in the flock, know how best to minister to their sheep (John 10:4, 14).[35] How much more effective is the ministry wherein the shepherds hold the confidence of congregants who know that their pastors, having baptized them, taught them, counselled and preached to them, led them in worship, married them to their spouses, baptized their children and lovingly buried their grandparents are fully invested in their lives!

The other happy development of such ministerial troth will usually be a mutual affection[36] between pulpit and pew that makes obligation sweet and actually tends to perpetuate pastoral longevity. Consider a delightful episode in the life of one of George Whitefield's converts, the Rev. John Fawcett, in the year 1772:

> After he had been a few years in the ministry, his family increasing far more rapidly than his income, he thought it was his duty to accept a call to settle as pastor of a Baptist church in London, to succeed the celebrated Dr. Gill. He preached his farewell sermon to his church in Yorkshire, and loaded six or seven wagons with his furniture, books, etc., to be carried to his new residence. All this time the members of his poor church were almost broken hearted, fervently did they pray that even now he might not leave them; and, as the time for departure arrived, men, women, and children clung around him and his family in perfect agony of soul.

---

that has known those texts from childhood. But I have never been disappointed. I have always found the texts to speak in fresh ways first to me and then also, I hope, to my congregation" (*Christ of Christmas*, 9).

35. Richard Baxter, unpacking the implications of Acts 20:28-29 for ministers, urges: "It is, you see, *all* the flock, or every individual member of our charge. To this end it is necessary, that we should know every person that belongeth to our charge; for how can we take heed to them, if we do not know them? We must labour to be acquainted, not only with the person, but with the state of all our people, with their inclinations and conversations" (*Reformed Pastor*, 90).

36. Brown observes, "With us mutual affection being the great bond of union between a minister and people, it must be much more painful and afflicting to a congregation to have their dearly beloved pastor torn from them by the number or influence of a larger congregation. . . . Fears of such violent tearing away of their pastors, who knows how soon, hinders people to fix their love upon them as they ought; and thus ministers' usefulness, and people's edification, bid fair to be much hindered" (*Necessity and Advantage of Earnest Prayer*, 27).

> The last wagon was being loaded, when the good man and his wife sat down on one of his packing-cases to weep. Looking into his tearful face, while tears like rain fell down her own cheeks, his devoted wife said, "Oh, John, John, I cannot bear this! I know not how to go!" "Nor I, either," said the good man; "nor will we go. Unload the wagons and put everything in the place where it was before." The people cried for joy. A letter was sent to the church in London to tell them that his coming to them was impossible; and the good man buckled on his armor for renewed labors on a salary of less than three hundred dollars a year.
>
> He then took his pen and wrote the words,
>
> > *Blest be the tie that binds*
> > *Our hearts in Christian love.*
>
> as expressive of the golden bond of union that knit pastor and people so closely and tenderly together.[37]

In 1793, Fawcett was invited to become president of the Baptist Academy in Bristol, but he similarly declined and remained committed to the flock at Wainsgate, Yorkshire, for the rest of his active ministry.

Such pastors follow hard after their own dear Shepherd's example of enduring hardships while dying to self for the joy that is set before them.[38] Ministering after Christ with such confidence, contentment, and commitment, devoting themselves to live and die with their flock as providence allows, they enjoy the fruit of their labors in this life and, even more, in the next.

In one of the those engaging glimpses Jesus gives us into glory, we spy the welcoming arms of friends who were made "by means of unrighteous wealth" (Luke 16:9). How much sweeter and more precious must be the heavenly reunion of faithful shepherds and the sheep for whom they righteously spent themselves in this life! "Upon the death of John MacEwan, the faithful old pastor of the congregation in Sliddery in Scotland, one minister commented: 'his work is over and he is happier now. He has crossed the Jordan and dwells in the promised land, and no doubt he will be waiting somewhere near the entrance to see, sooner or later, one of his own flock from Sliddery coming in.'"[39]

---

37. Long, *Illustrated History*, 170–71. The hymn was sung "with great emphasis and significance at the reunion of the Old and New School divisions of the Presbyterian Church, in 1859."

38. See the helpful section entitled "Growing Through Hardships" in Burns et al., *Resilient Ministry*, 44–47.

39. Rayburn, "Ministry by the Generation," 18:07.

How many heavens must Samuel Rutherford's heaven be today, whose heart of love for them overflowed in a letter to his parishioners,[40] from which Anna Cousin poetically channeled the immortal lines:

> *Oh, if one soul from Anwoth,*
> *meet me at God's right hand,*
> *My heaven will be two heavens*
> *in Immanuel's land.*[41]

---

40. "My witness is above; your heaven would be two heavens to me, and the salvation of you all as two salvations to me" (Rutherford, *Letters*, 438–45).

41. Rutherford, *Letters*, 742.

5

Insights from the Westminster Standards for Today's Preaching and Preachers[1]

FOR MANY YEARS A statue of John Knox stood outside St. Giles Church in Edinburgh, Scotland. From the pulpit of St. Giles, the man known as "The Trumpeter of God" heralded the truth of the gospel, braved death to oppose a Catholic monarchy, and led the Reformation whose fruit we are. Yet soot and pollution were allowed to dark-streak the statue, and now the figure appears not only stained, but neglected. The impression is not altogether mistaken or unintended. Most people in the nation of our faith's flowering are now more embarrassed than appreciative of the trumpet calls for truth that once resounded from St. Giles. While gazing on the statue (now more a site for tourists than one of national pride), one cannot help but question how the Reformation that the forsaken statue represents could have any lasting significance. The answer to such a question still trumpets not from the mute figure's lips, but from his fingertips. Long ago, the sculptor determined to depict Knox with the finger of one hand curled into the core of the pages of his Bible, while the finger of the other hand points to the Bible itself. The sculptor portrays what Knox can no longer say, yet what we still believe: "This Word of God is the foundation of our

---

1. The author long-served as president of Covenant Theological Seminary, whose founding president was Robert G. Rayburn, the father of "Rob," the pastor we honor in this Festschrift. I offer thanksgiving to God for President Robert Rayburn, who taught the principles of expository preaching, and for his son, who exemplified the finest of those principles in a long and faithful Tacoma pastorate, and was also my St. Louis Sunday school teacher in my high school years. This essay previously appeared in Covenant Seminary's *Presbyterion* and is republished here in revised form with the author's permission.

faith, the source of truth that will never fail and the fount of hope that does not stain, rust or fade away."

The statue of Knox trumpets the message that the Westminster Standards still echo regarding our preaching: the necessity of the primacy of the Word. Webster's Dictionary describes primacy as "the state of being first in importance." For the Reformers, the primacy of the Word meant that the Bible was the first and final judge of all spiritual matters. In this essay, I will briefly explore *why* the primacy of the Word was so important to the Reformers, then turn to *how* that primacy is expressed in the Westminster Standards.

Competing Primacies

For the Reformers, the primacy of the Word stood in contrast to two other primacies of their era: papal primacy and scholastic primacy.

Papal primacy is articulated in the *Catholic Encyclopedia* in these terms: (a) that St. Peter was Bishop of Rome, and (b) that those who succeed him are also in supreme headship.[2] The primacy of the Pope was, in general terms, the principle that the authority of the Roman prelate not only governed the church, but also was the means by which to interpret Scripture. The church established Scripture, rather than Scripture establishing the church. Tradition—given authority by the station of the Pope as the Vicar of Christ on earth—determined what Scripture should mean, rather than Scripture determining what tradition should be. The Reformation standard of *sola Scriptura* was both derivative of, and twin of, the battle for the primacy of the Word.

The other challenge to the primacy of the Word was the pre-Enlightenment advocacy of the primacy of reason. In Central Europe in the seventeenth and eighteenth centuries, the weight of medieval papal authority was being challenged not only by ecclesiastical Reformers, but also by secular philosophers. Rationalists such as Descartes (1596–1650), Spinoza (1632–1677), and Leibnitz (1646–1716) were dismissing the need of revelation *and* the Spirit in order for truth to be known. Reason was sufficient. And for the empiricists who came after them—Locke (1632–1704), Berkeley (1685–1753), and Hume (1711–1776)—reason, combined with the revelations of experience and observation, would not only unlock truth, but also throw off the shackles of church authority that had kept truth unattainable.

The Reformers' stand for the primacy of the Word was an implicit rejection of both papal and scholastic primacy. Luther, for example, well

---

2. Joyce, "Pope," 260.

expressed the primacy of the Word relative to papal authority when he wrote, "Nor was Christ sent into the world for any other ministry but that of the Word, and the whole spiritual estate, apostles, bishops and all priests, has been called and instituted only for the ministry of the Word."[3] Less often discussed is Luther's parallel understanding of the primacy of the Word over reason: "The mind is unable to judge the truth . . . the mind has been taken captive."[4]

With this Reformation history behind them, the Westminster Divines were determined to express their commitment to the primacy of the Word, and this commitment had specific effects upon what the Standards teach about preaching. In short, the Divines' conviction regarding the primacy of the Word led to a derivative commitment to the primacy of preaching. This primacy of the preached Word was a result of the Divines' understanding of:

1. the primacy of the Word's authority;
2. the primacy of the Word's message; and
3. the primacy of the Word's ministry.

The Primacy of the Word's Authority

For the Divines, the Word's primacy (i.e., supreme status) as a spiritual authority rests on the understanding that the Bible is simply and unequivocally the Word of *God*.

Inherent Authority

Chapter 1 of the *Confession* (note the priority order) lists the many "incomparable excellencies" by which the Bible "doth abundantly evidence itself to be the Word of God" (*WCF* I.5). As the Word of God, the Bible bears inherent authority and needs no other institution to establish or validate its rule over our belief and conduct. The Divines write, "The authority of the Holy Scripture . . . dependeth not on the testimony of any man, or Church, but wholly upon God (who is truth itself) the author thereof" (*WCF* I.4).

Since the Bible has no peer authority, it must be interpreted in light of its own statements. While acknowledging that all matters are not equally clear (*WCF* I.7), the *Confession* says, "The infallible rule of interpretation of Scripture is the Scripture itself" (*WCF* I.9). Then, lest any make the argument

---

3. Luther, *Works*, 2.314–15.
4. Luther, "Pagan Servitude," 341.

that the Bible is true but does not adequately address all the spiritual challenges we face, the Divines add, "The whole counsel of God concerning all things necessary for his own glory, man's salvation, faith and life, is either expressly set down in Scripture, or by good and necessary consequence may be deduced from Scripture" (*WCF* I.6).

Final Authority

Concluding that the Bible is God's authoritative Word regarding *all* things necessary for life and godliness has a foundational implication for our preaching. We must go to God's Word to discern what we must say to God's people. The Bible is the source of our sermons. No other source has sufficient authority or scope to ground our message, neither church tradition nor human reason.

So concerned were the Divines with protecting the unique authority of the Scriptures that they were careful to guard against their own words being used as a final authority. They write, "All synods or councils, since the apostles' times, whether general or particular, may err; and many have erred. Therefore they are not to be made the rule of faith, or practice; but to be used as a help in both" (*WCF* XXXI.4; cf. XXV.5 and XXXI.2). Even where there is controversy, we are required to resort to Scripture to settle the matter. The *Confession* says, "The supreme Judge by which all controversies of religion are to be determined, and all decrees of councils, opinions of ancient writers, doctrines of men, and private spirits, are to be examined, and in whose sentence we are to rest, can be no other but the Holy Spirit speaking in the Scripture" (*WCF* I.10; cf. I.8, XX.2, and *WLC* 3).

Preaching Authority

When we preach from the Bible, we preach with its unique authority; when we do not preach from the Bible, we preach without authority. The Larger and Shorter Catechisms identify "the word, sacraments and prayer" as the "outward and ordinary means whereby Christ communicateth to us the benefits of redemption" (*WSC* 88; *WLC* 154; cf. *WCF* XIV.1). With these statements, the Divines remind us that the presentation of the Word has so much authority that our God and his benefits become as present to the church in preaching as he is in sacrament and prayer. Thus, when we preach apart from his Word, we deny his people his presence in their midst. But, when we preach the truth of his Word, his voice yet resounds in the church.

Thus, we are able to be very bold because we speak the oracles of God, not the traditions or opinions of men.

These emphases of our Standards caution us against the temptation to make any statement of men—even men we greatly respect—the source of our sermons. It is the truth of the Word, and not individuals' or movements' perspectives on the Word, which has the authority of God. We are on slippery ground when we begin to make statements about the Word the subject of our messages instead of the Word itself. Occasionally in Reformed churches where various forms of doctrinal or catechetical formulation are honored—and where there are concerns that our traditions are being lost—there arise movements to make preaching on some feature of the church's historical standards mandatory.[5] This has always backfired. Parsing man's statements rather than Scripture's leads to preoccupation with historical debates about what men meant, rather than authoritative declarations of "Thus saith the Lord." Only the latter is the "outward and ordinary means whereby Christ communicateth to us the benefits of redemption."

Spiritual Authority

The understanding that our Lord presents himself to his people by the Word that we preach also reminds us that the authority that is inherent in the Word is spiritual. The Word is not made effectual by our gifts or arguments, even though reverence for God and his Word requires us to prepare "as one approved, a workman who does not need to be ashamed and who correctly handles the word of truth" (2 Tim 2:15). The Divines emphasize the inherently spiritual nature of the preaching task. Though they say the Word displays its truth by its "many incomparable excellencies," nonetheless "our full persuasion and assurance of the infallible truth, and authority thereof, is from the inward work of the Holy Spirit bearing witness by and with the Word in our hearts" (*WCF* I.5; cf. *WCF* VIII.8 and *WLC* 4).

The Word works only as the Spirit that inspired it impresses the truthfulness of the Word upon the heart of the hearer. Thus, the *Larger Catechism* refuses to allow us to consider the preaching of the Word merely a task of sufficient eloquence or of the mechanics of research and recital. Instead, we

---

5. Robert Godfrey rightly critiques Philip Schaff's conclusion that the Divines intended for the Larger Catechism to be used for pulpit exposition. While the Divines would not have forbidden occasional preaching on a theme or passage of the Catechism, they would still have expected the message to be an expression of scriptural truth. Further, the Assembly's *Directory* specifically says of the minister that "Ordinarily the subject of his sermon is to be some text of Scripture." See Godfrey, "Westminster Larger Catechism," 131. See also Anderson, "Liturgy of the Westminster Assembly."

are urged to "preach sound doctrine, diligently, in season and out of season; plainly, not in the enticing words of man's wisdom, but in demonstration of the Spirit, and of power" (*WLC* 159).

The Primacy of the Word's Message

By following the lead of Scripture in pointing away from human giftedness as the true source of pulpit power, the Westminster Divines force us to consider the power of the Word itself. But we need to be careful to understand how power accompanies the preaching of the Word. The Reformers were not simply advocating the primacy of the Word's *authority*; they were advocating the primacy of the Word's *message*.

The Primacy of the Word's Meaning

Worship prior to the Reformation was characterized by the primacy of the *mass* rather than the message. The understanding that grace was communicated *ex opere operato* through the Eucharist made the preaching of the Word secondary and, in common experience, superfluous. Grace was conferred by the sacrament, and the sermon, when it was delivered, was most often in Latin, a language the common people did not understand.

Such theology and practice starved the people for the Word and substituted an almost superstitious sacramental practice for the Spirit working by and with the Word. Preaching showed the effects of the substitution. Before the Reformation, months could pass before an assigned priest (Catholic or Anglican) would make the rounds to actually preach in local parishes.[6]

By placing emphasis on the primacy of the Word, the Reformers necessarily placed a renewed primacy on preaching. But if you convince a man that he can present the very Word of God, which communicates the benefits of redemption, there is another danger that may arise. The Westminster Divines also needed to guard against the dangers of bibliolatry—the assumption that the paper and ink or the order of the words on the page somehow had spiritual power. Catholic practice, Jewish cabalas, and ancient versions of the Omega Code (a film presuming a mysterious, ancient code hidden in the Torah) were well known, and even the pre-Reformation Waldensians tended to deemphasize preaching and focus on the mere reading of the Word to access its power.

---

6. Cf. Calvin's criticism of Roman Catholic homiletics in his *Tracts and Treatises*, 1.40.

The Westminster Divines had no intention of denying the inherent power of the Word. They write, "The holy Scriptures are to be read with an high and reverent esteem of them; with a firm persuasion that they are the very Word of God" (*WLC* 157). But they also write, "The Spirit of God maketh the reading, but especially the preaching of the word, an effectual means of enlightening, convincing and humbling sinners" (*WLC* 155; cf. *WSC* 89).

The primacy of the Word's message, rather than the primacy of the Word's reading or recitation, was the Reformers' concern. They wanted the people to understand what the Word meant, and thus, the Westminster Divines advocated the study of the Word in the original languages, but they called for proclamation of the Word both "plainly" (*WLC* 159) and "in the vulgar tongue of every nation" (*WCF* I.8). The plain meaning of the Word was to be the prime message of the sermon. The message was the thing!

The Primacy of the Word's Content

But what was to be the content of the message? The message was to: (a) *encompass* the whole counsel of God; (b) *center* on the Word, the Incarnate Word; and (c) *motivate* by love for God.

Encompassing

The Westminster Divines wanted no portion of the Scriptures excluded from preaching. The *Larger Catechism* says, "They that are called to labour in the ministry of the word, are to preach sound doctrine... making known the whole counsel of God" (*WLC* 159). The whole counsel of God included all the matters of salvation and sanctification. With remarkable evangelical fervor, the *Confession* says,

> Repentance unto life is an evangelical grace, the doctrine whereof is to be preached by every minister of the Gospel, as well as that of faith in Christ. (*WCF* XV.1)

But the emphasis upon the doctrines of grace did not annul the necessity of preaching the moral requirements of the law:

> Although true believers be not under the law, as a covenant of works, to be thereby justified or condemned; yet it is of great use to them... in that, as a rule of life informing them of the will of God, and their duty, it directs and binds them to walk accordingly... (*WCF* XIX.6)

By including the necessity of preaching grace (as our sole basis of eternal hope) and the law (as our necessary guide to personal worship, safety, and service, rather than our basis of eternal hope), the authors of the Westminster Standards steer us between the errors of preaching that is either only evangelistic or merely moralistic. Their aim was to produce preaching that bore the fruit of both life and godliness. But how the Divines kept the testaments together so that neither license nor legalism would be produced by their preaching is one of the special contributions of the Standards.

Centering

The balance of law and gospel is maintained, not only by insisting that preaching's scope be the whole counsel of God, but also by holding the center with the message of the Son of God. The Incarnate Word was to be the unifying theme of the inscripturated Word. What enabled the Reformers to preach from any district of Scripture was the understanding that all scriptural roads lead to the person and/or work of Christ.[7] As long as he remains central, every text finds its proper place and emphasis (*WCF* VII.5; *WLC* 34 and 43).

The *moral law* not only guides our obedience and displays the blessing of God upon faithfulness, but also gives believers and others "clearer sight of the need they have of Christ" (*WCF* XIX.6). The *ceremonial law* also had the purpose of "prefiguring Christ, His graces, actions, sufferings, and benefits" (*WCF* XIX.3). All of the Bible has this Christ-pointing purpose:

> Although the work of redemption was not actually wrought by Christ till after His incarnation, yet the virtue, efficacy and benefits thereof, were communicated unto the elect, in all ages successively from the beginning of the world, in and by those promises, types and sacrifices, wherein He was revealed, and signified to be the Seed of the woman, which should bruise the serpent's head, and the Lamb slain from the beginning of the world being yesterday and today the same, and for ever. (*WCF* VIII.6)

Note that the Divines are concerned more with saying that the "virtue, efficacy and benefits" of Christ are revealed to the elect in all ages, rather than that the *person* of Christ is revealed in all. The Scriptures consistently and successively

---

7. The use of the word "Christ" here should be understood synecdochically—as in Calvin—to refer not only to the person of Jesus, but also to the many facets of God's redemptive work that find their fulfillment in Christ but are often prefigured, foreshadowed, or reflected by aspects of God's grace revealed in diverse ways throughout Scripture.

reveal God's grace. This grace finds its ultimate expression in Christ's incarnation, but aspects and benefits of his gracious nature and work are previously revealed and successively maintained throughout Scripture.

The application of these insights regarding the Bible's consistent revelation of Christ's person and/or work are inescapable: preaching that is not Christ-centered (i.e., grace-revealing) is neither true to Scripture nor to our Reformed heritage. This does *not* mean that we must discern how Christ incarnate is revealed in every passage. Rather, our aim is to proclaim how God's grace is being revealed so that God's ultimate redemptive work is rightly contextualized, comprehended, and applied. The goal of expository preaching that is true to the redemptive nature of all Scripture is to reveal the aspects of God's grace that are being revealed in the text being expounded. Christ is the fulfillment and accomplisher of this grace. The grace in every text that reflects his person and work (rather than exegetical gymnastics that attempt to disclose his actual person in every text) marks preaching consistent with the Westminster Standards and Scripture.

Motivating

To maintain the Christocentric nature of preaching, the Reformers knew that it would not be enough to simply impose an interpretive scheme upon all Scripture and then require all ministers to preach accordingly. For the center to hold, it would also be necessary to provide the rationale (or motive) that would cause the heart to long for and seek out this preaching center. That motivation was mined from deep in the heart of the biblical and Reformed distinctives that are dearest to us.

The Divines write, "The moral law doth forever bind all" (*WCF* XIX.5). Yet they understood that the Christian "doth daily break them [i.e., God's commands] in thought, word and deed" (*WLC* 149; *WSC* 82). In addition, the Divines write, "We cannot by our best works merit pardon of sin . . . by reason of the great disproportion that is between them and the glory to come, and the infinite distance that is between us and God" (*WCF* XVI.5; cf. *WLC* 78). As a consequence, our best works are actually deserving of God's judgment, and preaching that exhorts behavior change or moral rectitude, independent of God's grace in Christ, only encourages what will lead to God's reproof (*WCF* XVI.5 and 6). Preaching the law's demands without the enablement or provision of grace damages God's people rather than promotes their obedience.

So what will keep us striving to do the works that the law binds us to do, an effort that we cannot adequately maintain and merits us nothing? The answer is love for God in Christ. The "obligation" of the moral law "neither doth Christ, in the Gospel, any way dissolve, but much strengthen" (*WCF* XIX.5), because the "Spirit of Christ [is] subduing and enabling the will of man to do that freely, and cheerfully, which the will of God, revealed in the law, requireth to be done" (*WCF* XIX.7).

The "general uses" of the law are to provide "a rule of life" (*WCF* XIX.6) for all men, even though none can do all that is required. Yet, what drives the performance of the rules for the regenerate is what the *Larger Catechism* calls the "special use" of the law: showing believers that they "are bound to Christ for his fulfilling of it, and enduring the curse thereof in their stead, and for their good; and thereby to provoke them to more thankfulness, and to express the same in their greater care to conform themselves thereunto as the rule of their obedience" (*WLC* 97). The special use of the law is intended to make us more thankful that Christ fulfilled the law on our behalf and suffered for our disobedience in our stead, so that we desire to please him by obeying his commands.

Full apprehension of the mercy of God in Christ, which the law and the gospel combine to reveal, creates the thankfulness that causes the regenerate heart to do freely and cheerfully what the law requires to be done—even though there is no merit in the obedience. Love for Christ engendered by his grace becomes the motive of the Christian life so that we are always "yielding obedience unto Him, not out of slavish fear, but a childlike love and willing mind" (*WCF* XX.1). Thus, what keeps our preaching true to the whole counsel of God and centered on the gospel of Christ, is the understanding that apart from Christ, there is no proper motivation for the transformation we exhort when we proclaim the commands of God. What further strengthens our commitment to preach Christ consistently is the understanding that we have no ability to do what God commands apart from him. The *Confession* reminds us that Christians' "ability to do good works is not at all of themselves, but wholly from the Spirit of Christ" (*WCF* XVI.3).

Christ is the subject of all the Scriptures, his provision the proper motivation of all our obedience and his Spirit the enabler of all our goodness. What implication does this have for our preaching? Christ's grace always anchors our message. If that sounds strangely un-Reformed, it is only because the Westminster Standards are categorized according to theological topics rather than a homiletical method. However, when the subject of preaching arises, the grace threaded throughout Scripture becomes the superstructure undergirding all subjects and texts addressed. In the chapter explaining God's covenant (note the singular) with man, the *Confession* says of the covenant of grace, "This covenant was differently administered in the time of the law and in the time of the gospel; under the law it was administered by promises, prophesies, sacrifices, circumcision, the paschal lamb, and other types and ordinances . . . all foresignifying Christ to come" (*WCF* VII.5; cf. *WLC* 34). The subject of the covenant in the OT was Christ.

And what about the NT? "Under the New Testament, when Christ the substance was exhibited, the same covenant of grace was and still is to be administered in the preaching of the word, and the administration of the sacraments" (*WLC* 35; cf. *WCF* VII.6). Even as the sacraments represent the covenant of grace, so also preaching administers the covenant of grace to the church. When we understand that preaching is to administer the covenant of grace to the church, we stop questioning whether grace should be integral to all our preaching and begin asking how to make it so. The Divines answer this question, at least in part, by reminding us that all the Scriptures testify of God's provision (in various ways and under various dispensations) by making us aware of our spiritual deficiency and of his holy sufficiency and saving supply. All Scripture rightly understood and contextualized beacons the necessity and hope of God's grace.

In a church and a secular culture dominated by moral license, the Reformed church is committed to maintaining faithfulness to the law of God. But this concern can lead to a focus upon the law that is not faithful to our history or to the Westminster Standards. When the grace of Christ is absent from our message, the power of the gospel is absent from our ministry. Yet when we realize that God's provision (ultimately provided in Christ) is the message of the entire Scripture and the hope that we can provide in every sermon, then preaching becomes for us and for our people the joy that supplies the power of obedience and sustenance of peace.

The Primacy of the Word's Ministry

This emphasis upon the grace of God throughout the scope of our preaching not only echoes the traditional Reformed emphasis upon the doctrines of grace, but it also underscores a final element of the primacy of preaching in the Westminster Standards: the primacy of the Word's ministry. The Reformers valued and elevated preaching because it was seen as the primary means by which God ministered to his people in the church.

The Primacy of the People's "Necessities and Capacities"

The idea of the primacy of preaching's ministry may jar us a bit. Almost cliché in our circles is the notion that we preach for the glory of God—that while we preach to people, God is the audience; and while the people's obedience is our concern, his glory is our goal. The Standards are somewhat less idealistic, but more biblical. Consider where the *Shorter Catechism* starts: "What is the chief end of man?" The Westminster Divines did not consider it compromise to say that "man's chief end is to glorify God *and* enjoy him forever" (*WSC* 1, emphasis added). In a similar way, the Standards refuse to allow the glory of God to be the sole, chief end of preaching. "They that are called to labour in the ministry of the word, are to preach . . . with fervent love to God *and* the souls of his people; sincerely, aiming at his glory, *and* their conversion, edification, and salvation" (*WLC* 159, emphasis added). We are not allowed to forget God's people when we preach of God. Their good and his glory constitute the chief end of preaching.

The Westminster Divines capture this dual obligation of preaching out of love for God's glory and his people's good in a phrase of pastoral genius and heart. Having commended the constant preaching of sound doctrine and the whole counsel of God, and having cautioned against preaching enticing words of man's wisdom, the Divines then say that pastors should preach "wisely, applying themselves to the *necessities and capacities* of the hearers" (*WLC* 159, emphasis added). Yes, we must consider what people need to hear, but we must also consider what they are capable of hearing. If someone were to say this today, he would be accused of "dumbing down" his messages or pandering to the people's ignorance. But the blessed Reformers, while not using the terms, were reminding us of the necessity of audience analysis. We must consider our people's necessities and capacities the way Jesus did when he said, "I have much more to say to you, more than you can now bear" (John 16:12).

Of course, there is the necessity of having people grow and mature from milk to meat, but simply beating babies with steak or trying to impress the learned with our wisdom is not what faithful gospel preaching requires. For Christ's sake and his people's sake, we must consider what people are capable of hearing, as well as what they need to hear. At some point in each of our ministries, we must decide if we are going to preach to preachers or to people. Do we desire more to nurture others with the Word or be worshiped for our eloquence?

We can discern some of the Westminster Divines' priorities on ministering to God's people by the guidelines they gave for preaching in *The Directory for the Publick Worship of God* that accompanied the Standards.[8]

---

8. For an introduction to the background and uses of the *Directory*, see Murray, "Directory for Public Worship." The subcommittee that composed the *Directory* consisted of "five senior Puritan figures—Stephen Marshall (chairman), Herbert Palmer, Thomas Goodwin, Thomas Young and Charles Herle, together with the Scottish commissioners

Concern for the whole counsel of God, and the non-avoidance of difficult issues necessary for individual and corporate maturity, led the Divines to advise reading a chapter of the Bible consecutively from both Testaments in every worship service, and giving the minister the option of expounding on the portion of the Bible previously read in the service.[9] But pastoral prudence was also weighed against this heavy instruction in order not to break the pious backs (or ears) of listeners. The minister is counseled to "let the introduction to his text be brief," to be willing to give "a brief sum" of a long text or "a paraphrase thereof, if need be."[10] The sermon is not "to burden the memory of the hearers in the beginning with too many members of division, nor trouble their minds with obscure terms of art."[11] The Divines advise that "regard is always to be had unto the time, that neither the preaching, nor other ordinances, be straitened, or rendered tedious."[12]

Pastoral concern for the "necessities and capacities" of hearers surfaced in numerous aspects of the Divines' homiletical instruction. The Divines clearly wanted to advocate an expository method that focused on the Scriptures themselves. In the section entitled "Of the Preaching of the Word," the *Directory* says, "Ordinarily, the subject of the sermon is to be some text of Scripture." Out of concern for hearers' necessities, the Divines prescribe that this text be studied in the original languages; but out of concern for hearers' capacities, the Divines advise "abstaining also from an unprofitable use of unknown tongues" in the sermon. The preacher is to focus on "raising doctrines from the text," making sure that doctrines are "grounded" in the text and cover "the scope of the text." But even this expository ethic is to be guided by a pastoral heart. The preacher "needeth not always to prosecute every doctrine which lies in his text," but rather is wisely to choose what "he findeth most needful and seasonable" by his "residence and conversing with his flock." As ministerial tasks make him aware of the most pressing needs of his congregation, the pastor is to concentrate his message on "those doctrines which are principally intended [by the biblical writer]; *and* make most for the edification of the hearers" (emphasis added).

---

and anyone else from the Grand Committee who wished to attend" ("Directory for Public Worship," 175).

9. *Directory*, "Of the Publick Reading of Holy Scripture."
10. *Directory*, "Of the Preaching of the Word."
11. *Directory*, "Of the Preaching of the Word."
12. *Directory*, "Of the Publick Reading of Holy Scripture."

The Primacy of the People's Edification

According to the *Directory's* section "Of the Preaching of the Word," sermons are to be characterized by "sparingly citing sentences from ecclesiastical writers or other human writers, ancient or modern, be they never so elegant." The goal is the hearers' understanding of, and growth in, the Word of God, not the display of the preacher's eloquence or erudition. At least a dozen times this section of the *Directory* urges plainness or clarity of expression in preaching in order that "the meanest [humblest] may understand." By these statements, the Westminster Reformers pressed away from both medieval extravagances and Puritan excesses in preaching. The Westminster sermon was neither to be ornate oratory-driven by allegorical methods (medieval homiletics), nor intricate doctrinal exploration topically launched from hints in isolated verses of Scripture.[13] What is most true to the Word and needful to the hearers drives the Westminster homiletic. Preachers are advised "neither to raise an old heresy from the grave, nor to mention a blasphemous opinion unnecessarily" since "propounding or answering vain or wicked cavils . . . doth more hinder than promote edification." The message of the text governs the content of the sermon, but the edification of the hearers governs how the content is prioritized, organized, and delivered.

We do not have to guess what the Westminster Divines believed would be the most edifying homiletic. Distinguishing their preaching from some in their time, and from some in ours, the Westminster preachers advocate three components for the sermon: the doctrinal division of the text (i.e., explanation), illustration, and application.[14] In the history of preaching, the validity of each of these standard components has been occasionally challenged. The Westminster tradition, however, not only reclaims the expository method advocated by Calvin, but it also maintains the homiletical method that is most ancient and consistent in the history of preaching.

For explanation, the preacher is "to regard more the order of the matter than of words [of the scriptural text]." The sermon is to be structured and expressed in such a way "that the hearers may discern how God teacheth it [i.e., the truth] from thence [i.e., the text]." In addition, "the

---

13. A practice typical among Puritan preachers, but not characteristic of the best of Puritan preaching.

14. These three specifically identified components catch our ear because of their echo of the homiletic categories of this age. They were the essential building blocks of expository sermons taught to the author by Robert G. Rayburn, and echoed in my own instruction across three decades of training preachers. For further discussion of the background of these categories, see Chapell, "Insights," 15–16.

arguments or reasons are to be solid," but also the "illustrations . . . ought to be full of light, and such as may convey the truth to the hearers' heart with spiritual delight." I confess a special appreciation for this last phrase that speaks so clearly of the pastoral concern of our Standards and so soundly answers those who believe that *really* Reformed preaching allows no content but propositional argument.

Receiving almost as much discussion as doctrinal development in the *Directory*'s section "Of the Preaching of the Word" is the preacher's obligation to apply the Word of God. The Divines say of the preacher, "He is not to rest in general doctrine, although never so much cleared and confirmed, but to bring it home to special use, by application to his hearers." Then they add words that ring true for every preacher who has discovered that, while explanation taxes our energies and challenges our minds, application remains the hardest necessity of preaching. The Divines say that the preacher must discuss application, "albeit it prove a work of great difficulty to himself, requiring much prudence, zeal, and meditation." The *Directory* will not allow us simply to describe duties, but says that the preacher must "teach also the means that help in the performance of them." Furthermore, "It is also sometimes requisite to give some notes of trial . . . whereby hearers may be able to examine themselves whether they have attained those graces, and performed those duties." In other words, not only does application require the preacher to tell God's people *what* to do based on the Word; he also needs to explain *how* to do what the Word requires.

This emphasis upon application underscores the primacy of the ministry of the Word in the minds of the Westminster Divines. By focusing on the edification of God's people, there is no compromise of God's glory in their minds. Instead, they are maintaining their understanding of the priorities of the Word. Those priorities are clearly stated in the answer to the third question of the *Shorter Catechism*: "The Scriptures principally teach what man is to believe concerning God and what duty God requires of man." The primary goal of the Scriptures cannot be divided between the glory of God and the obedience of his people. Because God is glorified in the obedience of his people, the proclamation of their duty is as integral to Scripture's message as the proclamation of God's glory. We preach faithfully when the glory of God *and* the good of his people remain inseparable in our sermons and have joint primacy in our hearts.

The Primacy of the Pastor's Heart

What may show the heart of the Reformers more than these specific suggestions about preaching are the adverbs they used to describe the preaching task. The simplicity and godliness of what the Westminster Divines believed would best serve the glory of God and the good of his people still inspires us today:

> They that are called to labour in the ministry of the Word, are to preach sound doctrine, diligently ... faithfully ... wisely ... zealously, with fervent love to God and the souls of his people; sincerely, aiming at his glory, and their conversion, edification, and salvation. (*WLC* 159)

Great power of intellect and grasp of doctrine were theirs, and yet, when the Westminster Divines wrote of preaching, their words were remarkably trusting in God's Word and Spirit and remarkably loving of God's people. This is a very simple and compassionate faith that remains ours to treasure and to proclaim.

6

The New Covenant and Redemptive History

I THANK GOD FOR THE opportunity to honor Dr. Robert S. Rayburn with this essay, which builds on his PhD thesis, and takes the argument further. I can never repay the debt I owe to Dr. Rayburn for his forming of me spiritually, intellectually, and ministerially; I dare to hope, at least, that this essay shows something of why my deep respect is well placed.

Most Christians, because of the way they read the NT, and especially Hebrews, think of the new covenant as denoting an era in redemptive history: the old covenant was given through Moses, while the new covenant was initiated with Jesus' ascension. This way of reading the Bible, however, presents us with many challenges: the relationship of law and grace and the place of good works in the believer's life; the role of the community of God's people; the nature of Christian ministry and worship; and so on.[1]

With so many topics in play, there is a vast secondary literature; in this essay I will focus on the primary sources in the Bible, to see if we can achieve greater clarity. Since the OT prophecies came first, they provide the proper framework for thinking about the NT passages.[2] Thus we will

---

1. For a fine presentation from this more conventional perspective, see Williams, "New and More Glorious Covenant."

2. For the sake of convenience I observe the convention of referring to the "*Old* Testament" and "*New* Testament." This terminological convention for a corpus of writings embodies several difficulties, including a theological stance (*old* and *new* connected with an interpretation of Jeremiah 31, the subject of this essay) and a canonical ambiguity (does the corpus include the Apocrypha, which books belong in the Apocrypha, and if so, with what authority?). Precision would have us distinguish "the Hebrew Bible" (TaNaK, Law-Prophets-Writings), "the quasi-canonical Second Temple Jewish writings," and the Christian apostolic writings. Eastern and Western Christians disagree over what books belong in the Apocrypha, and also on what form of the books of the TaNaK are authoritative (Greek or Hebrew). I take for granted the primacy of the *Hebrew* TaNaK and of the Greek apostolic writings as Scripture, without neglecting the

aim to imitate the first readers of the NT by reading it in the light of the OT.³ My basic thesis is that the Biblical material on the new covenant refers chiefly to the *subjective* response of faithfulness, and not to an *objective* redemptive-historical era as such.

This is what presents us with the problem, however: the basic position for which I will argue is not very hard to establish for Jeremiah (and the parallels in Ezekiel), but it will take a little thought to see how the NT authors are using the OT texts.⁴ The kind of interpretation that I favor actually has an antecedent in Augustine, and shows up from time to time in Western Christian exegesis; more recent proponents include J. Oliver Buswell and Wilber Wallis. Further, the doctoral theses of Robert Rayburn and Joshua Moon have done a great deal of the hard work, and I am appropriating and refining their conclusions.⁵

1. Definitions and Distinctions

We begin by making clear just what we are, and are *not*, talking about.

Redemptive history is simply the story of God's redemptive dealings with his people: calling them and constituting them as his own, making promises to them of life and blessing, instructing them how he wants them to know and love him, and preserving and shaping them for his purposes, particularly that they might be a fit vehicle of blessing to the world. A key

---

role of the other materials in helping us to interpret.

3. Strictly speaking, it is not as simple as that. After all, the reading of a later text might offer support for a proposed reading of the earlier one. Hence the model that sees interpretation as a feedback loop is better than that of a straight line. For more on this point, see my discussion in *Reading Genesis Well*, especially chapter 8.

4. For example, I find that Bright's exegesis of Jeremiah 31:31–34 is helpful in places (e.g., "Exercise in Hermeneutics," 188–97). However, when he relates this to what Hebrews says (e.g., "Exercise in Hermeneutics," 198), it loses its connection to his exegesis of Jeremiah, and is very superficial in its treatment of Hebrews (largely because he does not assess his own assumptions); and when he offers a contemporary application (e.g., "Exercise in Hermeneutics," 198–210), he does so by de-historicizing Jeremiah's text.

5. See Wallis, "Pauline Conception of the Old Covenant," where he expounds his view and refers to Buswell; see also Wallis, "Irony in Jeremiah's Prophecy," 107–10. For the history of interpretation, see Moon, *Jeremiah's New Covenant*. Moon provides his own exegesis of his title passage, which largely agrees with the position I take here—although the origin of Moon's work as a thesis (University of St. Andrews, 2007) means that it does not develop the connections with Ezekiel that I will mention. Rayburn, "Contrast Between the Old and New Covenants," gives a detailed exegetical treatment of passages in Paul and Hebrews that refer specifically to Jeremiah 31. I differ from Wallis and Rayburn chiefly in my perception of the nature of the communicative situation in Hebrews, and in what I see to be redemptive historical concerns.

word here is *covenant*—God graciously chooses his people and pledges himself to be their God, and he grants them the privilege of being his people and of living in his favor and presence.

God's covenants have both what we might call an objective and a subjective side. With a covenant, God objectively establishes a corporate entity as his people, who receive both privilege and responsibility, and specifies how they are to be administered. On the subjective side, the members of the people are expected to embrace the covenantal grace from their hearts. Those who do embrace the covenant are the faithful; they are, generally speaking, a subset of the whole covenant people.

Since God makes his covenants known in history, it is possible that he might develop the way he administers his covenant people and what they are to believe over time. The loyal covenant member will practice his faith according to the developments; he will not try to "turn the clock back" to a previous stage. This is what I mean by *redemptive-historical development*. For example, after Genesis 17, circumcision is the external mark of the covenant, and anyone who fails to observe it has "broken the covenant" (which means that he has failed to appropriate the benefits of the covenant in his own heart). After 2 Samuel 7, the house of David was the channel of God's covenantal working, and salvation was tied to it—and thus prophets to the *Northern* Kingdom foretold their return to David (Hos 3:5; Amos 9:11–15).

We may look at these developments in various ways: we can describe them as successive covenant*s*, or as a composite single "covenant" (the Bible can speak both ways), or we can see them as historical expressions of one "covenant of grace" (as the *Westminster Confession* does, using theological language rather than Biblical). In each case, we need to see the organic relationship between each successive stage. That is, it is the same God who made each covenant; there is one people of God, and the individual partakes of the blessing by embracing the covenanted grace with personal faith and perseverance (which makes him a living participant in the people of God).

Generally speaking, in the Bible successive covenants do not replace the earlier ones: they usually build on the earlier ones and make them more specific. For example, the Sinai Covenant did not replace the Abrahamic covenants; its purpose was to constitute Israel, the people of God and heirs of his promises to Abraham, as a church-state nexus—this will be the context in which they are to live out their privilege and calling as the people of God. The Davidic Covenant did not replace the Sinai Covenant; it specifies how the theocracy is to be governed, and how the people will eventually fulfill their mission and bring blessing to the world.[6]

---

6. In Genesis 12, 15, and 17, we find the basic promises to Abraham: land, offspring,

Hence, even though the objective *content* of faith may change over time (according to the mighty works of God and the particular stage of administering the covenant people), the subjective side of it is basically similar through the ages. This is why texts like Romans 4 can insist that Christian believers, even if they are gentiles, have the same kind of faith and spiritual experience as OT believers such as Abraham and David: we, like they, depend on being counted righteous, with sin not counted against us (vv. 6–8)—long before the objective basis of that counting (the work of Jesus) came along. It is also why Hebrews 11 can parade OT figures as exemplars of faith who will, along with us, be made perfect in glory (vv. 39–40). Indeed, it is part of Hebrews' apologetic for Christian perseverance that "good news came to *us* just as to *them*" (4:2)—what we have received is just as much from God's gracious hand as what they did (that *they* received grace, then, is taken for granted!).

These factors come out clearly in Romans 11:17–24, where Paul uses the image of the olive tree whose branches have been cut off, with other branches grafted in. The tree is an image for the covenant people of God; the cut-off branches represent Jews who were members of the covenant people externally, but who lacked genuine faith (v. 20), while the grafted-in wild branches are gentiles who have come to faith. Gentile Christians have been made members of Abraham's family (Rom 4:11), sharing full-status citizenship with Jewish Christians (Eph 2:19; 3:6), with Jesus as their common King (Rom 1:1–6). In this arrangement, whatever kind of continuing validity the Sinai Covenant will have, it cannot be any longer applicable in its sense of establishing Israel as a church-state nexus. Therefore the basic dynamic of faith, obedience, ministry, sacraments, covenant family, membership in the people of God, the mission of God's people in the world, and worldview is consistent throughout the ages of God's people.

This model helps us in another way: the pattern we see is *not* that of a later covenant *replacing* an earlier one. Hence a reading that sees the new covenant as a replacement for previous arrangements falls outside this pattern, which means that such a reading needs stronger argumentation than is ordinarily given it. At the same time, if we have a reading that shows its coherence with the pattern, then so much the better for this other reading!

---

blessing, and privilege. The Mosaic Covenant did not replace any of these, but provided a setting in which they would be realized: e.g., Genesis 17 institutes circumcision as the rite of entry into the visible people of God, and Exodus 12:22–49 makes it a requirement for participation in the Passover meal. Further, 2 Samuel 7:9 echoes Genesis 12:2; in 2 Samuel 7:11 the "rest" echoes Deuteronomy 12:10; and the father-son relationship of 2 Samuel 7:14 makes sense in light of Israel's sonship in relation to God (Exod 4:22–23; see also the "firstborn" in Ps 89:27).

It will be helpful here to describe how this notion of redemptive history affects exegesis. My conception of redemptive historical interpretation requires that it be firmly tied to the intent of the Biblical texts, and not simply an add-on. More specifically, I see the Biblical authors as self-consciously describing an unfolding story, and calling their audiences to live in a way that is fitting to their stage of that story, to advance the mission of God's people.[7]

The story, briefly put, is this: the one true God made the world as the ideal arena for humankind to live—to love and serve one another, to rule the world wisely, and to enjoy their relationship with God. The fall into sin of Genesis 3 corrupted humankind, which means that humans bring their defilement into their relationship with God, with each other, and with the world. Redemption has the purpose of healing this defilement in humankind, of restoring them to, and confirming them in, their proper functioning. Even the selection of a particular people, the offspring of Abram, was for the sake of the blessing coming to the rest of humankind (Gen 12:1–3). Israel's role among the nations was that of a priestly people (Exod 19:6); that is, they would display to the whole world the wonders of the true God and the delight of knowing him, by means of their faithfulness to the covenant, their renewed humanity (see Deut 4:6–8).

The shape of the OT story derives from the objective and subjective sides of God's covenants: on the objective side, God intends to use the corporate entity, the *people*, to bring his light to the whole world. On the subjective side, most of what we see in the OT is what results when the majority of the members of the people do not embrace the covenant, which leads to a polluted communal life and testimony. Judgments in the OT fall upon the corporate entity, the people, in order to bring the unfaithful members to repentance and true faith, or else to remove them from the people. At the same time, God intends to use the people of Israel as his vehicle by which he will bless the whole world; he will keep that commitment by purging the people and establishing the faithful. Thus these judgments are never to be seen as the end of Israel's story. (For a particularly clear exposition of this point, see Isa 1:24–28.)

The messianic hope in the OT developed with these ends in view. As I have observed elsewhere,

> The OT develops its idea of a Messiah (eventually clarified as the ultimate heir of David) in the light of these components. The earliest strands of the Messianic idea speak of an offspring

---

7. For a fuller (but still succinct) exposition of my views on this matter, see my "Theology of the Old Testament," 29–31.

who will undo the work of the Evil One and bless the Gentiles by bringing them into his kingdom (Gen. 3:15; 22:17–18; 24:60); the idea that kings will descend from Abraham (Gen. 17:6, 16) and Jacob (Gen. 35:11) becomes focused on the tribe of Judah, to which the obedience of the peoples will be brought (Gen. 49:10). The kings in David's line carry this idea forward. They are to embody the people: just as the people as a whole is God's son (Ex. 4:22–23), so also the Davidic king is God's son (2 Sam. 7:14; Ps. 89:26–27). The promise of a lasting dynasty for David (2 Sam. 7:16) becomes the expectation that a final heir of his line will one day arise, take his Davidic throne (in "the last days"), and lead his people in the great task of bringing light to the Gentiles (e.g., Ps. 2:8; 72:8–11, 17 [using Gen. 22:18]; Isa. 9:6–7; 11:1–10; see note on Isa. 42:1–9, concerning the Servant of the Lord).[8]

The "priestly" work of the Messiah, which has figured so prominently in Christian discussions, is certainly there in the OT, but it is presented as something that is folded into his *Davidic* (and therefore *royal*) messianic role (cf. Ps 110:4; Isa 52:13—53:12). The letter to the Hebrews, which devotes so much space to Jesus as the new high priest, begins with precisely this recognition.[9]

Now it is clear that the first Christian Pentecost marks a major redemptive-historical development. The OT had held out the anticipation that the gentiles would become partakers of the true faith, as the heir of David brought them under his sway. The resurrection-ascension of Jesus is his coronation (Matt 28:18; Acts 13:33; Rom 1:4; 1 Cor 15:25), so this era has begun. Further, the outpouring of the Holy Spirit equips the church for its mission of expanding Jesus' reign through the world.[10]

---

8. Collins, "Theology of the OT," 30. The note referred to on Isaiah 42:1–9 is part of the commentary in the *ESV Study Bible*.

9. See Heb 1:2, 5 (using the Davidic "son of God" idea); Heb 1:3 (drawing on Ps 110:1, where the Davidic Lord sits at God's right hand).

10. See my "Ephesians 5:18." In my view, the baptism and filling of the Spirit, which are on display in Acts 2, are not new kinds of spiritual experience, but instead a new level of equipping for service. In other words, the baptism and filling of the Spirit do not pertain to the inner life or sanctification of the believer, but to the realm of spiritual gifts being supplied and empowered. At this point, I will simply note that Acts 2 is the fulfillment of the promise in 1:5, 8, and Peter's speech is in the realm of what Paul calls "spiritual gifts." Further, "filled with the Spirit" is an OT expression, appearing in Exodus 28:3; 31:3; 35:31; Deuteronomy 34:9; and probably Micah 3:8. It pertains to *being equipped and enabled to serve the purposes of the people of God* (which is what spiritual gifts are).

Thus in the NT we certainly do encounter developments from the era of the OT, and differences with it. David's greater son has arrived and is on his throne—these promises have been fulfilled. However, he has not yet done everything promised: that is what the present era is for. The mystery revealed through the apostles, the secret that was not made known to previous generations, is "that the [believing] Gentiles are fellow *heirs*, members of the same body" (Eph 3:6): the Pentateuchal category of "strangers and aliens" (gentile converts who could not be full citizens of national Israel) has been eliminated (Eph 2:19).

In this light, we can see that the church-state nexus (theocracy) of OT Israel has now been eliminated, with its combination of ethnicity, citizenship, and covenant membership. On the other hand, features of that arrangement still supply important ways to understand what it means to be a member of God's people (as the Christians call themselves "brethren"). Further, the liturgical system of the OT has been impacted: the ultimate sin offering has been made, as Hebrews emphasizes. To reject this development, and to return to the old system, would be foolish apostasy (Heb 10:26–27, 36–39). This does not eliminate a "priestly" ministry, or the peace offering sacrifice—but that is a subject for another essay.[11]

Hence there should be no dispute over whether there are developments for our era: we ought to be careful, however, to see just what labels the Bible itself uses for them. In particular, we must not assume, just because we are used to reading the NT a certain way, that "new covenant" is the proper term for these developments.

This leads to a final point for clarification. The expression "new covenant" comes from Jeremiah 31:27–40 (v. 31), which we will discuss below. We should discern what the OT passage meant in its own setting, and *then* discern how NT authors used it. We need not assume ahead of time that the *only* way a NT author can use an OT text is to give the authorized interpretation of it; he may invoke it for analogy or example, or even to fill out its reference. We also need not assume that the way Paul uses the idea is the same as the way that Hebrews uses it.

2. The New Covenant in the Old Testament

The sole explicit new covenant reference in the OT is Jer 31:27–40. However, as I will explain, other passages from both Jeremiah and Ezekiel fill out the picture.

---

11. I have addressed this in "Eucharist as Christian Sacrifice."

To see the meaning of the passage to Jeremiah and his audience, we begin by discerning its context and structure. Our passage is part of Jeremiah 30–31, which can be called "the book of consolation" (some include chapters 32–33).[12] Jeremiah 31:27 begins a new section, since v. 26 has the prophet awaking and looking around.[13] We have three major segments, each introduced with "Behold, the days are coming, declares the LORD" (vv. 27, 31, 38). In the first segment (vv. 27–30), God promises to restore Israel and Judah after the exile (under the image of sowing). The people of God—the entity—will survive, and the members of it will not be cast off simply because their ancestors were unfaithful. The members of a later generation will have their own chance for covenantal faithfulness.

In the second segment (vv. 31–37), God promises to make a new covenant with Israel and Judah. God's commitment to this ethnic group is as enduring as the fixed order of the moon and stars. They will once again display covenant reality (see further discussion momentarily).

In the third segment (vv. 38–40), God promises that Jerusalem will be rebuilt, never again to be uprooted or overthrown. Some take this last expression, "any more forever" (v. 40), to be a reference to the consummation;[14] but three factors argue against that. First, the terms translated "any more forever" need not be unqualified or unconditional—if a future generation should prove unfaithful, Jerusalem would again suffer. Second, the very specific topographical terms of these verses suggest physical Jerusalem. Third, the terms "uprooted or overthrown" in verse 40 point back to "pluck up and overthrow" in verse 28. Hence I take this paragraph to refer to the same restoration from exile that verses 27–30 speak of. (Perhaps, though—as in verses 31–34—the time period is seen as stretching from the restoration off into the future. This would make physical Jerusalem the concrete expression of the enduring entity, the people of God.)

Consider further the use of the formula, "Behold, days are coming." It generally introduces a prediction for the future, without specifying whether it is near or far future. It can come with a promise of judgment (1 Sam 2:31; Jer 48:12; 49:2; 51:47, 52; 4:2; 8:11); it often precedes a promise of the Babylonian exile (Isa 39:6 [2 Kgs 20:17]; Jer 7:32 [cf. 19:6]; 9:24). In a number of

---

12. See Bright, "Book of Jeremiah," 263.

13. Most editions of the Hebrew text indicate a paragraph break between verse 26 and verse 27.

14. For example, Keil wrote: "It is very evident that this prophecy does not refer to the rebuilding of Jerusalem after the exile, but . . . announces the erection of a more spiritual kingdom of God in the Messianic age. . . . This prophecy, then, reaches on to the time when the kingdom of God shall have been perfected" (*Jeremiah*, 287).

cases, all in Jeremiah, it is part of an oracle that promises the return after the exile to Babylon (Jer 16:14; 23:5, 7; 30:3; 33:14).

All of this points to the "days" that are "coming" in verses 27 and 38 being the time after the exile. Perhaps, then, the same is true of the "days" of verse 31 (though of course they may extend well beyond what we call the "post-exilic era")? Several factors show that this is right. First, we have the immediate context of the pericope, verses 27–40. Second, the larger context also looks to the restoration after the exile, and couples that with spiritual renewal (see, for example, vv. 23–25).

Now let us look at some of the specifics of the prophecy of Jeremiah 31:31–34. The actual content and context of Jeremiah's prophecy show that his concern was not with redemptive-historical changes (though they are not necessarily excluded), but with the problem of God's covenant people lacking inward covenant reality: they were satisfied with having the covenant as an external administration only, without genuine circumcision of the heart. Hence the new covenant, as he told of it, was a situation in which this failure would be cured.

This comes through from the fact that the expression "they broke my covenant" (Jer 31:32, *heferu et-beriti*)[15] is properly interpreted in Greek by the LXX (see also Heb 8:9) *ouk enemeinan en tē diathēkē mou*, "they did not continue [or *abide*] in my covenant."[16] It refers to people who reject the provisions of covenant membership that God offers—people who refuse to live faithfully.[17] We further see it in the fact that the benefits—setting the law within them, writing it on their hearts, forgiveness, knowledge of God—were all intended for a faithful Israelite to experience.[18] The connection with the exile and restoration of Judah (vv. 27–28, 38–40) shows that these epochal events lie between the prophet's time and the "coming days" he spoke of.

---

15. For the same term, see Jeremiah 11:10; verses 1–13 provide a full indictment, not simply of sins, but of unfaithfulness (and therefore unbelief); cf. also 7:21–28.

16. A possible backcloth for one of John's characteristic expressions, *menō en* ("to abide in"; e.g., John 8:31; 15:4; 1 John 2:6; etc.); for *emmenō* with either *en* or the simple dative in the LXX, cf. Deut 27:26; Ben Sira 2:10; 6:20; 28:6. The nuance is that of covenantal perseverance. I have discussed the Johannine terms in "What the Reader Wants," 347–48, and in "Abiding in the Vine," 46–49.

17. See, e.g., Gen 17:14; Deut 31:16, 20; Jer 11:10.

18. For specific terms see, e.g., Prov 3:3; 7:3 (writing on the heart; contrast Jer 17:1); Isa 1:3; 1 Sam 3:7 (where *not* knowing the Lord is a reproach); Ps 25:11 (forgiveness). For the expression "I will be their God and they shall be my people," see Gen 17:7–8 (note also Jer 11:4; 24:7; 30:22; Ezek 34:24, 31; 36:28). For internality in general, see Deut 6:5–6; 10:16; 30:6, 14 (and in Jeremiah, see 4:4; 9:25–26).

We can add to this the reference in 32:36-44, which repeats many of the words and themes of 31:31-34, and explicitly connects them to the restoration. Here are some clear echoes from that passage (vv. 38-41):

> ³⁸And they shall be my people, and I will be their God. [See 31:33.] ³⁹I will give them one heart and one way, that they may fear me forever [see 31:31-33], for their own good and the good of their children after them. ⁴⁰I will make with them an everlasting covenant [see 31:31], that I will not turn away from doing good to them. And I will put the fear of me in their hearts [see 31:33], that they may not turn from me. ⁴¹I will rejoice in doing them good, and I will plant them in this land in faithfulness [see 31:28], with all my heart and all my soul.

Jeremiah takes up this theme in 50:4-5:

> ⁴In those days and in that time, declares the LORD, the people of Israel and the people of Judah shall come together, weeping as they come, and they shall seek the LORD their God. ⁵They shall ask the way to Zion, with faces turned toward it, saying, "Come, let us join ourselves to the LORD in an everlasting covenant that will never be forgotten."

The return from exile will be accompanied by spiritual renewal among the people, designated as a "new" or "everlasting" covenant.

Students of Jeremiah and Ezekiel commonly bring these texts from Jeremiah together with a set of texts in Ezekiel (11:14-21; 16:59-63; 34:25-31; 36:22-38; 37:26-28), as addressing the same topic.[19] This makes sense, both because of their related subject matter and because the two prophets, Jeremiah and Ezekiel, have so much in common. For example, both men came from priestly families (Jer 1:1; Ezek 1:3); both carried out their prophetic ministries on the verge of the Babylonian exile, and on into it (Jeremiah in Jerusalem, Ezekiel in Mesopotamia); both employed "acted sermons"; both denounced the wicked "shepherds" (leaders) in Judah; and both foretold the destruction of Jerusalem and proclaimed hope for restoration.

A more specific rationale for taking these texts together is the fact that all of these passages from Jeremiah and Ezekiel are set in the context of the Babylonian exile (in some cases, as impending; in others, as already occurring). They all explain that the reason for the exile is the sorry situation among God's people (specifically, Judah as what it left of Israel) in which people have the privileges of covenant membership but do not embrace

---

19. For helpful exposition of this theme in Ezekiel, see Greenberg, *Ezekiel 21-37*, 735-38.

those privileges by a living and obedient faith. The purpose of the exile is to purge the unfaithful from the people (see Isa 1:24–28); afterwards God will reestablish the survivors in the promised land, and bring about a genuine internalization of the law. This will enable Judah to carry out its calling among the nations, as the gentiles go from blaspheming the God of Israel because of his people's unfaithfulness (Ezek 36:20, 22) to knowing the true God (Ezek. 36:36). The coming of the heir of David (Jer 33:14–17 [cf. 23:5, 7]; Ezek 34:23–24) is closely tied to this: his task is to lead God's people in living faithfully in order to bring light to the gentiles.

A further feature of these prophecies, in both Jeremiah and Ezekiel, is what we may call their "ethnocentricity"—i.e., they are focused on what God will do for "the house of Israel and the house of Judah" (Jer 31:27, 31, cf. vv. 36–37; 50:4); they are also focused on the return from Babylon as a key event in the outworking of the promises. The blessing-to-the-gentiles theme comes in as a consequence of this (Ezek 36:36; 37:28).

Many scholars trace the origin of this theme of exile followed by restoration to Deuteronomy 30.[20] This is likely, since there are distinct echoes of the Mosaic text in the passages from Jeremiah and Ezekiel. For example, Deuteronomy 30:3 speaks of God restoring their fortunes and having mercy/compassion on them, and these words are picked up in Jeremiah 33:26 and Ezekiel 39:25. It also speaks of God gathering his people from the places they have been scattered and looks forward to the Lord circumcising the hearts of his people.[21]

The return from Babylon, coming in waves as it did, is portrayed as part of the fulfillment of this line of prophecy. Indeed, when the post-exilic Zechariah wants to reassure the restoration community of God's continuing commitment to them, he reiterates that "they shall be my people and I shall be their God" (Zech 8:8), using the words found in Jer 32:38; Ezek

---

20. The debate over whether Deuteronomy 30 is a prediction of Israel's ultimate failure and restoration need not detain us here. E.g., Wright, *Climax of the Covenant*, 140, finds a prediction in this. On the other hand, Deuteronomy 28:15 begins describing the curses *should* the people be unfaithful: "But *if* [Hebrew *'im*] you will not obey"—that is, the issue is not one of inevitability. This dispute arises at least in part from the way Paul quotes from the passage; hence, a very traditional Jewish commentary on the Hebrew text does not even consider the option: see Mirsky, *Sefer Debarim*, 422–25. If we take Deuteronomy 30 as a "prediction," then we will appreciate that its context fits into Patrick Fairbairn's "conditional" category, that is, of passages whose aim is lead people to actions to avoid punishments or to realize blessings; see Fairbairn, *Interpretation of Prophecy*, 58–82. Hence, my argument does not rely on a specific take on this question.

21. See how the theme of scattering recurs in Ezekiel 11:17; 20:34, 41; 28:25 (see also Jer 23:3; 31:8; 32:37); the theme of internalization appears in Jeremiah 4:4.

11:20; 36:28; 37:23 (see also Jer 31:33; Ezek 37:27).[22] Judah's willingness to accept the reforms under Ezra and Nehemiah would be a further outworking of the promises (compare Neh 1:8–9 with Deut 30:3–4); but nothing corresponds to "they shall all know me, from the least of them to the greatest" (Jer 31:34)—the full remedy to the initial problem of presuming on privilege instead of embracing it—which, the pious would probably say, awaits an eschatological fulfillment. We may conclude, then, that the texts in Jeremiah and Ezekiel speak of a time after the exile when there would be covenant reality at long last.

In what sense, then, is this covenant "new"? To answer that, we must appeal to several points about the context of Jeremiah 31: first, the semantic range of the Hebrew word "covenant"; second, the parallels to "new" in these prophecies; and third, the general pattern of these new covenant prophecies in Jeremiah and Ezekiel of focusing on the subjective renewal after the exile. These will help us to see in what way the new covenant is "not like the covenant that I made with their fathers on the day when I took them by the hand to bring them out of the land of Egypt, my covenant that they broke."

Let us take first the lexical point about "covenant": as indicated above, God's covenants have an objective side and a subjective one. Usually in the Bible, the terms for the word "covenant" (typically Hebrew *berit*; Greek *diathēkē*) focus on the objective side, the means by which God administers his people. Occasionally, however, the focus is on the subjective aspect, namely covenant participation (as in Isa 55:3, see following discussion). Not surprisingly, the common Christian interpretation assumes that Jeremiah is using the term in the objective sense; but there are reasons to find the subjective sense to be more suited to the overall thrust of Jeremiah's prophecy.

Second, consider what else is "new" in this set of prophecies: a "new spirit" and a "new heart" (Ezek 11:19; 36:26; cf. 18:31).[23] This newness refers to the new subjective condition of heartfelt embrace of God's covenantal grace; that is, the newness corresponds to the general thrust of all these prophecies in Jeremiah and Ezekiel.

Since Jeremiah describes the new covenant as "not like . . . my covenant that they broke" (31:32), it makes sense contextually to find his focus to be on the subjective side; that is, on failed appropriation (which is what the term "broke" commonly refers to). Hence it works best to take the term

---

22. See Assis, "Zechariah 8," 6–7, on this echo.

23. Cf. Moskovitz, *Sefer Yehezqel*, 287, on Ezek 36:27. Interestingly, Ezekiel 11:19, with its contrast of the heart *of stone* (Greek *lithinos*) and heart *of flesh* (Greek *sarkinos*) is said (e.g., NA27 cross reference) to have influenced Paul's wording in 2 Corinthians 3:3 (a Pauline new covenant passage), which contrasts "tablets *of stone*" with "tablets *of fleshly hearts.*"

"new covenant" as a metonymy for "new situation in which the people embrace the covenant from the heart."

And what is the time period to which the passage refers? We have seen that it is "after the exile"; can we get more specific? Yes, we can, if we notice just what the text says. In verse 34, we read of every member of the covenant people genuinely knowing God, with no further need of a teacher. In verse 33, we see that this describes "Israel" (see also vv. 27, 31, 36, 37). There is no reason to believe that anything prior to the consummation meets these criteria. So, strictly speaking, as Rayburn observes, "the time of the new covenant is the time of final consummation";[24] on the other hand, we see foretastes of this in various episodes since the restoration. For example, the positive response to Haggai and Zechariah is unlike anything before the exile; and it is likely that Malachi paved the way for the marvelous spiritual renewal under the leadership of Ezra and Nehemiah (see Ezra 10; Neh 8–11). The response that Jews gave to the apostolic preaching in Acts is astounding in view of the religious and cultural obstacles of the time.

Jeremiah's new covenant prophecy is well integrated, then, into the whole, not only of Jeremiah, but also of his shared themes with the contemporary Ezekiel, and with the post-exilic presentation.[25]

---

24. Rayburn, "Contrast Between Old and New Covenants," 159.

25. Seeing this will help us evaluate a unique and creative proposal from Walton; see his *Ancient Near Eastern Thought*, 257–58. (The back cover commendation for this reading by my mentor, Alan Millard, makes this proposal even more worthy of our attention.) Walton begins with the fact that the Lord will write on the heart in Jeremiah 31:33, whereas the other texts (as Prov 3:3) have the human person writing on his own heart. This leads him to find a parallel with "extispicy" texts from the ancient world, in which revelation from the gods is supposedly written on the internal organs of a sacrificial animal; the texts supply instructions for how to read these revelations. Thus, in Walton's reading, Jeremiah is speaking of his people being a medium of God's communication to themselves, and perhaps to the world.

Walton's argument illustrates the benefits and potential pitfalls of comparative studies; in this case, it does not do justice to the way the actual wording of the Hebrew text fits in with its Hebrew context. Walton properly acknowledges that "Jeremiah in no sense seeks to reproduce the literary structure or ritual setting of an extispicy procedure"; surely that should make us pause before finding any connection. But his treatment of the Hebrew text itself fails to account for its features. For example, God bade the first humans to "be fruitful and multiply" (Gen 1:28; see also Jer 3:16; 23:3); in further evocations of this text, he promises to his chosen that he will "make them fruitful and multiply them" (as in Gen 48:4; see also Ezek 36:11). Further, in Jeremiah already the "writing on the heart" has to do with the depth of penetration (Jer 17:1). Finally, the coherence of the texts in Jeremiah and Ezekiel, with their concern for internalizing the law after the exile, tells against this reading. The significance of the Lord writing becomes plain (see also Deut 29:4 and 30:6 on the Lord's operation on the hearts of his people).

Let us set our conclusions about these texts beside Christopher Wright's discussion of the "new covenant."[26] He notes that "the scope of the new covenant is at first very clearly national."[27] He sees a set of texts from Isaiah as adding the element of the inclusion of the gentiles, however (see below). He finds that "the new covenant would reaffirm that central, warm and possessive relationship" between God and Israel and includes "a new experience of forgiveness,"[28] without implying that such forgiveness was not previously available. He finds that it will involve a new obedience to the law. He notes that some suppose that here we have an individual stress, as opposed to the more corporate stress of previous times; but argues that this is a misinterpretation: "the people of God *as a whole* will be characterized as a community who know him."[29] He notes that this obedience stems from knowing God, and that it is far from being limited to personal piety, but actively promotes the well-being of the poor and needy.[30]

Wright includes a fine passage about obedience:

> 'The law written in the heart' means much more than a new upsurge of sincerity in keeping it. We have already seen that the Old Testament from the beginning had called for obedience from the heart. The popular parody of the Old Testament as a religion of external legalism is far from the truth. The heart, as the seat of the will and intelligence (not just emotions), was of great importance, in the law, in the Psalms and in the book of Proverbs. Ezekiel goes further in emphasizing that such obedience of the heart involves not just a new law, but a new heart itself, a veritable heart transplant performed by the Spirit of God. Only such a spiritual miracle will produce the obedience called for (Ezek. 36:26ff.).[31]

My only quibble is that I do not know where "new law" came from; there is no hint of that in either Jeremiah or Ezekiel—nor does the NT, properly understood, imply any such thing.

Wright goes on to find a messianic element in the new covenant, because he sees a reference to this covenant in Isaiah 42:6 and 49:8 (where the servant of the Lord is to be a "covenant for the people"). Hence he links the new covenant prophecy with those that speak of a new Davidic king,

---

26. Wright, *Knowing Jesus*, 93–107; see also his *Message of Jeremiah*, 323–39.
27. Wright, *Knowing Jesus*, 94.
28. Wright, *Knowing Jesus*, 97.
29. Wright, *Knowing Jesus*, 98.
30. Wright, *Knowing Jesus*, 98–99.
31. Wright, *Knowing Jesus*, 99.

though as he acknowledges, Jeremiah's "famous new covenant passage is entirely Sinaitic in flavour." He further adds "a new abundance of nature" to his list of features, because "the prophets look forward to the renewal of the land of Israel itself (Jer. 31:11-14, Ezek. 34:26-9, 36:8-12)."[32] As elsewhere in the Bible, the land of Israel functions in part as a token of the future new creation."[33] This last feature is better explained by reference to the conventions of figurative language in OT prophecy.

3. The New Covenant in Isaiah?

Christopher Wright, then, associates the new covenant with a messianic theme, which implies an objective, redemptive-historical component to it, and his case deserves serious consideration. While he has, in my judgment, nailed many of the features of the new covenant, he has not shown that we *must* count the servant passages in Isaiah in the list of new covenant texts. It is this, together with his assumption that the word "covenant" must refer to an objective administration of God's grace (and thus the subjective metonymy mentioned above never gets considered), that supports his reading that Jeremiah's new covenant referred to a redemptive-historical development. If, in fact, it looks unlikely that we should include Isaiah's servant passages under this rubric, then we have less reason to suppose that Jeremiah referred to such a redemptive-historical era.

The texts in Isaiah that have been associated with the new covenant are 42:6; 49:8; 54:10; 55:3; 59:21; and 61:8. It is, at first glance, reasonable to consider these texts, since they all use the word "covenant" and they all refer to God's intention to restore and renew Judah after the exile, and to fulfill his mission through his people. Let us consider the way in which these texts connect with the new covenant themes in Jeremiah and Ezekiel.

It looks like 54:10; 59:21; and 61:8 do in fact link up with the new covenant idea. In 54:10 we find that the Lord has a "covenant of peace" with his people, which shall not be removed (hence his intention to restore Jerusalem after the exile).[34] In 59:21 we find a description of the Lord's covenant with his people, that his Spirit and word will not depart from them or from their offspring. This comes in the context of their restoration, and it also speaks of their mission.[35] Finally, in 61:8 we read again of an "everlasting covenant,"

---

32. Wright, *Knowing Jesus*, 100.

33. Wright, *Knowing Jesus*, 100-101.

34. Cf. Ezek 34:25; 37:26 for the "covenant of peace" after the exile.

35. I argue below that apparently Paul used Isa 59:20-21 along with Jer 31:31 to describe God's future for the Jews in Rom 11:26-27.

that God *will make* with his people (after the exile), as a result of which "their offspring will be known among the nations" (v. 9).[36] By traditional notions of authorship, in which these parts of Isaiah come from the early seventh century BC, while Jeremiah and Ezekiel are from the late seventh to the mid-sixth century BC, this would mean that Isaiah has provided some of the groundwork that Jeremiah and Ezekiel developed. In all cases, the covenant referred to is a new situation of covenant authenticity for God's people, which is what enables them to bring blessing to the nations.

In Isaiah 55:3, the Lord invites "everyone who thirsts" (v. 1) to come to him, "and I will make with you an *everlasting covenant,* my steadfast, sure love for David." It makes sense to take this as using the *subjective* appropriation sense of "covenant" (as in Jer 31:31).

We are left with Isaiah 42:6 and 49:8, from two of the Servant Songs (42:1–9; 49:1–13). Isaiah's servant of the Lord is, in my judgment, a messianic (i.e., Davidic) figure.[37] In 42:6 and 49:8 the servant will be "a covenant for the people." The "people" here are Israel, as opposed to the gentiles (compare 42:6 with 49:6–8). The servant will serve as a "covenant" in the sense of being a covenant representative (a Davidic, and therefore messianic, role); he will lead the people in the great task of bringing light to the gentiles (42:1–4; 49:6–7).[38] Isaiah promises that, after exile, there will be return; the return has the purpose of establishing a purified and faithful people. Out of this people will come the great servant, who will successfully bring the knowledge of God to the gentiles. True to the characteristics of biblical prophecy, Isaiah gives no timeline for this, and he can describe a process that will take a long time, as if it were a single event. This is like what we find in Jeremiah and Ezekiel; and, like them, Isaiah does not *equate* the new covenant situation with the messianic period.

Now, Wright himself acknowledges that the servant passages do not include the dimension of writing the law in the heart, and appeals to the "strong emphasis on the full acceptance of the law and the reign of justice in its visions of the mission of the servant to the nations."[39] Certainly that strong emphasis is there; but it deals with something other than the problem addressed in Jeremiah and Ezekiel. This is further evidence that Isaiah was speaking of something else.

---

36. For "everlasting covenant," established after the exile, see Jer 32:40; 50:5; Ezek 16:60; 37:26.

37. For discussion, see my commentary on Isaiah (forthcoming).

38. The expression "light for the nations" (Isa 42:6; 49:6) probably lies behind Jesus calling himself the "light of the world" (John 8:12), thereby making it a messianic claim.

39. Wright, *Knowing Jesus,* 99.

Mind you, to say that the two are separate topics hardly means that the topics are unrelated—after all, the means by which the gentiles would come to know the true God was to be the authentic covenant life of Israel. Hence the reference in Jeremiah 33:14-16, about the intention to raise up the messianic branch, does not prove that Jeremiah's new covenant is in itself the messianic era; after all, the story must continue if the future Davidic ruler is to arise, and that, I take it, is the point: he will arise after the exile.

I conclude, then, that Isaiah 55:3 is the closest to Jeremiah 31:31 semantically (that is, in the sense of the use of "covenant"); while Isaiah 54:10, 59:21, and 61:8 all connect with the new covenant class of prophecies in Jeremiah and Ezekiel, speaking of the return from exile and the renewal of covenant authenticity. The key texts Isaiah 42:6 and 49:8, however, do not come into play, and therefore the new covenant is not an explicitly messianic idea.[40] This fits well with my assessment of Jeremiah and Ezekiel: they are referring to a subjective situation of covenant reality, and not commenting (for or against) on any objective development in covenant administration.

4. The New Covenant in Second Temple Judaism

The places in which Second Temple Jewish authors mention the new covenant show that they apparently read these prophecies along the lines that I am suggesting.

Take, for example, the book of Baruch, which was ostensibly written in Babylonian exile by Jeremiah's companion (Bar 1:1-4), although the extant Greek version is commonly dated to the second century BC (or even later). This work invokes the hope of restoration that will result from spiritual renewal in exile (Bar 2:30-35 and 3:5-8, echoing passages such as Jer 24:7; 32:40; 31:33).[41]

Jubilees 1:22-25 (ca. 161-140 BC) also envisions Israel's return to faithfulness, leading to God circumcising their hearts (echoing Deut 10:16; 30:6); the overall tone of the book is optimistic about the author's own time.[42]

---

40. We may argue that it is *implicitly* so, in that Isaiah 55:3 refers to the "steadfast, sure love for David." We remember that at this point the covenant is tied to the house of David, with its promise of an ultimate king. We might further observe that part of the servant's mission is to "bring Jacob back to" the Lord (Isa 49:5), so his work is not unconnected with the "new covenant." But this is hardly the same as saying that the new covenant refers to an age such as the messianic age.

41. See Tov, *Book of Baruch*, 25, 27.

42. See VanderKam, *Book of Jubilees*, 132-34, 139-41; he shows that it is likely that Paul had some awareness of its themes (147).

Additionally, the community at Qumran saw themselves as having entered the new covenant (cf. *Damascus Document* 6:19; 8:21; 20:12).[43]

Some have suggested that these Second Temple texts point to a "continuing exile" motif—that is, the notion that the "exile" did not really end with the events recorded in Ezra and Nehemiah.[44] As the returnees confessed, "we are slaves this day" (Neh 9:36). The matter deserves its own treatment, which I cannot give here. For now I have only two comments on that point:

1. The Second Temple works portray the "new covenant" as either imminent or already realized in the second century BC;
2. As I argue in the next section, I take Paul to be showing that his Jewish contemporaries had not yet received the fullness of what was foretold (see ensuing discussion on Rom 2:14–15).

That is, if I have read Paul rightly, he is not disputing the general line of interpretation found in these sources, which seems sound, but instead the application (which is unduly optimistic).

5. The New Covenant in Paul (and Luke)

The apostle Paul speaks of the new covenant explicitly in only two places: 2 Corinthians 3, and 1 Corinthians 11:25 ("the new covenant in my blood," see also Luke 22:20). The term shows that Jeremiah's prophecy is in the background. He probably alludes to it in Galatians 4:24, where Sarah and Hagar are allegories for "two covenants." Further, it seems likely that Paul is alluding to the prophecy of Jeremiah 31:31–34 in at least two more places: Romans 2:14–15 ("the work of the law written on their hearts") and 11:27 ("this will be my covenant with them," combining with Isa 59:20–21).[45]

It is clear that in 2 Corinthians 3:5–6 Paul is using the term "new covenant" in the way we found it in Jeremiah:

> ⁵Not that we are sufficient in ourselves to claim anything as coming from us, but our sufficiency is from God, ⁶who has made us sufficient to be ministers of a *new covenant*, not of the

---

43. Hebrew text in Rabin, *Zadokite Documents*, and Lohse, *Die Texte aus Qumran*.

44. Notably Wright, *New Testament and the People of God*, 268–72.

45. There is, of course, an extensive secondary literature on the way these texts use the OT, not least in Beale and Carson, *Commentary*, but space limitations forbid a thorough interaction here.

letter but of the Spirit. For the letter kills, but the Spirit gives life. (emphasis added)

He defines the "ministry of the new covenant" as being one of the Spirit, as opposed to of the letter. Now Paul makes this same contrast of letter and Spirit in Romans 2:28–29:[46]

> [28]For no one is a Jew who is merely one outwardly, nor is circumcision outward and physical. [29]But a Jew is one inwardly, and circumcision is a matter of the heart, by the Spirit, not by the letter. His praise is not from man but from God.

You can see here that "the letter" corresponds to being a Jew only outwardly, while "the Spirit" makes sure that one is a Jew inwardly, by circumcision of the heart.[47]

Paul goes on to refer to his "ministry of the Spirit" (2 Cor 3:8)—in view of the evidence above, that is because its fruit is covenant reality in those who hear. He contrasts this with the "ministry of condemnation" (v. 9), which Moses carried out—namely because in the passage Paul alludes to (Exod 34:29–35), the people had been unfaithful to the covenant (and not because condemnation was the content of Moses' revelation).

When in Galatians 4:24, Paul says, "these women [namely Sarah and Hagar] are two covenants," he goes on to define what he means in terms of subjective condition: slavery (following the Judaizers) and freedom (faith). In other words, he does not refer to redemptive-historical entities.

The eucharistic references (Luke 22:20; 1 Cor 11:25) are difficult, but the key is to note what Jesus did *not* say: he did not say "this cup *inaugurates* the new covenant," or "this cup *commemorates* the new covenant inaugurated in my blood," or any such thing.[48] He declares that the cup *is* the new covenant, just as the bread *is* his body. I have suggested elsewhere that[49]

> The cup is participation in the sacrifice—in other words, the sacrament expresses the reality of participating in Christ's sacrifice,

---

46. Some NT specialists call this a "redefinition" of the people of God: e.g., Berkley, *Broken Covenant*, 216; and Seifrid, "Romans," 639. However, it seems to me to be a standard theme in the Hebrew Bible itself.

47. As noted, it looks like the wording of 2 Corinthians 3:3 ("not on tablets *of stone* but on tablets *of fleshly hearts*"; ESV margin) derives from Ezekiel 11:19 (LXX; "and I will pluck out the heart *of stone* from their flesh and I will give to them *a fleshly heart*").

48. Contrast Wright, *Knowing Jesus*, 163, who takes the words in just this way. The purpose of a peace offering is not to *inaugurate* a covenant, but to convey participation in the fellowship with God that is the purpose of the covenant (this is why a peace offering may be used at the inauguration, e.g., Exod 24:8).

49. See discussion in Collins, "Eucharist as Christian Sacrifice," 13.

that is, of embracing the covenant from the heart.... The cup "is" the new covenant in the same way as the bread "is" the body of Jesus (see 1 Cor 11:24-25; Luke 22:19-20)—sacramentally.[50]

The apparent allusion to the new covenant in Romans 11:27 follows the interpretive line that I am advocating here. That is, the present era is, to Paul, the time during which "the fullness of the Gentiles" will "come in" (Rom 11:25); and although there is controversy about the proper interpretation of "all Israel will be saved" (11:26), it makes the most sense in the light of Paul's reading of the prophets to suppose that he anticipates a future conversion of the Jews (probably to be followed by further blessing to the Gentile world: vv. 12, 15).[51] In verses 26-27, Paul quotes from Isaiah 59:20-21 and, while his wording seems to be a straightforward adaptation of the LXX of Isaiah, many also find an echo of Jeremiah 31:33.[52]

The first line of Romans 11:27 (*hautē autois hē par' emou diathēkē*, "and this will be my covenant with them"), which comes from Isaiah 59:21 (LXX), also evokes Jeremiah 31:33 (LXX 38:33; *hautē hē diathēkē, hēn diathēsomai tō oikō Israēl meta tas hēmeras ekeinas*, "this is the covenant that I will make with the house of Israel after those days"), which, as argued above, deals with the same topic. If this is so, and if Paul's expectation in Romans 11:13-32 really is that the ultimate remedy will come to the Jewish people as a whole at some unknown future time (which in turn would bring further blessing to the gentiles), then it appears that Paul read this line of prophecies in the way I have described them. This reading of Paul, well-represented in the history of interpreting Romans 9-11, becomes even more reasonable when we discover that the Second Temple Jewish texts do provide a context for this reading.

In Romans 2, Paul is addressing the question of why the family of Abraham did not achieve its calling to be "a guide to the blind, a light to those who are in darkness" (v. 19). He argues that the reason is that Israel failed to embrace the covenant privileges. Part of this argument comes in 2:14-15, where Paul describes the moral performance of "Gentiles, who do not have the law," who "by nature do what the law requires"; such people "show that the work of the law is written on their hearts." Paul describes them this way in order to show that his fellow Jews, for all their vaunted new

---

50. Collins, "Eucharist as Christian Sacrifice," 13n50, explains: "A sacrament is a sacred rite of the covenant that uses symbolism, but also conveys what it symbolizes—for spiritual nurture (1 Cor 10:16-18) or for punishment (1 Cor 11:29-30), depending on the condition of the worshiper."

51. For versions of this reading of Romans 11, compare the Romans commentaries of, say, Murray, Cranfield, and Schreiner, as over against that of, say, N. T. Wright.

52. See, for example, the NA27 cross reference; Seifrid, "Romans," 677.

covenant experience, have not attained to what the prophets envisioned; that is, "the work of the law written on their hearts" is an ironic allusion to Jeremiah 31:33, to argue that when gentiles outperform Jews in the moral sphere, this means that the Jews have not really grasped the covenant properly.[53] Paul is not denying the line of interpretation that his fellow Second Temple Jews might have had for these prophecies in Jeremiah and Ezekiel, though he is denying the kind of application the prophecies seem to have been given; the Second Temple material mentioned above shows why Paul might have needed to do this.

In sum, we gain insight into Paul if we read his discussion in the light of what we saw in Jeremiah.

6. The New Covenant in Hebrews

The letter to the Hebrews makes the most extensive use of covenant contrast in the NT. In 7:22, Jesus is "the guarantor of a better covenant" (in contrast to the Aaronic priests); in 8:6-13, we have Jesus as the mediator of a "better covenant" (followed by a citation of Jeremiah 31:31-34); in 9:15, Jesus is "the mediator of a new covenant," who provides for "the transgressions committed under the first covenant"; and in 12:24, we again read of Jesus as "the mediator of a new covenant." It is easy—and common—to see this as a contrast between Sinai and Calvary, and this lies behind the typical Christian view that the new covenant is the covenant inaugurated by the death and resurrection of Jesus, but let us first see if that is the best way to read the book.

Hebrews appears to be a book written to a specific group of Hellenistic Jewish Christians[54] who had endured some troubles for their Christian profession (10:32-33; 12:4), but who are now tempted to give up the struggle for the seemingly easier path of "normal" Judaism (10:23, 35-39; 12:3; 13:10-16; see also 6:1-12). The author is supplying reasons to ground his exhortation for them to persevere, which is the only way they can receive the benefits of God's promises (11:25-26; 12:9-11, 25) and of genuine membership in the heavenly people of God (11:39-40; 12:18-24). We can infer that their argument involves a claim that God had instituted the sacrifices in the first place,

---

53. For full discussion of these verses, and the likely allusions to Aristotle in them, see my "Echoes of Aristotle."

54. Support for this identification comes from the fact that the book is filled with LXX citations and allusions, and a scholarly type of exegesis. It further makes little or no reference to the gentiles. For helpful conversations on this point, I thank my former student, Christopher Richardson, whose 2009 Aberdeen PhD thesis was published as Richardson, *Pioneer and Perfecter of Faith*.

so we might expect him to be happy if his people continued to use them; this explains why the author would insist that these things do not work in any kind of automatic fashion (as in Heb 10:1–4). From this we can see that the letter to the Hebrews is not a treatise on salvation, perseverance, and apostasy *in general*: it is addressed to the needs of a particular group of Jewish Christians, facing a particular set of challenges. The Jewishness of the audience makes the new covenant passages from Jeremiah and Ezekiel relevant to them.

Christian readers generally take this letter to the Hebrews as implying that the primary reference of the new covenant is the era initiated by Jesus' death and resurrection, with its change of sacraments, dissolution of the church-state nexus that the law of Moses instituted, and its new openness to people of all ethnicities. At this point, we will simply observe that none of these issues comes up in the course of that letter.[55]

Our author argues that the first tent (the one built in Exodus) was made as a copy of the heavenly one (Heb 8:5, echoing Exod 25:40 [LXX]). This is not a negative assessment: Moses obediently made the tent, and that tent was the earthly contact of the heavenly sanctuary, where God is especially present. That tent had an important function for the people of God, but it served its purpose in redemptive history (part of which was to cultivate subjective faith toward the one who would accomplish the objective basis of the covenant). To think that using the first tent would be an acceptable way of relating to God, now that Christ has offered his sacrifice, would be to use that tent for a purpose that God never gave it: rejecting the ultimacy of Christ's sacrifice, for which the OT had paved the way. It appears from the book that our author feared that his audience might be tempted to do just that, reasoning that since God had ordained these ordinances they would still achieve their purposes. Such an attitude would be a true defection from God's own revelation; it would be a mark of an unbelieving (and unregenerate) heart. No wonder the author cautions his readers against continuing to sin "after receiving the knowledge of the truth" (10:26), and spurning the Son of God and profaning the blood of the covenant by which a person is sanctified (10:29), and urges them, "See that you do not refuse him who is speaking" (12:25). He is optimistic that, once the audience comes to see things his way, they will follow his instructions (6:9–12; 10:32–39; 13:22).

In all of this, the author does not speak ill either of the OT or the faithful among the ancient people of God. He takes the OT as God's word

---

55. As Rayburn observes, "Remarkably the author is little interested in the present fulfillment of Old Testament prophecy. Indeed, the idea of fulfillment plays almost no role in the argument. For this author, the Old Testament is not a collection of prophecies now fulfilled in Christ so much as a contemporary Word of God to be heard, believed, and obeyed" ("Hebrews," 1131).

that addresses "us" today (namely, the author and his audience of fellow Jewish Christians; Heb 3:13), a word that is shot through with "good news" (4:2). The OT faithful are the examples for "our" faith (11:2), and they are the community whom "we" may be privileged to join. Its principles—especially that it is possible to be a member of God's people in name but not in heart (3:12–4:1)—apply just as much to the first-century readers as it did in Jeremiah's day.

Further, he introduces his citation of Jeremiah 31:31–34 in a way that lays the blame, not on the Sinai administration, but on the people. He says:

> ⁷For if that first covenant had been *faultless*, there would have been no occasion to look for a second. ⁸For he *finds fault* with them when he says:
>
> Behold, the days are coming, declares the Lord,
> when I will establish a new covenant with the house of Israel
> and with the house of Judah. (Heb 8:7–8)

In verse 7, the "first covenant" is not "faultless" (*amemptos*), but that is not a reference to the revelation at Sinai, since he goes on to say that "he finds fault [*memphomenos*] with them"—that is, with the unbelieving people. In other words, the author is using the Jeremiah passage in line with what I take to be its original intent, with "covenant" in its subjective sense, and applying it to the situation that he faces: for one of these Jewish Christians to fail to keep following Jesus, and to draw back to Judaism simply in order to avoid conflict, would be unbelief as rank as any found in the OT itself.[56]

The best way to make sense of the letter to the Hebrews, then, is to suppose that its author has used the Jeremiah passage properly, and has applied it to the situation his audience faced. For the audience not to hold on to Jesus would be for them to think that they have the right to decide how God is to be worshiped—which is just what unbelief had consistently done in the OT (only there it was blatant idolatry and syncretism). True faith—the covenant written on the heart—makes God's revelation the primary thing.[57]

A further bit of evidence in this discussion is the fact that Hebrews makes no reference to the servant passages in Isaiah that some think add a messianic element to the new covenant (see section 3, "The New Covenant in

---

56. If we read things this way, we do not have to conclude with Rendtorff (and many others) that the author of Hebrews has used the passage in Jeremiah contrary to its first intention: see Rendtorff, "New Covenant?"

57. Note how, in Hebrews 2:1–4, the author reminds them that the message about Jesus was properly attested as being from God and having redemptive-historical weight. They have no excuse for not knowing that a redemptive-historical development has come to them.

Isaiah?"). In fact, the only relevant items of the list of Isaianic texts mentioned above are Isaiah 55:3 and 61:8, which mention the "eternal covenant"; these may have contributed to the wording of Hebrews 13:20 ("by the blood of the *eternal covenant*").[58] But this only strengthens the argument here, since these texts speak of God's plan to renew his people in faithfulness after the exile.

I conclude, then, that Hebrews does not imply that the new covenant of itself is a redemptive-historical development in the way that Christ's incarnation, death, and resurrection-ascension are (1:1–4); rather, the author focuses on the subjective condition of the new covenant being that which enables his audience to embrace the particular redemptive-historical development in their time and to persevere.

7. New Covenant Ecclesiology

A number of authors with Baptist convictions have argued that the new covenant establishes a ground for present church practice, namely their understanding that only those we believe to be regenerate are eligible for church "membership." I will take Stephen Wellum as a worthy proponent of this position.[59]

In Wellum's understanding, Jeremiah's prophecy (Jer 31:29–34) "entails that *all* those within the 'new covenant community' are people, by definition, who presently have experienced regeneration of heart and the full forgiveness of sin."[60] That is, the situation I described above, in which not all of the members of the people embrace the covenant from the heart, no longer applies in the "new covenant community." Now, Wellum never considers the exegetical question of whether that does indeed follow from Jeremiah; he never therefore deals with the possibility mentioned here that there is an ultimate fulfillment, still in the future. Quite apart from that, though, Wellum's description certainly does not match what we find as the NT authors deal with the actual churches to which they write. For example, Paul can cite examples from Israel's wandering in the wilderness, examples whose very point is that one can be a member of the people without the heart reality of true faith (1 Cor 10:1–5). In fact, Paul goes on to say that "these things took

---

58. The expression "by the blood of the covenant" appears in the LXX of Zechariah 9:11, which probably suggests that the benedictory formula in Hebrews 13:20-21 is a composite of allusions to OT passages.

59. Here I cite Wellum, "Baptism." See also Gentry and Wellum, *Kingdom Through Covenant*, 506–13. The *Southern Baptist Journal of Theology* 20.1 (2016), of which Wellum is the editor, contains several articles reflecting this same perspective.

60. Wellum, "Baptism," 105 (emphasis original).

place as examples for us, that we might not desire evil as they did" (1 Cor 10:6). That is, the same principles at work in the old era bear upon gentile as well as Jewish Christians in our era. Paul can also remind the churches that the members must "continue in the faith, stable and steadfast," if they wish to finally be presented "holy and blameless and above reproach before [God]" (Col 1:22–23). The author of Hebrews insists that "good news came to us [first-century Jewish believers in Jesus] just as to them [the people of Israel following Moses]," and he is concerned that "no one may fall by the same sort of disobedience" (Heb 4:2, 11)—referring to events whose very dynamic is the situation in which some covenant members "believe in" the Lord, while others do not (see Num 14:11, 22–24, 38), with the implication that the same dynamic applies to this new audience.

Hence, it does not follow that the empirical Christian communities are "by definition" only composed of people "who presently have experienced regeneration of heart and the full forgiveness of sin." Jesus' parable of the sower and the soils (Luke 8:4–15 and parallels) explains why this is so: there are people who "receive the word with joy," but only "believe for a while" (Luke 8:13). There is no hint that a human administrator of God's people could have told the difference between these and the fruitful ones, nor that he should even try to erect a pattern of church life designed to do so; therefore, Wellum's thesis fails.

8. Conclusions

What, then, shall we say to these things? As I indicated earlier (in section 1, "Definitions and Distinctions"), there are certainly redemptive-historical developments connected with the resurrection-ascension of Jesus and the gentile mission. In terms of the succession of covenants in the OT, it would seem that the fruition of the Davidic covenant (the enthronement of the heir of David and the beginning of his worldwide empire) has been accompanied with the dissolution of the Sinai covenant (i.e., the people of God are no longer defined by a particular ethnic group living under a theocracy). At the same time, these are *developments*—which implies that the basic covenant principles are still in play, as we gentile Christians are joined to the same people of God as Abraham, Moses, Joshua, and all OT believers. The term "new covenant" does not of itself describe these developments—though it can be used to describe the subjective condition necessary to lay hold of them, because we too must make a personal response of owning our place in the covenant.

7

The Catholicity of John Calvin

IT IS THE GREATEST pleasure for me to contribute to this *Festschrift* in honor of my dear friend Rob Rayburn. Rob and I have been friends for almost forty years. We first met in Aberdeen, Scotland, when Rob was pursuing his doctoral studies. From the first, we became what that eminent theologian Anne of Green Gables would have called "kindred spirits and bosom friends." Our friendship has meant much to me both personally and theologically. I can say that I prize and cherish his friendship—and that of his dear wife Florence. What follows is my tribute to a faithful and much used servant of God.

What does it mean to be Reformed? The answer might seem obvious. However, the sixteenth century Reformation embraced Wittenberg as well as Geneva, Edinburgh as well as Canterbury, and Basel as well as Zurich, to name but six centers of Reformation activity. "Reformed" not only had a geographical diversity, it also contained a measure of theological diversity. Martin Luther, Martin Bucer, John Calvin, Heinrich Bullinger, John Knox, and Thomas Cranmer all espoused the central doctrines of the Reformation but had their theological differences, differences that at times were animated and polemical. A similar Reformed diversity held in the centuries that followed. While there were deep theological congruencies between John Calvin, John Owen, Thomas Goodwin, John Bunyan, Jonathan Edwards, and Charles Hodge, there were also marked differences, sometimes of emphasis, sometimes of substance.

The Westminster Confession of Faith[1] was the mature reflection of a century of Reformed theological thought. The Divines who constructed the Confession and its Catechisms were conscious they were engaging in a Re-

---

1. The Westminster Assembly was called by the English Parliament and met from 1643–1652, though almost all of the substantive matters were concluded by 1649. The Confession of Faith was completed in 1647 and ratified by the Scottish, though not the English, Parliament.

formed ecumenical endeavor. This consensual engagement was highlighted in the debate on God's eternal decree.[2] The discussion focused on "whether God's decree to elect some people also includes a decree to reject others."[3] The "keynote"[4] of the discussion was expressed by George Gillespie: "When that word ('same') is left out, is it not a truth, and so every man may enjoy his own sense?"[5] Gillespie was seeking to "bridge the gap" between those in the Assembly who believed God's decree of predestination concerning the elect and the non-elect was unitary and those Divines who argued that the predestination of the elect and the predestination, or preterition, of the lost were separable. There is an underlying awareness that there were both infralapsarians and supralapsarians in the Assembly. The point is that Gillespie, a non-voting Scottish commissioner, desired to make the wording of the Confession of Faith nonspecific on this matter. Edward Reynolds immediately followed Gillespie and declared, "let us not put in disputes and scholastical things into a Confession of Faith."[6] Commenting on this, B. B. Warfield in his scholarly work on the Westminster Assembly made this observation: "Obviously it was a generic Calvinism they were intent on asserting and not any particular variety of it."[7] In other words, catholicity as much as particularity was a note that the Westminster Divines sought to express in the Confession and Catechisms that they produced.

From its inception, the Reformed faith has been a multifaceted faith. To be sure, it has a well-defined core of non-negotiable doctrines; but it does not have, and has never had, one public face or particular theological expression. The Continental Reformed tradition, centered upon the Three Forms of Unity (the Heidelberg Confession, the Belgic Confession, and the Canons of Dort), is no less "Reformed" than its British and American Reformed counterpart within the Westminster tradition.

This historical fact helps us to appreciate the instinctive and determined catholicity of John Calvin. Calvin was a man of strong theological convictions. He spent his life tirelessly promoting and defending the great doctrines of the gospel recovered for the church by the grace of God. He was no compromiser, but he recognized that the Reformed faith did not have one pristine expression (though he thought his own exposition of the

2. See Van Dixhoorn, *Minutes*, 3.688–97.
3. Van Dixhoorn, *Minutes*, 3.689.
4. Warfield, *Westminster Assembly*, 136.
5. Quoted in Warfield, *Westminster Assembly*, 136. See Mitchell and Struthers, *Minutes*, 151.
6. Mitchell and Struthers, *Minutes*, 151.
7. Warfield, *Westminster Assembly*, 136.

Reformed faith in his *Institutes* came nearest!). In his *Letters, Commentaries, Treatises,* and supremely in his *Institutes,* Calvin displayed a Reformed catholicity that was by turns humbling and breathtaking.

Calvin's passion for peace and unity in the church permeated all his reforming initiatives. He served the cause of Christ at a time when Protestants were visibly and acrimoniously divided, and from the outset he sought to heal those breaches. In a letter to Archbishop Thomas Cranmer, Calvin expressed his passionate commitment to help heal the divided body of Christ. He wrote,

> This other thing also is to be ranked among the chief evils of our time, viz., that the churches are so divided, that human fellowship is scarcely now in any repute among us, far less that Christian intercourse which all make a profession of, but few sincerely practice.... Thus it is that the members of the Church being severed, the body lies bleeding. So much does this concern me, that, could I be of any service, I would not grudge to cross even ten seas, if need were, on account of it.[8]

Calvin would have been mystified how Reformed Christians today could appear to be so indifferent to Christ's "bleeding body."

Calvin's pursuit of visible church unity appeared first in his tireless attempts to find a solution to the vexed question of the presence of Christ in the Eucharist. In seeking a solution that would satisfy Zwinglians and Lutherans, Calvin was zealous and yet flexible. His flexibility was evident in his commitment to the *Consensus Tigurinus* (1549, often called the "Zurich Agreement") in which he and Heinrich Bullinger reached agreement on twenty-four articles relating to the Lord's Supper.

Calvin had long desired to have his conviction that the sacraments are divinely-ordained instruments for conferring grace (*sacramenta conferunt gratiam*), but not apart from faith and the ministry of the Spirit, become the standard view of the Reformed churches. Bullinger was, however, unhappy with Calvin's language, fearing it could lead to misunderstanding and worse. In the interests of Reformed unity, Calvin agreed that the word *instrumentum* should not appear in the *Consensus*.[9] Bruce Gordon comments, "No one who

---

8. Calvin, *Tracts and Letters,* 5.347–48.

9. Article Seventeen reads: "The Sacraments Do Not Confer Grace. By this doctrine, that fiction of the sophists is refuted which teaches that the sacraments of the new law confer grace on all who do not interpose the obstacle of mortal sin. For besides the fact that nothing is received in the sacraments except by faith, it is also necessary to hold that the grace of God is certainly not so tied to them that whoever has the sign receives the thing itself. For the signs are administered to the reprobate as well as to the elect, but the reality only reaches the latter." Calvin had taught that both believers

had seen the consequences of Charles' victory over the Schmalkaldic League could allow disputes over terminology to doom the church. Calvin was prepared to shift to reach agreement in the cause of unity."[10]

It would be wrong, however, to see this as a matter of personal graciousness on Calvin's part. Calvin was motivated, even driven, by a passion for Protestant church unity. Calvin greatly respected Bullinger. But it was not respect for Bullinger that led Calvin to agree to the omission of the word *instrumentum* from the text of the *Consensus*. It was Calvin's biblical catholicity that persuaded him to leave aside a passionate personal conviction in the greater interest of Protestant church unity. Gordon rightly attributes Calvin's accommodation, even concession, to Bullinger; not to a "cave in,"[11] but to the catholicity of a man who cherished the hope of Protestant church unity.

Second, Calvin pursued peace and unity among the Protestant churches by his pastorally wise and doctrinally acute advice to churches pursuing scriptural purity. In his letter *To the English Exiles at Frankfurt* in January 1555, he urged them to recognize the perilous times in which they were and to lay aside "contentions about forms of prayer and ceremonies." Calvin was not saying that these matters were of no importance. He was, however, reminding the English exiles not to behave "as if you were at ease and in a season of tranquillity, and thus throwing an obstacle in the way of your coalescing in one body of worshippers." To do so, he added, "is really too unreasonable."[12]

Calvin was sympathetic to the concern of the exiles. He spoke of the ceremonies to which they were being required to submit as "silly things," however "silly things that might be tolerated." He told the exiles that, regarding matters such as "external rites," he himself was "indulgent and pliable," though at the same time he was quick to add, "I do not deem it expedient always to comply with the foolish captiousness of those who will not give up a single point of their usual routine." Calvin believed the exiles, and indeed all true believers, should be aiming "at something purer," a church shaped by the teaching of Holy Scripture alone. This, however,

---

and unbelievers receive the Supper as a sign and a seal. To believers, the Supper is a sign and seal of God's covenantal grace. To unbelievers, the Supper is a sign and seal of God's covenantal judgment. See the recently translated sermons of Calvin on Acts 1–7 (*Sermons*, 64).

10. Gordon, *Calvin*, 179. The Schmalkaldic League was a defensive alliance of Lutheran princes within the Holy Roman Empire during the mid-sixteenth century.

11. Gordon, *Calvin*, 179.

12. Calvin, *Tracts and Letters*, 6.117-18.

he was quick to acknowledge would take time, and "faults would not be corrected on the first day."[13]

The same godly patience is evident in his letter to Edward Seymour, Duke of Somerset and Lord Protector of England from 1547–1549. Calvin expressed his concern that the Reformation in England was proceeding too slowly, but continued, "I willingly acknowledge that we must observe moderation, and that overdoing is neither discreet nor useful; indeed, that forms of worship need to be accommodated to the condition and tastes of the people. But the corruptions of Satan and of the Antichrist must not be admitted under that pretext."[14]

This last note was emphatic in Calvin's condemnation of the Nicodemites.[15] Unlike Martin Bucer, who thought that a compromise might be reached with the Roman church, Calvin was adamant that true believers must leave the "Great Harlot." He viewed Rome as "Babylon" and beyond internal reform. As such, all believers must totally reject her and come out from her. Calvin's opposition to the Nicodemites seemed too harsh and "inexpedient" on the part of some of his fellow Reformed Christians. For Calvin, however, the issue first and foremost was not what would best further the cause of reform, but what would most honor God. It would be right to leave the Roman church, even if that decision did not politically or ecclesiastically appear to advance the gospel. Truth must always trump consequences.

Although he saw no prospect for biblical reform in the Roman church, Calvin was relentless in his pursuit of wider church unity among the Reformed. There is a striking passage in the *Institutes* (4.10.30) where Calvin reflected on the fact that God's word did not specify "in outward discipline and ceremonies to prescribe in detail what we ought to do (because [God] saw that this depended upon the state of the times, and he did not deem one form suitable for all ages)."[16] Calvin was quick to acknowledge that "we ought not to charge into innovation rashly, suddenly, for insufficient cause." However, he continued, "But love will best judge what may hurt or edify; and if we let love be our guide, all will be safe." Calvin's readiness to "let love be our guide" is a vivid illustration of his accommodating spirit. He always had his eye on the "bigger picture." Where doctrines fundamental

13. Calvin, *Tracts and Letters*, 6.118.

14. Calvin, *Tracts and Letters*, 5.193.

15. This was the term Calvin used to describe those evangelical believers who, like Nicodemus in John 3, hid their attachment to Jesus under a cloak of "darkness." Calvin could not understand how a true believer could hide their gospel allegiance and remain within the Roman church, practicing "idolatry," for fear of persecution. See Eire, *War Against the Idols*.

16. The example Calvin cited was "kneeling when solemn prayers are being said."

to the true worship of God and the truth of the gospel were at issue, Calvin was immoveable, even implacable. Where issues like kneeling for prayer threatened to bring disorder and even division into the church, he called for moderation and a sense of proportion.

Third, in pursuit of Protestant church unity (a unity that for Calvin was more doctrinal than organizational), Calvin "travelled extensively, frequently visiting Berne, Zurich and Basle, as well as journeying further afield to Frankfurt and Strasburg."[17] In addition, he received a constant flow of visitors from all over Europe and wrote letters to refugees, statesmen, princes, struggling Christians, pastors awaiting execution, bishops, and at least one archbishop. Calvin knew, because he believed it was imperative for him to know, what God was doing throughout Europe. He was driven by an instinctive catholicity that compelled him to seek the good and promote the good of the true body of Christ wherever he found it.

Why is this "churchly passion" for visible unity among Bible Protestants so apparently absent from evangelical, Reformed church life today? Is it due to a doctrinal commitment to radical independency? Is it a reaction against the ecumenical movement with its theological indifferentism? Does the pursuit of church unity seem a luxury the church can ill afford in an age of aggressive unbelief, moral relativism, and religious pluralism? According to Jesus Christ, the King and Head of the church, the church's visible unity will be a compelling testimony to a watching world "that you have sent me" (John 17:21, 23). The concern for and pursuit of church unity is not a luxury Christians can politely, or even impolitely, ignore, unless they want to live in public opposition to the prayer of their King and Head.

When one looks at the lives of the great men and women God has raised up to bless, revive, and renew his church throughout the ages, they almost all exhibited a catholicity of spirit toward other true believers that is both breathtaking and unsettling. Whatever else Calvin can be accused of, being a doctrinal compromiser is not one of them. He may at times have been mistaken, but Christ's "bleeding body" mattered so deeply to him that he was always ready to wear himself out seeking its healing and unity.

What can Christians, and especially Reformed Christians, today learn from Calvin's Reformed catholicity?

First, it would be historically naïve and theologically wrong-headed to think that the Reformed faith, especially in its sixteenth-century expression, was monolithically homogeneous. Geneva was not Wittenberg; Basel was not Berne; Zurich was not Edinburgh! Yet there was a breadth of collegiality

---

17. Gordon, *Calvin*, 251.

and contact that should both humble and embarrass many who today profess to be Reformed Christians.

One of the remarkable features of "Old Princeton"[18] was its Reformed catholicity. In his inaugural address as associate professor of didactic theology in 1877, A. A. Hodge expressed what he believed was a marked feature of his father's (Charles Hodge's) theology:

> zeal for doctrine has in too many instances been narrow and prejudiced, mingled with the infirmities of personal pride and party spirit, and has hence led to the unnecessary divisions and alienations of those who were in reality one in faith, and to the conditioning of communion, and even of salvation, upon unessential points.[19]

James Alexander, the eldest son of Princeton's first professor, was not expressing a mere personal opinion when he wrote, "At judgement I heartily believe that some heresies of heart and temper will be charged as worse than heavy doctrinal errors."[20] Alexander was only reflecting, faithfully, the consistent teaching of the New Testament.

Perhaps the most striking illustration of Old Princeton's Reformed catholicity was seen in Charles Hodge's assessment of Friedrich Schleiermacher. He had gone to hear Schleiermacher preach and commented, "The words were biblical . . . [but] the ideas so vague and indefinite."[21] Hodge later attacked Schleiermacher's pantheism in his *Systematic Theology* and his rejection of the Bible as a "supernatural revelation from God."[22] However, in a famous footnote, Hodge wrote,

> When in Berlin the writer often attended Schleiermacher's church. The hymns to be sung were on printed slips of paper and distributed at the doors. They were always evangelical and spiritual in an eminent degree, filled with praise and gratitude to our Redeemer. Tholuck said that Schleiermacher, when sitting in the evening with his family, would often say, "Hush, children; let us sing a hymn of praise to Christ". Can we doubt that he

---

18. "Old Princeton" defines the years 1812–1929 when Princeton was wholly committed to biblical inerrancy and supernatural religion ("unembarrassed supernaturalism," to use B. B. Warfield's words). It was the bastion of Reformed theological learning and piety.

19. Quoted in Calhoun, *Princeton Seminary*, 49.

20. Alexander, *Forty Years' Familiar Letters*, 227.

21. Hodge, *Systematic Theology*, 2.440.

22. Hodge, *Systematic Theology*, 2.440–54.

is singing those praises now? To whomsoever Christ is God, St John assures us, Christ is a Savior.[23]

Whether Hodge was right or even wise to make such an assessment is not the point. Here is a hero of the Reformed faith whose catholicity is breathtaking. I am not sure many evangelical conferences, never mind Reformed conferences, today would invite someone to speak who had written so positively about Schleiermacher. In an age of theological reductionism and Reformed pietism (as distinct from true piety), it would serve the Reformed church well to be re-acquainted with its history and heritage.

Second, Christians, and especially Reformed Christians, have a divinely imposed obligation to "maintain the unity of the Spirit in the bond of peace" (Eph 4:3). Like Calvin, it should be the longing of Reformed churches to do all they can to help "heal the bleeding and broken body of Christ." This, of course, is easier said than done. To some, that course would lead to the charge of compromise. But surely John Murray was right when he wrote,

> The lack of unity among the churches of Christ which profess the faith in its purity is a patent violation of the unity of the body of Christ, and of that unity which the prayer of our Lord requires us to promote. We cannot escape from the implications for us by resorting to the notion of the invisible church. The body of Christ is not an invisible entity, and the prayer of Jesus was directed to the end that the world might believe. The unity prayed for was one that would bear witness to the world, and therefore belonged to the realm of the observable. The implications for visible confession and witness are unavoidable.[24]

Martin Lloyd Jones, perhaps the most influential Reformed preacher of the twentieth century, expressed the same concern: "Can we deny the charge that we, as evangelical Christians, have been less interested in the question of church unity than anyone else?" He continued, "We are always negative; we are always on the defensive; we are always bringing up objections and difficulties. I do not think we can deny this charge."[25]

Are Reformed churches, committed to the Westminster Confession of Faith and Catechisms and the Three Forms of Unity, always to live in "splendid isolation" from one another? Are we to exist in our little self-contained associations and fellowships, occasionally praying for one another (if we even do that) but never expressing our historic, biblical, confessional

---

23. Hodge, *Systematic Theology*, 2.440n1; Tholuck was one of Hodge's teachers in Berlin.

24. Murray, *Collected Writings*, 2.335.

25. Lloyd-Jones, *Knowing the Times*, 249.

unity in Christ? There should be no illusion that a meaningful Reformed collegiality would be easy to cultivate. Suspicions abound, and some suspicions are well-founded! Our Lord Jesus was not being naive when he prayed, "[may] they all be one, just as you, Father, are in me, and I in you, that they also may be in us, so that the world may believe that you have sent me" (John 17:21). The Son of God in our humanity prayed for his church to be one. He shed his precious blood on Calvary's cross to redeem his church and make it one. Should it not be the daily prayer and labor of his church to exhibit that oneness to an unbelieving world? What will this mean? What do you think? This much is certain: until evangelical, Reformed Christians rediscover the God-honoring grace of gospel catholicity, godly church unity will ever remain an elusive mirage.

In his gospel, Mark recounts a significant incident in the ministry of Jesus and his disciples. John, one of the disciples, said to Jesus, "Teacher, we saw someone casting out demons in your name, and we tried to stop him, because he was not following us." Jesus sternly replied, "Do not stop him, for no one who does a mighty work in my name will be able soon afterward to speak evil of me. For the one who is not against us is for us" (Mark 9:38–40). It is said that a long journey begins with one small step. Church unity, visible, observable, church unity may seem a long way away. What is surely undeniable is that Christians can begin that long journey with the small but significant step of treating other believers as believers, however imperfect their theology. If the Father has elected them, if the Son has redeemed them, if the Spirit indwells them, they are family, "warts and all."

Ever since I first met my dear friend Rob Rayburn (it is hard to think it is almost forty years ago), I have been both struck by and impressed with his godly catholicity. Rob is a pastor-scholar, to whom the Lord has given stellar gifts. In this he follows in the footsteps of Calvin. But even more, Rob is a Christian whose heart's desire is to call no one master but Christ. It is this combination of Christian and pastor-scholar that I have so valued these past almost forty years. I cherish his friendship, made all the richer by Florence. May the Lord richly bless his life and ministry until we are all caught up into the nearer presence of our great King.

8

Gospel Harmony: American Popular Sacred Music, 1871–1969

How Mass Evangelism and the Jubilee Choral Tradition Inaugurated a Revolution in Gospel Music across Ecclesiastical and Racial Lines.

Allergy alert: Parts of this paper have the smell of sawdust.

I never shall forget that day,
Coming for to carry me home,
When Jesus washed my sins away,
Coming for to carry me home.

—"Swing Low, Sweet Chariot"
   As sung by the Fisk Jubilee Quartet, 1909[1]

Oh happy day, oh happy day,
When Jesus washed, oh when He washed,
When Jesus washed, He washed my sins away—
Oh happy day.

—"Oh Happy Day"
   As sung by the Edwin Hawkins Singers, 1969[2]

1. From the album *Swing Low, Sweet Chariot: Fisk Jubilee Singers in Chronological Order, vol. 1 (1909-1911)*. The couplet in the original collection of Fisk Jubilee songs is: "The brightest day that ever I saw / When Jesus washed my sins away" (Seward, *Jubilee Songs*, 160). The Fisk Jubilee Quartet in 1909 inserted the more singable rhyming phrase that shows up in other spirituals (e.g. Dett, *Religious Folk-Songs*, 49, 195, 207, 232). It is to be regretted that subsequent publications did not follow their lead, but either print the non-rhyming version or, more often, omit the couplet altogether. To their credit, the original couplet is reproduced in Boyer, *Lift Every Voice*, and Carpenter, *African American Heritage Hymnal*.

2. From the album *Let Us Go into the House of the Lord* (1968). The lyrics are drawn

A. Moody-Sankey and the Fisk Jubilee Singers

I BEGIN THIS ESSAY WITH the year 1871 because of the coincidence of two events that are the backdrop for the appeal of popular sacred music over the course of the next century. Ira D. Sankey joined D. L. Moody early in 1871 as the evangelist's song-leader in Chicago, and the Fisk Jubilee Singers began their first national fundraising tour on October 6 of that same year, setting the stage for a revolution in congregational singing and public listening to gospel music through the marvels of the phonograph, and later the radio.

The Moody-Sankey evangelistic team was famous for making the preacher and the song-leader equal in their mission of urban evangelism. Moody preached the gospel; Sankey sang the gospel and got the crowd to sing it along with him. Endowed with a powerful baritone voice, Sankey led the music facing the audience, seated in a high chair that towered above a reed pump organ positioned on the stage next to the pulpit. The arrangement was entirely innovative and highly effective in its day. Since the harmonium, as the instrument was called, was relatively inexpensive and not affected by temperature or humidity, it was ideal for their year-round campaigns.

Sankey tells the story of how he was recruited by Moody in his autobiography.[3] As a delegate to the International Convention of the YMCA meeting in Indianapolis in 1870, Sankey was asked to breathe life into a meeting that had dragged on far too long by singing something. At the first opportune moment he stood up and launched solo into a familiar gospel hymn, which the assembly lustily joined in evident relief. Moody was in the audience, and afterward insisted that Sankey leave his current business and join him in Chicago because, he told him, "I have been looking for you for the last eight years." Sankey was politely noncommittal, so the next day Moody arranged an impromptu street meeting in the late afternoon. He set up a large storage box and asked Sankey to mount it and sing something. Here's how the scene played out:

> "Am I a soldier of the cross?" soon gathered a considerable crowd. After the song, Mr. Moody climbed up on the box and began to talk. The workingmen were just going home from the mills and the factories, and in a short time a very large crowd

---

entirely from Philip Doddridge's 1755 hymn "O Happy Day, That Fixed My Choice." In the spring of 1969, the track of "O Happy Day" as a single became a runaway R&B and pop music hit, eventually winning a Grammy and selling upwards of seven million copies. It is regularly cited as marking a new epoch in the history of gospel music, e.g., Boyer, *How Sweet the Sound*, 5.

3. Sankey, *My Life*. Sankey died in 1908.

had gathered. When he had spoken for some twenty-five minutes he announced that the meeting should be continued at the Opera House, and invited the people to accompany us there. He asked me to lead the way and with my friends singing some familiar hymn. This we did, singing as we marched down the street, "Shall we gather at the river."[4]

Moody's purpose in concocting the surprise event was to illustrate the decisive contribution Sankey's singing could make to urban evangelism. After a long period of deliberation and a visit to Chicago, Sankey finally accepted the invitation and moved to Chicago early in 1871, where he served alongside Moody until his church burned to the ground in the Chicago fire on October 8-9, which happens to have been the Sunday and Monday on which the Fisk Jubilee Singers gave their first concerts on tour in Cincinnati. The Monday concert was their first paid event. "Out of money and in debt as they were, they donated the entire proceeds, which amounted to something less than $50, to the Chicago relief fund."[5] Who could have predicted that the two groups, after this "baptism by fire," would both shortly begin their first tours of Great Britain and collaborate in singing the gospel in Scotland, of all places, where hymn singing was frowned upon and Sankey's beloved harmonium was dismissed as a "kist of whistles."

The Jubilee Singers arrived in London in early May of 1873 and gave their first concert to an audience gathered by invitation of the Earl of Shaftesbury, president of the Freedmen's Mission Aid Society, the English auxiliary of the American Missionary Association (AMA). A great deal of credit goes to the AMA, which was founded in 1846 to protest slavery and to educate the slaves when most of the other mission agencies had acquiesced in the institution. They persevered in that endeavor in the face of severe persecution, and they eventually succeeded in planting seventeen academies and normal schools in the South, as well as seven institutions for collegiate and theological education, including Fisk University in Nashville and Hampton Institute in Virginia.[6] In the Reconstruction era, the well-trained Jubilee Singers of Fisk and Hampton succeeded in "the emancipation of Negro music from the chains of false and often low ideals set upon it by popular minstrelsy,

---

4. Sankey, *My Life*, 20–21.
5. Marsh, *Jubilee Singers*, 17.
6. The other five institutions of higher education founded by the AMA were Berea College in Kentucky, Atlanta University in Georgia, Talladega College in Alabama, Tougaloo University in Mississippi, and Straight University in New Orleans. For a full account of the work of the AMA in the nineteenth century, see Richardson, *Christian Reconstruction*.

and in the establishment of it as a wonderful thing, a gift, and art, a glorious contribution to this nation and the world."[7]

The initial program was a huge success, and the Duke and Duchess of Argyll arranged a visit to their lodge the next day, to which Queen Victoria had also been invited.

> Soon after her Majesty's arrival the Duke informed them that she would be pleased to see them in an adjoining room. At his request they sang first, "Steal away to Jesus;" then chanted the Lord's Prayer, and sang "Go down, Moses."[8]

The Queen was duly impressed and communicated her satisfaction and gratitude through the Duke. Later she commissioned a floor-to-ceiling portrait of the original nine singers in commemoration of the tour as a gift of England to the University. Their interaction with Prime Minister Gladstone and his wife was equally productive for the University. But the capstone of the London tour was the concert in Charles H. Spurgeon's Tabernacle. The singers visited the morning service there on the Sunday of the week that the concert was to be given (on Wednesday). As they waited to meet the great preacher in his receiving room, some present asked them to sing something. They responded with the hymn "O Brothers, Don't Stay Away." Spurgeon was so moved by it that he called them into his room and requested that they sing it again in the evening service, at the beginning of which he announced:

> After the morning service I heard the Jubilee Singers sing a piece, "O brothers, don't stay away, for my Lord says there's room enough in the heavens for you." I found tears coming in my eyes; and looking at my deacons I found theirs very moist too. That song suggested my text and my sermon to-night. Now as a part of the sermon, I am going to ask them to sing it, for they preach in the singing; and may the Spirit of God send home this word to some to-night—some who may remember their singing if they forget my preaching.[9]

The Jubilees sang their invitational hymn and Spurgeon preached on the text "It is done as thou hast commanded, and yet there is room." In giving notice of the Wednesday concert, Spurgeon (with typical humor)

---

7. Dett, "Emancipation," 176. Dett was a classically trained concert pianist and composer who served as Director of the Music Department at Hampton Institute from 1926–1936. He published *Religious Folk-Songs of the Negro* in 1927, and in 1930 led the Hampton Singers (forty voices) on a six-week European tour.

8. Marsh, *Jubilee Singers*, 50.

9. Marsh, *Jubilee Singers*, 60.

used the catchphrase of the evening as an exhortation: "O brothers, don't stay away." An estimated crowd of seven thousand showed up early hoping there was still room.

The Moody-Sankey team began their campaign in Newcastle on August 25. The Jubilee Singers met up with them there and joined in their evangelistic endeavor. As Marsh reports, "Their songs were found to be especially adapted to promote the revival." After they had been prayed for in one of the noonday prayer meetings, a bit of drama unfolded that Moody often recalled.

> A moment's pause, and there went up in sweet, low notes a chorus as of angels. None could tell where the Singers were—on the floor, in the gallery, or in the air. The crowd was close, and the Singers—wherever they were—were sitting. Everyone was thrilled, for this was the song they sang: *There are angels hovering round / To carry the tidings home.*[10]

The services at Newcastle were filled to overflowing, and it was there that Sankey organized the first campaign choir. People were heard singing new songs such as "The Sweet By and By" and "Christ Arose" in the shipyards and other public places. Sankey notes, "It was the beginning of a revolution in Great Britain in the matter of popular sacred songs."[11]

The Moody-Sankey team opened in Edinburgh Sunday evening, November 23. After the invocation, Sankey asked the packed venue to join in singing "Old One Hundred," which the psalm-singers did with a will. Sankey followed with a solo rendition of "Jesus of Nazareth Passeth By." The intense silence during his singing of the gospel song indicated to him that it had been effective. This was confirmed in his mind when, after the sermon, he sang "Hold the Fort" and invited the crowd to join him on the chorus, "which they did with such heartiness and power that I was further convinced."[12]

Still there was room for doubt. In a later service in Barklay Free Church (with a borrowed reed organ), Sankey reports: "As I took my seat at the instrument on that, to me, most memorable evening, I discovered, to my great surprise, that Dr. Horatius Bonar was seated close by my organ, right in front of the pulpit." Bonar was Sankey's ideal hymn writer, yet he belonged to a church that practiced exclusive psalmnody and took exception to a "kist o' whistles" in church. "With fear and trembling," Sankey reports, "I announced as a solo the song, 'Free from the law, oh, happy condition.'" At the close of the service, he was rewarded as "Dr. Bonar turned toward me

---

10. Marsh, *Jubilee Singers*, 67.
11. Sankey, *My Life*, 53.
12. Sankey, *My Life*, 61.

with a smile on his venerable face, and reaching out his hand he said: 'Well, Mr. Sankey, you sang the gospel tonight.'"[13]

As was the case in Newcastle, the Jubilee Singers enthusiastically participated in the evangelistic endeavor, sometimes assisting in as many as six meetings in a day and joining Sankey on the platform to sing "Steal Away to Jesus" and other spirituals from their repertoire. Steve Turner quotes from one contemporary account in his definitive history of the hymn "Amazing Grace": "Mr. Moody pronounced the benediction, and Mr. Sankey and the sweet Jubilee Singers burst out from supercharged hearts into joyful, triumphant praise, the likes of which have never been heard."[14] At least not in a church in Scotland!

B. Torrey-Alexander and the Bendigo Pianist

Moody was succeeded as preacher on the sawdust trail by his protégé R. A. Torrey, whose song leader was Charles Alexander, a dynamo of a musician who knew how to get a crowd singing. He used the whole stage as his podium, sometimes spontaneously dividing the voices into male and female or antiphonal sections, sometimes provoking them to greater volume in getting them fired up for the sermon, sometimes relaxing them by telling jokes. He was the ringmaster of the circus tent crowd, and he used the position to great advantage for the gospel.

Alexander much preferred the piano to the reed organ because of its percussive and tonal qualities. Torrey and Alexander arrived in Australia in 1902 for a series of meetings sponsored by a wide variety of denominations. They began in metropolitan Melbourne, then moved on to rural Bendigo, where they scoured the music halls for a pianist to join them in their evangelistic endeavor. They found just who they were looking for in a talented young pianist named Robert Harkness, who signed on to accompany the singing that was a major attraction to their services.

At the first meeting, Harkness immediately regretted his decision. He had no sympathy with the mission and he hated the simplistic gospel songs he had to play. He began to contemplate how he could get out of his commitment. After Alexander called unwanted attention to him as the pianist, Harkness decided to get back at him a bit. As he explained in print a couple of years later,

---

13. Sankey, *My Life*, 62.
14. Turner, *Amazing Grace*, 151–52.

> Two thousand people were singing the Glory Song, and after practicing the chorus a few times I decided to introduce a few chords and runs into the music which did not appear in the printed copy. I thought in this way Mr. Alexander would be rather disgusted with my efforts, and would perhaps give me a chance to get out of my position. To my surprise, when he heard the additional chords, he turned round, and motioning with his hand, cried out: "That's fine; keep it up." I was determined, however, to test him further, and towards the end of that hymn I entered a more lavish series of improvisations. This only served to please him the more, for, as he explained to me afterwards, it was just what he wanted.[15]

Harkness later became a committed Christian, composed several gospel hymns—he is proudly remembered in Victoria as "the Bendigo hymnwriter"[16]—and produced a method for learning his piano style. It was first offered in 1939 as *Home Correspondence Course in Gospel Song Piano Accompaniment* ("Sixty lessons under the personal supervision of Robert Harkness") for which correspondents were awarded a diploma upon completion. Two years later it was published as *The Harkness Piano Method of Evangelistic Hymn Playing: A Home Study Course*, reissued in a reprint edition by Lineas in 1962.

Harkness's method was taken to the highest degree of perfection by Rudy Atwood, the pianist for the choir and quartet of Charles E. Fuller's Old Fashioned Revival Hour for over twenty years beginning with the initial "international" broadcast in 1937. The style is wonderfully illustrated by the quartet arrangements of "The Old Account was Settled Long Ago," "The Lily of the Valley," and "My Heavenly Father Watches Over Me." Through the influence of Harkness, the piano became the instrument of choice to accompany congregational singing in evangelical churches, as well as tent meetings on the sawdust trail.[17]

---

15. Harkness, *Torrey Alexander Mission*, 20–21 (cited in Steeves, "Origin of Gospel Piano," 48). The Glory Song was called this because the chorus begins, "O that will be glory for me."

16. Cole, *Robert Harkness*. The best-remembered composition by Harkness is "He Will Hold Me Fast," in *Alexander's Hymns No. 3* (1915) by Alexander. It is also included in Townsend's *Gospel Pearls* (1921) along with "The Ninety and Nine" and "I Am Praying for You" from Ira D. Sankey's *My Life*.

17. Dr. Robert G. Rayburn, founding president of Covenant College and Seminary, began his calling in ministry as a revival pianist, a talent that remained with him throughout his career as a pastor, military chaplain, and theological educator.

C. African American Churches and the Chicago School of Gospel

The revolution in popular sacred music was taken to a new level by black composers and promoters in the early twentieth century.[18] This was especially true of the Baptist and Pentecostal (Holiness) churches in Chicago, though the movement actually began in a multiracial congregation of the Methodist Episcopal Church in South Philadelphia pastored by the Rev. Dr. Charles A. Tindley. The church, located on East Bainbridge when Tindley was installed as pastor in 1902, moved to a prime location on South Broad (purchased from Westminster Presbyterian) in 1904 and changed its name to East Calvary Methodist Episcopal Church. The website *Hymnary.org* has this biographical note:

> Tindley was known for being a captivating preacher, and for also taking an active role in the betterment of the people in his community. His songs were an outgrowth of his preaching ministry, often introduced during his sermons. Tindley was able to draw people of multiple races to his church ministry; likewise, his songs have been adopted and proliferated by white and black churches alike.[19]

This is highly reminiscent of the model established by the Moody-Sankey and Alexander-Harkness evangelistic teams. To supplement the standard Methodist Episcopal hymnal, Tindley arranged for the AME Zion church to publish *Soul Echoes: A Collection of Songs for Religious Meetings* (1905, 1909) featuring his compositions along with some of the more popular hymns of the day. The Chicago-based National Baptist Convention (NBC) followed its lead in 1921 with the publication of *Gospel Pearls: Edited and Compiled for Special Use in the Sunday School, Church, Evangelistic Meetings, Conventions, and All Religious Services by the Music Committee of the Sunday School Publishing Board.* The committee roster is quite illuminating.[20]

Heading the list is Willa A. Townsend, Director, a highly trained classical musician and music educator in Nashville, Tennessee. When her

---

18. See Darden, *People Get Ready*, and Reagon, *We'll Understand It Better*. Reagon was Director of the Smithsonian Institution Research Project that studied the pioneering composers of the movement.

19. The allusion is to such popular hymns as "Leave it There," "Nothing Between [My Soul and the Savior]," "Stand by Me," and "We'll Understand It Better By and By."

20. Mrs. Willa A. Townsend, Director; Dr. J. D. Bushell; Prof. R. A. Austin; Prof. J. H. Smiley; Prof. J. W. Work; Prof. F. J. Work; Prof. W. M. Nix; Prof. E. W. D. Isaac Jr.; Mrs. Carrie Gooker Person; Miss Lucie E. Campbell; and Mrs. Geneva Bender Williams.

husband, A. M. Townsend, was appointed president of Roger Williams University, she undertook the directorship of the university chorale. As a hymnologist and songwriter in her own right, Townsend was the ideal choice to chair the NBC publications committee. *Gospel Pearls* included her arrangements of "Wade in the Water" and the old gospel shout, "[My Soul is a] Witness for my Lord." They were republished six years later in *Spirituals Triumphant: Old and New*, which also published her arrangement of "Nobody Knows [the Trouble I've Seen]." It includes as a third stanza the call-and-response couplet comprised of words found in many versions of "Swing Low, Sweet Chariot":

The brightest day I ever saw,

Oh, yes, Lord!

When Jesus washed my sins away,

Oh, yes, Lord![21]

Also listed is Lucie E. Campbell, a Memphis public school teacher who served as music director of the Sunday School and Baptist Young People's Union Congress of the NBC from 1916 until her death in 1963—just short of half a century. She was a major promoter of gospel songs at the annual meeting of the NBC in Chicago, typically introducing one of her own compositions. *Gospel Pearls* includes "The Lord is My Shepherd," her musical setting of the Twenty-Third Psalm. Though Campbell preferred classical forms for her compositions, she endorsed the blues and jazz innovations of Thomas A. Dorsey and even composed a classic in the genre, "Jesus Gave Me Water" (1946), which became a hit record by Sam Cooke and the Soul Stirrers.[22]

The committee responsible for *Gospel Pearls* presents its selections under three headings: worship and devotion (seventy-five hymns), revival (sixty-eight hymns), and spirituals (twenty hymns). Apart from the spirituals and about a dozen hymns by contemporary black composers,[23] *Gospel Pearls* shares a common canon with the other popular evangelical songbooks of the day. It includes, for example, E. O. Excell's arrangement

21. Boatner and Townsend, *Spirituals Triumphant*, 44.

22. Campbell's other best-known compositions are "Something Within" (1919) and "He Understands; He'll Say, 'Well Done'" (1933).

23. Charles A. Tindley, "Leave It There," "Nothing Between," "Sweet Bye and Bye," "What Are They Doing in Heaven," "A Better Home," and "Stand By Me"; Lucie E. Campbell, "The Lord Is My Shepherd"; Thomas A. Dorsey, "If I Don't Get There"; Charles Price Jones, "I'm Happy in Jesus Alone"; Carrie Booker Person, "Ring It Out With a Shout" and "Someone Is Hitting the Home Trail Tonight."

of "Amazing Grace," first published in *Make His Praise Glorious* (1900) and adopted in all twentieth-century hymnals.[24]

Most of the hymns in the spirituals section of *Gospel Pearls* were arranged by the Work brothers, John Wesley Work Jr. and Jerome Frederick Work. Both were Fisk University graduates with continuing involvement in its choral tradition. John Wesley Jr. returned to the university to become professor of Latin and History and eventually founded the Fisk Jubilee Quartet, a step that took the choral tradition in a new direction. The Work brothers were avid preservers of African-American sacred folk music and published two collections of their arrangements: *New Jubilee Songs as Sung by Fisk Jubilee Singers* (1901) and *Folk Songs of the American Negro* (1907). In addition, John Work II (as he is sometimes referenced to distinguish him from his son, John Wesley Work III) published a treatise on *The Folk Song of the American Negro* (1915), "one of the earliest studies of African-American music undertaken by a descendant of an ex-slave."[25] After running into some opposition at Fisk over his positive views of slave music, Work accepted the presidency of Roger Williams University, which position he held until his death in 1925. He was replaced by A. M. Townsend, the husband of Willa A. Townsend, whose arrangements of "Wade in the Water" and "[My Soul is a] Witness for My Lord" are included in the spirituals section of *Gospel Pearls*. The inclusion of African-American sacred folk songs from the slave era alongside hymns handed down in the Protestant evangelical tradition signaled that they too were "gospel pearls" that belonged in the church's canon of songs of authentic religious experience, particularly experience borne of the trouble that nobody knows but Jesus.[26]

Easily the most recognizable name in the Chicago School of Gospel is Thomas A. Dorsey, often referred to as the Father of Gospel Music, a title he earned for the bluesy elements of his compositions and his dedicated promotion of black church choirs in the soloist-chorus form descended from the Jubilee tradition.[27] Dorsey had migrated to Chicago from his home in Atlanta—his father was a Baptist preacher accompanied by his mother on

---

24. Edwin Othello Excell was a prolific writer of gospel songs—he had been song leader and choir director for evangelist Sam Jones—one of which, "I Do, Don't You," was included in *Gospel Pearls* and was instrumental in Thomas A. Dorsey's conversion back to gospel music as his vocation.

25. Watson and Hornby, "John Wesley Work (II)," http://www.hymnology.co.uk/j/john-wesley-work-(ii).

26. The spirituals section, comprised almost exclusively of African-American folk hymns, is headed by Tindley's "Stand by Me."

27. The definitive Dorsey biography is Harris, *Rise of the Gospel Blues*. Sources include the Dorsey Papers and extensive interviews with Dorsey in Chicago (1976–1977) and his family, friends, and associates. See also Harris's essay, "Conflict and Resolution."

organ and piano—to pursue a career as a professional blues and jazz pianist. At the suggestion of a concerned uncle, he attended the 1921 National Baptist Convention, where he was so impressed by the response to evangelist W. M. Nix's forceful rendition of "I Do, Don't You" that at age twenty-two he determined to pursue a career in gospel music instead.[28]

That didn't happen, however, until after Dorsey had achieved notable success over the next decade as a blues pianist. The decisive turning point came in 1930 when a woman sang Dorsey's "If You See My Savior" ("Standing at the Bedside of a Neighbor") at the National Baptist Convention. Lucie Campbell provided him with a booth onsite where he sold over four thousand copies of the sheet music. The next year Dorsey accepted a call to organize a "junior" chorus at Ebenezer Baptist Church in addition to their established choir. This turned out to be Dorsey's strong suit in partnership with Theodore Frye. In January of 1932, a chorus of over a hundred members recruited and trained by Dorsey debuted at Ebenezer, directed by Frye with Dorsey accompanying on piano. Dorsey then accepted the position of music director at Pilgrim Baptist Church, a position he held until his retirement in 1983. Frye remained at Ebenezer, and the pair continued their collaboration in promoting the new choral group music.

In August of 1932 the team set out to organize a chorus in Greenville, South Carolina. Frye had to return to Chicago en route to fulfill a prior engagement. When Dorsey arrived in Greenville, a telegram was waiting for him with the news that his wife had gone into labor. He rushed back to be with her, but she died giving birth to a son before he could get there. To make matters worse, the child also died. The tragic double loss left Dorsey emotionally devastated and incapacitated to such an extent that he believed his musical career was over and that he would never play the piano again. His supportive friends, especially Frye, eventually persuaded him to sit down at the piano in the hope that it would bring him out of his catatonic state. As he ran his hands over the keys he began to experiment with an old hymn tune by an unknown composer that had become the setting for G. N. Allen's hymn, "Must Jesus Bear the Cross Alone."[29] As he improvised on the tune, words began to come to him to match the music. "Take my hand," he began. That evocative phrase echoes a powerful biblical image in Isaiah where the Lord says, "I will take you by the hand and keep you" (Isa 42:6). Dorsey originally had "blessed Lord" but gratefully changed it to "precious Lord" at Frye's suggestion. Dorsey went on to write

28. The first line of the hymn is this: "I know a great Savior, I do, don't you?" Set to music by E. O. Excell.

29. The anonymous hymn tune called Western Melody was first published in the *Plymouth Collection of Hymns and Tunes* compiled by Henry Ward Beecher (1855).

over a thousand gospel songs, but none more beloved than this one, which had a message of help in despair that has resonated with so many. When Frye and Dorsey introduced the hymn the next day at Ebenezer Baptist, the response was sensational. Dorsey had created a hit that fulfilled his vocational dream beyond all expectations.[30]

The year 1932 also marked the formation of the National Convention of Gospel Choirs and Choruses by Dorsey, in collaboration with blues singer Sallie Martin. The Chicago School of Gospel included composers, arrangers, and publishers, as well as performers. Sallie Martin toured with Dorsey and assisted him with his publishing business until they had a falling out and she teamed up with Kenneth Morris to found one of the most successful and comprehensive ventures of the school.

Kenneth Morris was born in the New York City borough of Queens. He studied classical piano from grade school through high school, though he preferred playing jazz with his Jamaican neighborhood peers. After high school, he attended both CUNY and the Manhattan Conservatory of Music. While a student at the latter, Morris organized an impressive jazz ensemble that landed a gig at the World's Fair in Chicago in 1934. Remaining in Chicago after the gig for health reasons, Morris sat in with local jazz musicians and came to the attention of Lillian Bowles, owner of Bowles Music House. Hired by Bowles as a scribe to put music in written form for composers without technical training, he actually arranged the music for them, including the first song recorded by Mahalia Jackson, "God's Goin' to Separate the Wheat from the Tares" (1937).

Morris worked for Bowles from 1937 to 1940, and then he teamed up with Sallie Martin to form the Martin and Morris Music Studio: Arrangers, Publishers, Distributors—Everything in Religious Music. In his 1987 autobiographical retrospective, "I'll Be a Servant of the Lord," Morris told how he came to arrange and publish the gospel classic "Just a Closer Walk with Thee."

> It was an arrangement that I made on an old spiritual.... I went to Kansas City to a conference of some kind, and one of the choirs there sang it. I asked them where they heard it, and they asked their choir director . . . where they had gotten it from. He didn't know; he had heard it all of his life. I had never heard it before. I am the one who made the arrangement; the first one that was put in print was mine. I took it to the National Baptist Convention in 1944 and presented it with my group, the Martin

30. It is well known that it was the favorite hymn of Dr. Martin Luther King Jr. It was sung at a church rally in Memphis the night before his assassination, and later at his funeral by Mahalia Jackson, as he had requested in advance for her to do.

and Morris Singers, and it simply clicked. After we left there, everybody was using it.[31]

As musicologist Robert Marovich notes, "'Just a Closer Walk with Thee' went on to became a jazz band favorite as well as a staple for black and white church congregations, singers, groups, and quartets."[32] The first known recording of Morris's arrangement is a slow version by the Selah Jubilee Singers (more about them later) in October of 1941. It was followed in December by an uptempo rendition by jazz guitarist and gospel singer Sister Rosetta Tharpe. A half century later, the black female ensemble Sweet Honey in the Rock recreated the original Martin & Morris quartet sound (with Sallie Martin on bass!) for the Smithsonian/Folkways & National Public Radio album *Wade in the Water*.

Recruited as choir director by the Rev. Clarence H. Cobb, founder and pastor of the First Church of Deliverance in Chicago, Morris inaugurated a new era in gospel music by having Cobb purchase a Hammond organ for the church in 1939, starting a revolution in the black church as piano and electronic organ quickly became the standard instruments of public worship. A prime example of the sound is one of Morris's later hits, "Dig a Little Deeper in God's Love," recorded in 1947 by Mahalia Jackson and the Jordanaires with piano and Hammond organ.

D. Thermon Ruth's Caravan of Gospel Quartets

The revolution in African American gospel music was not confined to the Chicago School. Likely the greatest twentieth century promoter of black gospel quartets (one-on-a-part harmonizing groups, sometimes with two lead singers, one singing falsetto) was Thermon Ruth whose base was New York and Philadelphia.[33] Not only did he organize the Selah Jubilee Singers at age thirteen, he worked closely with the Dixie Hummingbirds, another quartet organized by a juvenile church choir member in Greenville. The Hummingbirds were a regular feature of Thermon's "Gospel Caravan" at the Apollo Theater, often billed with the Sensational Nightingales or the Soul Stirrers on the famous Harlem marquee.[34] American poet laureate Billy

---

31. Reagon, *We'll Understand It Better*, 329–41, esp. 336.

32. Marovich, *City Called Heaven*, 177. "Dig a Little Deeper" was also famously recorded by the Fairfield Four in 1947.

33. See Ruth and Saylor-Marchant, *From the Church to the Apollo Theater*; this is part third-person autobiography by Ruth, part interview by Saylor-Marchant.

34. Zolten, *Great God A'Mighty!*, 245–59.

Collins captures the essence of the genre in his "Sunday Morning with the Sensational Nightingales."

> *I have always loved this harmony,*
> *like four, sometimes five trains running*
> *side by side over a contoured landscape—*
> *make that a shimmering, red-dirt landscape . . .*
> *Sunday morning in a perfect Georgia.*[35]

Thermon T. Ruth (1914–2002) was born in Pomaria, South Carolina, a really small town in the county of Newberry. It was his boyhood home for the first eight years of his life. Thermon's family migrated to Brooklyn in 1922. Five years later, the musically talented Thermon organized a gospel quartet drawn from the choir of St. Mark's Church (Holiness). For the next ten years, the quartet sang every Sunday night at St. Mark's. The services were broadcast live, and soon the quartet was singing regularly on four area radio stations, including WOR (710 AM) in New York City where Thermon held sway as a disc jockey. In 1937, Thermon took his quartet to Houston where they met, and were deeply affected by, the Soul Stirrers, whose name signaled that they were about something more than entertainment.

By 1939, Thermon's quartet was called the Selah Jubilee Singers and had landed a recording contract with Decca Records. Among their early releases was "I'll Fly Away" in 1941, apparently the earliest recording of that gospel classic popularized by the Chuck Wagon Gang with their unprecedented hit gospel record in 1949. The Selahs included a piano for this recording, which was fast becoming the norm for Southern white gospel quartets. The Selahs made this piece their own by speeding up the tempo, introducing creative chord progressions, using two lead singers, and incorporating ad libs to fill out the expression.

During the war, the Selahs were very popular on the USO circuit and at veterans' hospitals. Thermon contracted with the USO for performances in every state but Nevada, which they fulfilled through an eighteen-month national tour in 1945–1946. They then settled in Raleigh, North Carolina, where they broadcast a morning program five days a week on WPTF (680 AM) with performance dates at night. Ruth left the group for another in New York, best remembered as the Larks. In mid-December of 1955, they were featured on Thermon's breakthrough "Gospel Caravan" at the Apollo Theater

---

35. Collins, *Art of Drowning*, 18. The Sensational Nightingales were organized as a gospel quartet in 1942. Over the years, they have remained remarkably true to their evangelical mission, so much so as to be included in Tony Heilbut's dedication of *The Gospel Sound* to "All the gospel singers who didn't sell out."

in Harlem, which they took as an opportunity to sing the gospel to a wider audience. The Selahs existed as a group until 1955, when Ruth joined them for a recording session for Savoy. They were reunited for the final time in 1968 when they recorded for Veep-Gospel Records as the Jubilators.

Another five-member group promoted by Ruth in his Caravan was the Dixie Hummingbirds, organized as a gospel quartet in 1928 by twelve-year-old James Davis for the Bethel Church of God Holiness in Greenville. When they were a few years older, the "Junior Boys" became the "Sterling High School Quartet" and were much in demand as representative of the black high school founded by the Rev. Daniel Minus, a former slave, and named for anti-slavery activist Emeline Sterling. After graduation, they began to travel in the South as the Dixie Hummingbirds (Davis joked that they were named for "the only bird that could fly both backwards and forwards," just like their career) and to broadcast Sunday mornings on WFBC in Greenville. As the acclaimed author of their history remarks, "When they took to the radio, the Dixie Hummingbirds were connecting to a diverse audience and winning fans across racial lines."[36]

In 1938 the Birds traveled to New York City for a recording session with Decca, after which Davis recruited Ira Tucker of Spartanburg, SC as a second lead singer. The group migrated to Philadelphia in the 1940s to be nearer to the recording industry in New York City. They had remarkable success with Apollo Records, but broke ties with them after a few years in order to preserve their independence as a gospel musical group whose goal was to minister to the soul through popular sacred entertainment. Sometimes the line was finely drawn, as when in 1973 they provided backup for Paul Simon's "Loves Me Like a Rock." The next year the Birds released their own rendition that received a Grammy for "Best Soul Gospel Performance." More typical of their vocation would be "Rasslin' Jacob," a highly effective retelling of Genesis 32:24–26 in the Jubilee tradition, and two gospel songs by Thomas A. Dorsey, "If You See My Savior" and "Hide Me in Thy Bosom."

Perhaps the best measure of the fulfillment of their purpose is the testimonial of the Rev. Gadson Graham, who was pastor of a church in Lake City, South Carolina in the 1950s and remembers well the effects of the Birds's ministry of gospel music in the black community.

> They would come to our town, the Dixie Hummingbirds, they would come, and they would sing. . . . And this would give us inspiration. Whenever they came around, it was a tremendous uplift that helped us cope and deal with all of the negative things

---

36. Zolten, *Great God A'Mighty!*, 39.

that was going on at this time. Racism, social injustice, economic injustice.

The Birds would sing and it would just seem that heaven came open and God had come down. We just felt that we could deal more with what we had to deal with, after hearing them. . . .

The Birds, you got sincerity from them that you did not get from anybody else. Their singing was like a salve on a wound. Whatever hurt that you had experienced, when you put that hurt up against the singing of the Dixie Hummingbirds, it was like a soothing situation that made it possible for you to deal with whatever you had to deal with. They would sing that, and that's how they would send us home, rejoicing in what we were.[37]

Say amen, somebody.

---

37. Zolten, *Great God A'Mighty!*, 259.

9

A New Participation in an Old Identity

1 Peter and the Church's Inclusion into Israel

MANY RECENT STUDIES IN 1 Peter, like much of NT scholarship, have turned their focus to questions of the so-called "parting of the ways" between Judaism and Christianity: that is, how to discuss the relationships between "Jews" and "Christians"—however one might define the terms—in a way true to the complex realities of the first century. But 1 Peter is an odd bedfellow to Paul in these discussions and is generally taken to be of less interest and value to the questions normally asked. After all, there is no explicit discussion of what we most expect in the matter, at least upon reading Paul's letters: no mention of circumcision, no discussion of food laws, Sabbath, and nothing beyond rather standard ideas regarding the temple.[1] In fact none of what many assume the standard "boundary markers" of first-century Judaism emerge as concerns at all.

But the absence of an explicit polemic may allow us to better view the positive construction of an identity that is self-confessedly "Christian."[2] The term "identity" here will refer generally to the ways in which we pick someone (or some group) out, or more particularly the way(s) in which a group can construct for itself a sense of who they are, whether in the world, in history, or before God. As Richard Bauckham frames it:

---

1. This latter point is debated, but would take too much space to treat here. For a very different view of the temple language, see the attempt to construe the whole of 1 Peter as presenting an eschatological "new temple" idea (language I find nowhere justified in the epistle), see Mbuvi, *Temple, Exile, and Identity*.

2. Peter's use of "Christian" (4:16) might simply be a label used by outsiders (cf. Acts 11:26; 26:28), but he seems happy to embrace its appropriation by the believers.

(Identity) is understood not as a mere ontological subject without characteristics, but as including both character and personal story (the latter entailing relationships). These are the ways in which we commonly specify "who someone is."[3]

Through this letter, Peter aims to construct an identity meant to be shared by the believers in Jesus he addresses throughout the region of Anatolia. And the argument here is that the identity he constructs is that of sharers in the theological identity of Israel.

The structure of the argument here is rather simple, though each part could be pursued much further: first, that there is a particular theological identity of "Israel" constructed in the Hebrew Bible (HB); second, that Peter in the letter urges the believers to view themselves as having this "Israel" as their theological identity; third, that Peter places belief in Jesus as central to their sharing in that identity. While the details in each of these three parts can be debated, in general none are very controversial. But having them in hand allows us to see the importance of how one frames the dynamic of constructing this particular identity for these believers in Jesus. And so at the end we will suggest that, rather than the language of replacement or supersessionism—often attached to the dynamic of "giving" the identity of Israel to "the church" in 1 Peter—a better framework comes in the language of sharing or participating in the theological identity of Israel through faith in Jesus.

Israel as a Theological Identity

To claim that 1 Peter constructs for its audience the theological identity of Israel, we must first say something of what that "identity of Israel" might be. The question is not helped by the confusion surrounding modern Israel with all the various and contested definitions. But for all the complications, ancient and modern, it seems to me indisputable that central to the Torah is the construction of a theological identity of "Israel" as the people of God. When the Shema calls out, "Hear, O Israel!" (Deut 6:4) it refers to something beyond a simple political entity. Israel exists *as* something in the Torah. "Israel" in Deuteronomy 6 can be identified with a particular story of its ancestors and YHWH's actions toward them, its deliverance by God from Egypt, and its constitution as YHWH's people by covenant at Sinai. From Genesis to Deuteronomy we are given ways in which the people

---

3. Bauckham, *Jesus and the God of Israel*, 6n. One need not adopt the claim that because identity is constructed, it is therefore an "exercise of power and the strategies of exclusion" (so Lieu, *Neither Jew Nor Greek*, 214).

were meant to identify themselves generation after generation as a certain thing—as "Israel" in the sense used at Deuteronomy 6:4.

Sometimes that work of identity-construction is fairly explicit. One illustration is the "small credo" of Deuteronomy 26:5-10, where the worshipers are meant to take up a particular story as their own identity when they bring to YHWH the firstfruits of the land:

> A wandering Aramean was my father, and he went down to Egypt and lived as a stranger there few in number, and there he became a nation—great, mighty, and numerous. And the Egyptians treated us harshly, afflicted us, and subjected us to cruel service. And we cried out to YHWH, God of our fathers, and YHWH heard us and saw our affliction, and our toil, and our oppression. And YHWH brought us out of Egypt with a mighty hand and an outstretched arm, with great terror and signs and wonders. And he brought us into this place, and he gave us this land. (Deut 26:5-9)[4]

The story of the patriarch Israel's wandering is meant to shape the identity of future generations ("we") as the *children* of Israel. We can read nearly the whole of the Torah along these lines. As Birch says regarding the structuring of the book of Exodus: "For Israel, new identity is the necessary context for formation as moral community."[5] It is the possession of a new identity, distinct from the nations and determined by God's action. And it is an identity that gives rise to (and is embodied in) the laws and practices throughout the Torah. There is, in short, a theological identity of "Israel" constructed in the Torah. To be "Israel" was to be a direct participant in the story of Abraham, Isaac, and Jacob, in the people bound by covenant to YHWH and living in YHWH's land.

We could demonstrate the same idea in a negative sense through the prophets. Hosea, for instance, assumes just such an identity from the start: the Israel to whom he speaks is bound to YHWH (else they cannot be said to "whore against" him) who has acted in love toward them (e.g., 11:1-11). Generally, in Hosea and the Prophets, it may be that Israel fails to live according to its identity, but that failure consolidates the sense of a particular theological identity for Hosea's readers. They have failed to live up to a particular calling and status which is preserved and held out

---

4. All translations are my own, unless otherwise noted.

5. Birch, "Divine Character," 122. In the argument developed below, the similarity of his remark to another scholar's on 1 Peter is more than accidental: "Before giving them moral instructions, [Peter] gives them a moral vision that places them within a moral universe. He does this by depicting not simply a theological worldview, but a *narrative* theological worldview" (see also Dryden, *Theology and Ethics*, 64).

to later generations: "Return, O Israel, to YHWH your God" (Hos 14:1). So while various options exist for referring to that theological identity, I have chosen "Israel" as the most prominent in the HB and so the simplest for our purposes.[6]

The Identity of Israel in 1 Peter

The attribution of this theological identity to 1 Peter's audience begins from the moment of address in 1:1:

> To those who are chosen sojourners [*eklektois parepidēmois*] of the dispersion.

Scholars have debated aspects of these terms, most often around John Elliott's insistence on reading the language as "exile" rather than "sojourner," and his maintaining that it refers to an actual sociological category.[7] But while the latter point seems appropriate for the language of "dispersion," the terminology of the sojourner almost certainly comes from the narrative of Abraham. Bargaining for a cave in which to bury Sarah, Abraham tells the Hittites:

> I am a *stranger* [*paroikos*] and *sojourner* [*parepidēmos*] among you. (Gen 23:4; cf. Ps 39:12)

It might be that the first reading of 1 Peter would allow initial ambiguity to the reference, but that Peter means to evoke this text is confirmed by his repetition of the term at 2:11:

> Beloved, I urge you as *strangers* [*paroikous*] and *sojourners* [*parepidēmous*].

Nowhere else do we find the two terms together in the LXX than the story of Abraham. The use at 1:1 seems to anticipate that later, more explicit tie. To be a "sojourner" here (as in 2:11) offers a framework for these believers to understand their current life. These believers are now what Abraham

---

6. No name seems free of drawbacks, and here two strong objections exist. First is that in apostolic writings (at least) the term "Israel" seems generally reserved for the ethnic people rather than the theological identity—though some instances are hotly debated (cf. Rom 9:6, 27–31; 10:19–21; 11:2–25; 1 Cor 10:18; Gal 6:16; Eph 2:12; Phil 3:5). On the other side, the term in our own day is too easily equated or associated with the modern political entity. But "Jew(ish)" is even more fraught with challenges, and "Israel" has the benefit of being used in this theological manner in the HB. "Children of Abraham" might perhaps avoid the pitfalls, but is too clumsy for present purposes.

7. Elliott, *Home for the Homeless*.

was: sojourners in the land awaiting the full award of their promised inheritance.[8] As Abson Joseph puts it:

> As the Israelites were encouraged to see the patriarch's story as their own (Deut. 26.5), so the author of 1 Peter is inviting the audience to see Israel's story *as their own* (1 Pet. 1.1).[9]

In language that we will find throughout this study, they become participants in their own lives within a larger story. Abraham's story has become their own.

The qualifier "chosen" (*eklektos*) in 1:1 compliments this notion. The term is ubiquitous in apostolic writings as shorthand for the people of God and will play an ongoing role in 1 Peter.[10] But that should not diminish the function of the adjective to refer to the people of God (Israel), put so formatively in Deuteronomy:

> For you are a holy nation to the Lord your God, and the Lord your God has chosen (LXX: *exelexato*) you to be his treasured people from all the nations on the face of the earth. (Deut 14:2)

To be "chosen" referred to a status wrought by God's calling. And in every case it seems to continue to draw on the basic point that it is being chosen *from among* others—in Deuteronomy, chosen from among the nations. It refers to the particularity of Israel who could lay claim to being "chosen" in a way untrue of any other people. And Peter, like other early Christian writers, seems quite unabashed in applying the term to believers in Jesus.

But if these might be somewhat subtle clues in 1:1 that the identity of Israel is being urged on the audience, we are given a direct pronouncement with the identity-laden description of the believers at 2:9–10:

> You are a chosen lineage,[11] a royal priesthood, a holy nation, a people for his own possession, in order to show the excellence of the one who called you out of darkness, into his marvelous light.

---

8. Lieu seems not to consider this in declaring 1 Peter as "without reference to the promise of the gift of land." That promise seems explictly evoked by the terms of "sojourning" and even perhaps "dispersion." Cf. Lieu, *Christian Identity*, 230.

9. Joseph, *Narratological Reading*, 78.

10. See below on 2:4–9; cf. Matt 22:14; 24:22–31; Mark 13:20–22; Luke 18:7; Rom 8:33; Col 3:12; 2 Tim 2:10; Titus 1:1; 2 John 1; Rev 17:14.

11. Translating *genos* as "lineage," tied to a concern for common ancestry ("descendant, family, relatives, nation, people, class, kind," in Danker et al., *Lexicon*, 194–95). It is a notoriously difficult term to translate, with a wide usage in Greek literature. In biblical translations, it is often taken as "race," but modern usage is fraught with political-social dynamics far removed from the ancient texts. For a defense of ethnoracial translations, see Horrell, *Becoming Christian*, 133–63.

> Once you were not a people, but now you are God's people; once you had not received mercy, but now you have received mercy. (1 Pet 2:9–10)

Peter weaves together three (or four) texts, all of which demonstrate the one basic point that these believers have been made a part of the theological identity of Israel.

The first text is Exodus 19:5–6, where we find Israel standing at the foot of Sinai in one of the most formative moments in their story as a people:

> "And now, if you will indeed hear my voice and keep my covenant, you shall be to me a people treasured from among all the nations . . . and you shall be to me a *royal priesthood*[12] *and a holy nation.*" These are the words you shall speak to the children of Israel. (Exod 19:5–6, LXX)

The final line is important: these are words particular to Israel and impossible to attribute to another in the world of the HB. Peter does not choose general descriptors of value for the believers, but the particular epithets of the "children of Israel."

The exact reference for Peter's phrase "possession" (*peripoiēsin*) is debated, as it could be an adaptation of the term "treasured" (*periousios*) from Exodus 19:5 or from Isaiah 43:21 (*periepoiēsamēn*). The exact term is used in the LXX of Malachi 3:17, so some have suggested that it may be the text in mind.[13] I find the use of Exodus 19 and Isaiah 43 in the immediate context to suggest that they are better candidates, especially since precise verbal quotation seems less a concern in the ancient world. But whether one concludes that he takes the term from Malachi, Exodus, or Isaiah, the point remains the same: in each case the particular status of (faithful) Israel

---

12. The phrase *basileion hierateuma* is difficult, but the former term seems best taken as an adjective (thus "royal") qualifying the kind of priestly community they are to be rather than as two nominatives ("royal house, priestly community," as suggested by, e.g., Elliott, *1 Peter*, 406 (cf. Selwyn, *First Epistle of St. Peter*, 165–66). However, Elliott is certainly right that the latter term is not "priests" in an individual sense, but "priestly community." Whether he is right that it therefore "cannot apply to the believers as individuals" (*1 Peter*, 452) is another matter. The Masoretic Text has the terms in a construct relationship (*mamlekhet kohanim*).

13. "Then those who feared the LORD spoke with one another. The LORD paid attention and heard them, and a book of remembrance was written before him of those who feared the LORD and esteemed his name. 'They shall be mine, says the LORD of hosts, in the day when I make up my treasured possession, and I will spare them as a man spares his son who serves him. Then once more you shall see the distinction between the righteous and the wicked, between one who serves God and one who does not serve him'" (Mal 3:16–18, ESV).

is expressed through God's treasuring of his people. They are YHWH's possession, a claim that is unique to the theological entity Israel.

In weaving Isaiah 43 into this fabric, we find the same point made just as bluntly as the use of Exodus 19:

> I give water in the wilderness, rivers in the desert,
>
> to give drink to *my chosen lineage* [to *genos mou* to *eklekton*],
>
> the people I treasured [*periepoiēsamēn*] for myself
>
> that they might declare my *excellences* [*aretas*]. (Isa 43:20–21, LXX)

In Isaiah, the ones addressed are those who are redeemed from YHWH's judgment. But the language does not refer to a *new* status the redeemed receive—as if unknown to the faithful beforehand. It refers to Israel standing before YHWH (her identity), and so why it is that YHWH acts toward them in redemption. They are his "chosen lineage," whom YHWH formed for himself with the particular purpose of declaring his excellences in the earth, and *thus* he acts in favor toward them even after judgment. Once more, Peter chooses language of Israel's particular theological identity in the HB to construct the identity of these believers in Anatolia: they possess the identity of faithful Israel.

The final text used in 1 Peter 2:9–10 comes from Hosea, in which YHWH's judgment is pronounced in terms of the naming of the prophet's children, the last two of whom are "No-Mercy" and "Not-My-People."[14] Israel's infidelity has meant they can no longer lay claim either to the benefits of the covenant (mercy/steadfast love, Hos 1:6) or the covenant itself (Hos 1:10). Peter points to the overturning of that judgment held out by Hosea:

> And I will show mercy to "No-Mercy," and I will say to "Not-My-People," you are my people, and he shall say, "The Lord is my God." (Hos 2:25, LXX)

Those who, through their own infidelity, no longer hold a right to the covenant are by grace reconstituted into the covenant people. They are restored to the particular identity of those who are in covenant with YHWH. Paul will apply this language to the inclusion of gentiles (Rom 9:25–26), and in that context it seems an apt enough application: those estranged from the covenant are brought into it. Its use here sits even closer to its place in Hosea, fitting the repeated emphasis on these believers as new participants in

---

14. More precisely, both to the Hebrew and Greek, "Not-Mercied" as an adjective. But English lacks such an adjective, and "Not-Pitied" has different connotations.

the status of the faithful; they have moved from past unfaithfulness to the "now" of their belief and standing (1:18; 2:25).

Whatever other details remain, it seems clear that the identity constructed in 1 Peter 2:9–10 is explicitly the identity particular to Israel as we find it constructed throughout the HB. Peter weaves together the language of Israel—Israel as it ought to be—as providing the identity of those who have heard the message of Jesus and believed.

Identity as Israel in its Calling

This same point could be pursued across all the moments of Peter's attributions and epithets for his audience. But we can find the same dynamic as well in the exhortations and callings given to the Anatolian believers. We have already seen from the use of Isaiah 43 that Israel's theological status came with a calling. Israel was a people treasured by YHWH *so that* they might declare his excellences among the nations. To be Israel was to have an identity that issued out into a calling (Deuteronomy 6). And this same dynamic takes place in 1 Peter. Their identity issues out into a particular calling, and examining the latter gives us an indication of the former.

It would require greater space to tease out some of the more subtle aspects in which this works, such as the emphatic narrative of these Christians as those who have believed the prophetic word over against those who refuse to believe it (1 Pet 1:10–12; 1:22–2:8). The dynamic of Israel as meant to believe and heed the prophetic word, when in reality it often refused it, marks out not only the prophetic books of the HB but much of the history of Israel in the polemics of the Gospels.[15] In fact, the dynamic at play in 1 Peter seems very close to what we find in Luke 20:9–18, in which the owner of the vineyard has sent his servants (the prophets) time and again, only for them to be rejected. At last he sends the son whom they kill in order to take the vineyard as their own apart from the owner. What makes the parable particularly relevant is the concluding flourish in Luke's telling, in which Jesus looks at the people and cites Isaiah 28:16, in much the same role as we find it in 1 Peter 2:7. As those who believe the prophetic word, these Christians demonstrate their identity. They are directly called to faith and faithfulness by the prophets, addressed by the prophets of Israel because they have become sharers in Israel's identity (cf. 3:9–12). Such subtle cues would be worth exploring further, but for our purposes we can simply point

---

15. Cf. Amos 7:12–16; Mic 2:6–8; Jer 11:1–8, 38–44; Hos 9:17; 12:10–14 (on which, cf. Moon, *Hosea*, ad loc.); Matt 5:12; 21:33–41; 23:29–37; Luke 11:49–50; 13:34.

out the more blunt expressions in which the calling of these Christians ties them to the identity of Israel.

The most direct of these expressions is the citation of the holiness formula from Leviticus:

> As obedient children, do not be conformed to the passions of your former ignorance, but as he who called you is holy, you also be holy in all your conduct since it is written: "You shall be holy, for I am holy." And if you call on him as Father who judges impartially according to each one's deeds, conduct yourselves with fear through the time of your sojourning. (1:14–18, ESV)

As Karen Jobes remarks, his use of the holiness formula is striking (at least to us) largely because there seems to be neither apology nor concern for a supposed new epoch in redemptive history that would render such calls outdated for the church:

> He directly enjoins upon his readers what God had previously told his chosen people in the book of Leviticus. . . . He makes no distinction between the Jewish and the Gentile Christian in his application, nor does the span of time between Leviticus and his letter mitigate the relevance of God's ancient revelation of himself.[16]

The use of the holiness formula, so central to Leviticus, demonstrates that in 1 Peter the identity of these Christians gives rise to their calling. And that identity seems difficult to construe as anything but "Israel" in the sense described above. The nations around Israel in Leviticus 19 were *not* holy in the sense implied there. Like being "chosen," "treasured," or "called," their status as "holy" was particular to Israel. God dwelt in their midst, which was constitutive to what it meant to be "Israel" in the book of Leviticus. Peter does not cite the formula as a general concern, but as a direct confirmation of the point at issue: that these believers in Jesus were to see themselves as having the identity of Israel.

In fact, the whole of 1:14–18 can be tied directly to the calling of Israel in the HB: they have God (YHWH) as their "Father," to whom they must be obedient (cf. Deut 32:6; Exod 4:22–23; Hos 11:1); they must live before God, who judges each according to his or her deeds (Eccl 12:14); they must conduct themselves with "fear" (Lev 19:14, 25; 25:17, 36, 43; etc.) as "sojourners" (cf. earlier discussion on 1 Pet 1:1). It is not only that Peter is indebted to the HB for his language here anymore than is true at 2:9–10;

---

16. Jobes, *1 Peter*, 112–13.

but it is that he directly sets his audience into the same role in which Israel is placed throughout the HB.

The same dynamic of the calling and identity of Israel emerges in Peter's calling the wives to act like "the holy women" of old. The wives are described as Sarah's children, thus the offspring of Abraham (cf. Isa 51:2).[17] Again, the issue could be construed as mere moralizing, but he places the moral call into the framework of their identity (regardless of their biological lineage) as children of Sarah—the identity of Israel.

It is within this framework of an identity-exposing calling, and especially of an identity particular to Israel, that we can understand the exhortations not to live like "the Gentiles" (2:11–12; 4:3). So much does Peter frame the identity of these believers as "Israel" that he can simply consign all others to the category of "Gentiles." And it is the particularity of Israel's identity among the nations, constructed as the identity of his audience, that makes that dichotomy possible.

Identity as Christians

While the previous point could be pursued throughout the whole of the letter, it is worth remarking on the nature of its relationship to the standard "Christian" claims in the epistle. For Peter, none of this renders the work of Christ either pointless or less valuable, as if valuing the work of Christ meant devaluing the theological identity of Israel. In fact, it is the work of Christ—and belief in that work—which marks out these believers as participants in Israel's identity. So, picking up from 1:14–18, Peter says:

> Conduct yourselves with fear through the time of your sojourning knowing that you were redeemed from the futile ways of your ancestors, not with perishable things like silver and gold but with the precious blood of Christ, like that of a lamb without blemish or spot. (1:18–19)

God's "redeeming" of his people was fundamental to their identity, above all in the Exodus (Exod 6:6) but applied more broadly throughout the HB (e.g., LXX Ps 24:22; 25:11; 33:23). Peter ties the redemption directly to the

---

17. The use of the aorist here (*egenēthēte*)—"whose daughters you became"—might suggest once more the disjunctive between the past unfaithfulness and present status. Davids accordingly suggests it demonstrates that the audience "were not Jews, for a writer would hardly say a Jewish woman *became* a daughter of Sarah through conversion" (*First Epistle of Peter*, 121). But the disjunctive here would be no different than the use of Hosea 1–2 above, and the aorist may be used here more in its aspectual sense than temporal.

Passover sacrifice and is unabashedly "Christian" in its claims of the work of God in Christ.

In fact, in 1 Peter, the person of Christ unites the whole of the people of God: he was foreknown by God before the foundation of the world (1:20), the one by whose spirit the prophets spoke (1:11), and the one about whom the prophets spoke (1:10–12). That Christ is now "made manifest" only brings to fruition what has always been expected, so that "through him" they have become "believers in God" (1:21). Far from dispensing with Israel's theological identity, the coming of Christ and believing the message of his work confirms that identity. These Christians have come to "the Lord" to taste that he is good (2:3; cf. Ps 34:8), and that movement gives them their identity as a "spiritual house" and "holy priesthood" (1 Pet 2:5). That is, they receive the theological identity of Israel by coming to God through Jesus Christ (2:5), by which Peter means believing in Jesus as the prophets declared (2:6–8). Even their perseverance as faithful through suffering, the main exhortation of the letter, comes in imitation of Christ: first suffering, then glory. At every turn, the focus of their new identity as Israel turns on the person and work of Christ in whom they believed and in whom they now stand.

This is not to say that nothing different is asked of these believers than what we find already in the HB, at least in details. They are to imitate Christ in a way that is obviously more applicable to those who live after bearing witness to his sufferings, and they are to live out their lives appropriate to their own context under Roman imperial rule of the first century. But such things are not at odds with an identity as Israel, it simply fills out what it means to embrace that identity in their own situation. The basic principle here is no different from what we find in a number of instances in the HB itself: it was both the same and different to embrace being Israel before and after the temple, before and after exile, and so on. They are given the identity of Israel as it now lives in the "last times" (*eschatōn tōn chronōn*, 1:20), while still awaiting the finality of the "last time" (*kairō eschatō*, 1:5), and all in the context of their life under Roman imperial rule in Anatolia. That some differences of practice and speech might be different is expected and is in no way a threat, at least in principle, to the stability of identity.

1 Peter and Supersessionism?

The above description of 1 Peter's use of Israel's identity has not gone unnoticed in scholarly discussions, nor has the Christian nature of the claims. Both sit on the face of the letter. But how are we to frame both of them together? Perhaps most common is to see the dynamic as a simple matter of replacement theology or supersessionism: that the church has come along and replaced (or superseded) Israel before God. There are various ways of framing this family of ideas; one of the more explicit is from Paul Achtemeier:

> In a way virtually unique among Christian canonical writings, 1 Peter has appropriated the language of Israel for the church in such a way that Israel as a totality has become for this letter the controlling metaphor in terms of which its theology is expressed.

In some instances a term like "appropriation" might be innocent enough. But here the language only emerges in the assumed gap between "Israel" and "the church"—a point that becomes very clear:

> In 1 Peter, the language and hence the reality of Israel pass without remainder into the language and hence the reality of the new people of God.[18]

For Achtemeier, the church is the "new" that has replaced "without remainder" the implied "old" of Israel. Language that assumes some form of replacement theology can be found across the scholarly literature on 1 Peter. For Jacob Prasad, the use of Israel's identity is taken to mean that "now the Christians are the People of God, and whichever prerogatives the old People had are now possessed by the Christians."[19] In Selwyn's terms, "Israel had been the object of God's special affection . . . and this affection was now transferred to the Christian Church."[20]

In Paul Richardson's language, the dynamic of Israel's identity concerns the "transposition" of status, a "conscious attempt . . . to appropriate the *Ehrentitel Israels* [the epithets of Israel] for the new people of God."[21] His less-than-celebratory language for that idea becomes even more stringent in the oft-cited essay by Betsy Bauman-Martin, who excoriates Peter for "the appropriation of Judaism," complaining that it "constituted an imperialist move." She continues:

18. Achtemeier, *1 Peter*, 69.
19. Prasad, *Foundations*, 193–94.
20. Selwyn, *First Epistle of St. Peter*, 167.
21. Richardson, *Israel in the Apostolic Church*, 172–73. More circumspect but still unable to shake such language, cf. Hiršs: "Er will mit seinem Brief am ehesten eine Kontinuität vom Altem Testament zur eigenen Zeit und Situation herausstellen, vom alten zum neuen Volk Gottes" (*Ein Volk aus Juden und Heiden*, 5). Or again, though much of the work is helpful in just these concerns, Feldmeier cannot seem but share the same language (*Die Christen als Fremde*, 195): "Ein Merkmal des 1 Petr ist auch die starke Übertragung jüdischer Traditionen auf die christliche Gemeinde."

1 Peter is a supersessionist text, and that supersessionism itself might be better understood from a postcolonial viewpoint as a strategy that posits an "other" to better delineate one's own group, plunders the resources of a marginalized group to delineate the self in relation to the colonial power and leaves that other group in a position of no value or status.²²

While not quite so censorious, John Elliott's manner of phrasing these things leans in the same direction:

> By attributing divine election and other honorific predicates of ancient Israel (2:9) to the Christian sect, the author(s) of 1 Peter have thereby attempted to disenfranchise the Jews of their peculiar "claim to fame." The sect, it is implied, is now the exclusive representative of the chosen people of God.

And again:

> Not only does this passage imply that in view of faith in Jesus Christ Judaism's "privileges are annulled"; it also indicates that, through the expropriation of Judaism's distinctive honors, the Christian community saw itself as Judaism's superior replacement.²³

Even David Horrell, who has some room for criticism of Bauman-Martin's use of postcolonial criticism, seems happy enough to speak of the dynamic as "the appropriation—one might say expropriation—of the Scriptures and identity of Israel."²⁴

The above represents a large swathe of modern writers on 1 Peter, and the assumption in each case is that Peter's language of identity in a Christian context requires a transfer from one entity to another, from Israel to the church or from the Jews to Christians. The governing picture appears to be that one group existed who had a right and claim to that identity, and Peter then came along to strip that community (explicitly or implicitly) in order to clothe another group. Some might approve of the act, and others might disapprove, but in each case the same governing picture seems to be at play.

A few have tried to offer different governing pictures. One writer, taking the above material as evidence that Peter's audience is "Jewish" rather than "the church," goes on to suggest that Peter is speaking to "Jewish

22. She speaks as well of "transferring the identity of Jews to Gentiles," and similar phrases; see Bauman-Martin, "Speaking Jewish," 149–50, 152.

23. Elliott, *Home for the Homeless*, 127, 142n55. The in-line quotation is from Chevallier, "Israël et l'Eglise," 127.

24. Horrell, *Becoming Christian*, 228.

believers" in a way that is not addressing "the church" at all.[25] It is not replacement theology simply because it has nothing to do with non-Jewish believers. Another recent work suggests that Peter was unaware that these terms and epithets were ever really used for another people at all; that he saw the Scriptures as immediately applicable without reference to Israel as a historical reality.[26] But these are unconvincing suggestions. And so we are left with the question: how do we frame Peter's use of Israel's theological identity for an explicitly "Christian" audience if not in the terms of replacement theology that have dominated 1 Peter scholarship?

Participating in an Identity

Using the language of "identity" throughout this essay provides the grounds for a solution by peeking over the fence at the use of that language in christological discussions. Richard Bauckham has made much of the notion of Jesus as being "included" into the "divine identity" through his status and role in early Christian writings.[27] Whatever we might say of that notion in explaining early Christian views of Jesus, the language provides a way of speaking of participating and sharing an identity without replacement ideas. Jesus does not displace God by being granted a share in his identity, nor does he "appropriate" (much less disenfranchise or expropriate) God's identity. Such ideas fail to express the dynamic appropriately. Rather, by constructing an identity for Jesus that cannot be other than divine, Jesus is presented as sharing in and participating in divine identity—without replacement, transfer, or supersession.

The usefulness in our own situation is obvious: Peter constructs for these believers the theological identity of Israel to demonstrate that these believers have become sharers in that identity. They are included into an identity and made participants in it. This does not mean a disenfranchising of Israel, nor a transfer (or even appropriation) of identity from one group

---

25. Cf. Sibley, "You Talkin' to Me?"

26. So Sargent, on the use of Leviticus 19: "there is no evidence, both in the use of this citation here as well as in the theological narrative of 1.10–12, that the citation is understood to refer both to Israel at the time of the exodus as well as the communities in the present." Or on 2:9–10: "the fact remains that there is nothing in 1 Pet. 2.9 to indicate the presence of a citation: the language appears to function as Peter's own, without any sense of incongruity, and there is no citation formula. . . . It is not at all obvious that Peter understood the scriptural terms he employs in 2.9 to refer initially to people at particular instances in the past and now, in a secondary manner, to people in the present" (*Written to Serve*, 57 and 121).

27. Cf. Bauckham, *Jesus and the God of Israel*.

to another. These Christians are meant to view themselves as newly-made participants in a very old identity.

This will not, of course, resolve all fears of "supersessionism," variously defined as it is. After all, it is clear enough that Peter requires that his readers believe that the prophets did, in fact, speak of Christ's suffering; and he leaves no room for salvation elsewhere but in belief in Christ.[28] Many writers have spoken at length of how Peter "ignores" the "Jewish" communities around him.[29] What they mean, presumably, is the Jewish communities that remained unconvinced or actively rejected the claims of Jesus as the Christ. Yet put that way, we can see that 1 Peter does in fact address them, only not in felicitous terms (2:8). We see the modern take on this point in Bauman-Martin, who places her condemnation of 1 Peter squarely on the grounds that she is unconvinced of the claims about Jesus made in the letter—mainly ideas of pre-existence, resurrection, and being spoken of by the prophets.[30] What she calls supersessionism is, in fact, simply a claim about Jesus with which she disagrees. Those two categories should not be confused.[31] And in this context, Peter does not ignore those who reject the "good news" of Jesus (1:12, 25), which would have included many among "the Jews" of his day; he simply declares them to be among those who disobey the living word of the prophets.

Conclusion

I have to this point largely sidestepped the disputed question of Peter's audience—whether Jewish or gentile. But the question seems largely beside the point in the letter, however prominent in academic arguments. Peter

---

28. So, e.g., Michaels: "Peter never goes so far as to endorse . . . a 'two-track' approach to salvation, for to him Jesus is unmistakably the only way (1 Pet 2:6–8; cf. Acts 4:11–12)" (*1 Peter*, lv).

29. E.g., Michaels, *1 Peter*, xlix.

30. 1 Peter has "misrepresented, silenced and defined out of existence . . . the original holders of the covenant promise and constituents of the holy people"; it represents "distorting" and "destroying" Jewish history "as a means of establishing superiority and legitimating" Christian ideology; it is "intellectual-colonial 'plundering'"; "simple theft"; etc. See Bauman-Martin, "Speaking Jewish," 163, 170, 174.

31. As N. T. Wright laments in Pauline studies: "now, paradoxically, the word 'supersessionism' is being applied by some to any attempt to suggest that Paul believed Jesus to be the fulfilment of the covenant and the promises, so that the community of those who believe in Jesus is, for him, the single family promised to Abraham, able to be referred to in a shockingly straightforward manner as *Ioudaioi* (2:29), 'sons of Abraham' (Galatians 3:29), 'the circumcision' (Philippians 3:3), 'sons of God' (8:12–17) and similar Israel-titles" ("Romans 9–11," 50).

expressly cares little for the line of descent which one can claim, as if that established one's identity without regard for belief in the prophetic word (1:23). And the evidence can all be read either toward an ethnically Jewish or ethnically gentile audience. If the audience is Jewish, then the statements of their former life can all be coordinated with the same terminology found in the LXX for unbelieving/unfaithful Israel. The use of Hosea 1–2 at 2:10 would be a model: Hosea is speaking of Israel being disowned by YHWH in judgment, and a later generation (still "Israel") reconstituted through YHWH's grace. The "futile" (*mataios*) ways of their ancestors (1:18) could coordinate with the idolatry for which the term is used in the HB (LXX 1 Kgs 16:13; 2 Kgs 17:15; Ps 23:4; Hos 5:11; Amos 2:4). Their "straying like lost sheep" could be tied to Jeremiah 50:6 (LXX 27:6)—or less polemically to Isaiah 53:6. And the "darkness" from which they are delivered could similarly be coordinated with any of Isaiah 8:22, 9:2, or 50:10 (or again, less polemically, with 2 Sam 22:29 or LXX Ps 17:29).

Most of these renderings appear rather more polemical than normally imagined for 1 Peter, characterizing their life before hearing and believing the report of Jesus as the same kind of infidelity exposed by the prophets of old. And to my mind, that seems overly harsh—these are ones who believed the prophetic word about Jesus, after all. On the flip side, we could just as well understand all of the above as addressing a largely gentile audience: futile ways of ancestors, not part of YHWH's people, straying like sheep, a life pursuing pleasures (4:1–4). That we could read it in either case might indicate that there is very little difference to Peter for the point being made. What they are *now* matters, and that does not depend upon what they *were* (descent-wise). Again, it seems to me overly harsh to the character of the letter to find Peter defining all Jewish practice/belief prior to Jesus in such terms as above, and would come close to cutting off the branch on which he has built the argument.

And in truth an audience of both some from Jewish and some from ethnically gentile backgrounds, besides better fitting recent demographic suggestions, would allow the rhetoric sufficient freedom not to be taken as overly polemical toward one particular group.[32] It also has the added benefit of minimizing, though not eliminating, the challenge of mirror-reading a historical audience from polemics.[33] The emphasis in 1 Peter falls entirely upon the *new* identity of these Christians, given to them "now" over against who they were before. But the argument here is that this new identity is, in fact, quite old. They have been joined to Israel, made to share in the honor

---

32. For the demographic point, see Trebilco, *Jewish Communities*.
33. Cf. Barclay, "Mirror-Reading."

and calling of Israel's theological identity, which entails hearing and believing the prophets and, for them, following the pattern of Christ.

Tributary Conclusion

To those familiar with Robert S. Rayburn's life and work, the above suggestions will make sense as a modest attempt to work out his general viewpoint on the continuity of the covenant to a reading of 1 Peter.[34] No part of his influence on me has been as important or far-reaching in my theological development than his arguments on the unity of the Bible as Christian Scripture, and the unity of the people of God through the history of redemption. His arguments on that point have sat in my mind throughout all of my formative academic work and formed the impetus to my own PhD dissertation.[35] And while I continue to pursue the questions, I have only become more deeply convinced of the value and truth of his position. And more than this, they have made the whole of the Bible come alive to me as, from beginning to end, given for *me* to sit under and love. Dedicating this essay to him is the smallest token of gratitude.

34. Rayburn, "Contrast."
35. Moon, *Jeremiah's New Covenant*.

10

The Body is for the Lord

Physicality and Worship

WE WERE ENJOYING A lovely Easter meal when one of my friends mentioned he had recently read that a child who does not learn to bat by age four would never succeed at baseball, even in high school.[1] My firstborn son was three years old at the time. Suddenly my afternoon was ruined—we had not been working adequately on his batting stance! So this pastor, at the risk of breaking the fourth commandment, put his son to work immediately upon returning home with soft tosses until he finally broke down in tears and begged to take a nap! Fortunately, the Lord had mercy on my horrendous parenting and enabled my now twenty-two-year-old son to love Jesus and his dad. (He also mercifully allowed him to bat over .600 by his senior year in varsity baseball!)

Thanks to Malcolm Gladwell, those of us who are not experts in the mechanics of baseball understand why coaches insist that a star player must learn basic batting technique by the age of four: Because he has to start down the road toward the "ten-thousand-hour rule." Gladwell concluded from studies of elite performers, from golfers to rock bands, that the key ingredient to their success was "to have practiced, to have apprenticed, for 10,000 hours before you get good."[2] Gladwell's thesis provided the inspiration for hip-hop artists Macklemore and Ryan Lewis to write their hit "Ten Thousand Hours."

While there is debate over Gladwell's ten-thousand-hour rule, no one denies there is such a phenomenon as muscle memory or that an athlete can do "reps in his head," which in turn affects his future physical performance. As Christians, we understand why there is this phenomenon of interplay among our various modalities. We understand why the mind affects the

1. http://www.2createabaseballplayer.com/little-league-parents.html.
2. Gladwell, *Outliers*.

body and the body affects the mind and why prayer lowers your heart rate and why an anxious neighbor can increase your blood pressure. It is because God made us "living souls" or "body-spirits." God designed our mind, soul, and body to operate as an integrated system. Holistically, we bear the image of God.[3] Why then does the Western church consider any discussion about the body's effect on the soul in worship to be such a radical idea? Because we have been infected by Platonism, the idea that the body is the "prison house" of the soul. Moreover, we have unconsciously adopted a sub-biblical reductionism that views the purest worship activity to be unseen, un-affective, unphysical, intellectual, and internal; that is, "spiritual." Not only is such a view unbiblical, it is impoverished.

No two people have made a greater impact on my views of worship than Drs. Robert G. and Robert S. Rayburn. These two men set me on a course to enhancing my own as well as my people's experience of worship by faithfully embracing its biblical physicality. It was during a Day of Prayer at Covenant Theological Seminary that Robert G. Rayburn introduced a handful of us first-year students to the benefit of kneeling during prayer. With my body bent in prayer, my mind could not wander as it tended to do when I merely "bowed my head and closed my eyes." In a posture of humility, I also found it easier to remember that God is sovereign and I am not. With heart and mind softened by the elder Rayburn's instruction and example, I was primed to further discipleship by the younger Robert. As he and his congregation have learned to "respond to God in every way the psalmist did," I have passed the same along to my congregations. Rob taught me to lift my hands in prayer, kneel for confession of sin, don a robe, and utter a vocal "Amen." I must confess, however, I'm glad Rob has not taken up dancing. As his closest friends would say, that would be "unsociable!"

While I do wish to honor my dear friend and mentor with this essay, I know that the greatest way to honor him would be for this chapter to inspire more worshipers to respond like David to the Lord, in body as well as spirit.

Dr. Rayburn, as we lovingly referred to Rob's father, said in his groundbreaking book *O Come, Let us Worship*,

> Worship is the *activity* of the new life of a believer in which, recognizing the fullness of the Godhead as it is revealed in the person of Jesus Christ and His mighty redemptive acts, he seeks by the power of the Holy Spirit to *render* to the living God the glory, honor, and submission which are His due.[4]

---

3. For a detailed biblical and theological treatment of the subject, see Cooper, *Body, Soul, and Life Everlasting*.

4. Rayburn, *O Come, Let us Worship*, 20–21 (emphasis added).

I emphasize "activity" and "render" because I know from having studied with Dr. Rayburn that worshipers being active was an emphasis for him. His study of the constellation of vocabulary within the church (Hebrew, Greek, and Latin) led him to conclude that true worship cannot be passive. On the contrary, it is an engaged "dialogue between God and his people" from beginning to end.[5] Though he was speaking primarily of the Christian funeral, we could also borrow Tom Long's language to describe a church worship service as a "gospel liturgical drama."[6] Such language points to the dynamic I wish to emphasize in honor of Dr. Robert S. Rayburn—worship must be a holistic response to the gospel of Jesus Christ. Since we are accustomed to describing the spiritual nature of that response, I intend to underscore the importance of physicality in worship.

Platonic Baggage and Scripture's Anthropology

An OT worshiper, or any Jew in the NT era for that matter, would have wondered how we ever devolved to such a strict dualism and why we waste so much energy trying to dissect a human being into component parts like a body, soul, spirit, and mind. How did we fall to this state in which we habitually distinguish between body and soul, physical and spiritual, secular and sacred, temporal and eternal? While there are numerous possible sources for our contemporary dualism, the most convenient object of blame is Platonic philosophy,[7] which insisted that body and soul are distinct components within a person, to the denigration of the former. Thus, for example, Plato called the body the "prison-house" of the soul, claiming "the soul is imprisoned like the oyster in its shell."[8]

There are several inconclusive theories as to how Plato's ideas made their way into Christian thought.[9] Experts consider Philo to be a representative of Middle Platonism, a bridge between his two beloved traditions—Judaism and Plato.[10] Some posit that by the third century the church had succumbed to the constant barrage of gnostic ideas. Still others say Augustine reformatted Plato's dualism. Regardless of how the stream got poisoned, evangelical Christians in particular have been heavily influenced by a Platonic idea that the church's main mission is to "save souls" and that worship

---

5. Rayburn, *O Come, Let us Worship*, 118.
6. Long, *Accompany Them With Singing*, 78.
7. Renehen, "Greek Origins."
8. *Phaedo* 80–85 and *Phaedrus* 250c, respectively.
9. Anderson, *Earthen Vessels*, 236.
10. Scholer, "Introduction to Philo," xiii.

is a spiritual connection to heaven, which requires separating physically and mentally from "daily life."

The resulting view of heaven is that it is an immaterial, ethereal place where the Christian experiences God who is spirit. In this view, worship requires taming the body to keep it from distracting the "mind" and "heart" from "soul-work." That seemed to be William Temple's presupposition to his definition of Christian worship, which refers to all aspects of personhood except the body: "Worship is the submission of all our nature to God. It is the quickening of conscience by his holiness; the nourishment of mind with his truth; the purifying of imagination by his beauty; the opening of the heart to his love; the surrender of will to his purpose."[11] From the beginning to the end of Scripture, however, there is no evidence of God's despising anything physical or material. His first act was to create material reality, "In the beginning, God created the heavens and the earth" (Gen 1:1). At the conclusion of each day's work of unpacking the potential of the raw stuff he spoke into being, God pronounced his approval with "It was good." The crowning work of creation was God's crafting humankind out of the earth, which he declared "very good." It is noteworthy that after the trinitarian decision to "make man in our image," God executed that decision by making a physical being. God, a spirit, breathed life into the physical lungs of a man. There is no hint of God's maintaining his distance from a corrupt material world nor skittishness of pressing his divine lips against Adam's nostrils. God the Creator is no evil demiurge who bunglingly brought the material world into being.[12]

There is not a hair's breadth of division between the spiritual and the physical in a believer's daily life with the Lord. Every physical action and every material blessing or curse is only understood in relation to the reality of God. The cosmology of the OT is such that God is immanently coupled with every physical act and object. The absence of any dividing wall (not even a "thin place") is only further emphasized in the NT by the incarnation and work of Jesus Christ. Jesus' ministry was intensely physical as it was prophesied to be. In fact, it verified him as the messiah (Luke 4:16–18). He laid hands on lepers who had not been touched for years. He got close to unclean dead bodies. He made poultices with mud and his own spittle and applied them to blind eyes. He healed a bleeding woman and gave peace to a prostitute by allowing them to touch him. The stripes laced on his body by Roman whips healed our sins. His righteous corpse canceled the debt of our sin. Having achieved our justification, his body

---

11. Temple, *Readings*, 67.
12. On this see Jones, *Gnostic Empire*, 11–22, 43–47.

lived again. After his resurrection, he ate meals with his disciples. And that same body ascended to heaven where it remains with real wounds and lives to make intercession for us.

Paul's eschatology and understanding of the final state, likewise, are unabashedly fleshly. All bodies will be raised to be judged for what was done in them (2 Cor 5:10). Those outside of Christ will be punished in the body with which they rejected salvation. Those bodies united to Christ will be essentially the same which lived on earth, but they will be transformed to enjoy heaven forever. The resurrection of those bodies will be the catalyst to renewing the fallen creation (Rom 8:23). Real physical human beings will inhabit a real material creation, but liberated from all vestiges of the fall. Paul's somatic theology is summarized in his brief but brilliant line, "The body is for the Lord and the Lord is for the body" (1 Cor 6:13).

Corporate worship, then, could be called corporal worship, a weekly dry run for the way we will act physically in the consummated kingdom. This being the case, does it not behoove us to practice now for how we will live in the coming kingdom? When God calls to us, will we not speak back to him enthusiastically? When Jesus strolls by, will we not stand in respect and stretch out our hands to touch him? When he ascends his throne, will we not fall down in humility? When the angels lead in song, will we not shout praise with all our might? When he as our priest raises his hands to bless us, will we not lift ours to receive it? Current corporate worship is choreography for our future eternal movements with our bridegroom.

Scripture is replete with physical acts of worship. Worshipers raise hands in prayer and praise (Pss 28:1–2; 88:8–10; 134:1). God's people kneel, bow and fall down when they are humbled by the Lord (Rev 4:9–11; 5:8–14; Ezra 9:5–6; 2 Chr 6:12–14; Ps 35:13–14; Neh 8:5–6). In joy, worshipers dance or leap (Ps 149:3–4; Exod 15:20–21; 2 Sam 6:14–17) and clap and shout (Ps 47:1–2; 66:1).[13]

What would it look like to respond physically to the gospel as it is recapitulated in our worship? How would it change the way we act if we endeavored to respond to God as the psalmist did? There are numerous possible answers to such questions, since it may be argued that every liturgical act involves a physical dimension, from using one's vocal chords in singing to using one's ears to listen to a sermon. For purposes of this essay, however, I will focus selectively on those elements of a dialogically arranged worship service that more obviously engage our physical natures.

---

13. Allison, "Theology of Human Embodiment."

Prelude

The physicality of a worship service begins upon entering the sanctuary. In the OT, entering the space set aside for worship was to walk into the presence of God. Of course, a faithful Hebrew knew that God was everywhere present—"the earth is the Lord's" (Ps 24:1). However, a sanctuary, the tent of meeting, the holy place or the temple was viewed as an earthly outpost, an embassy of God's throne room. Therefore, to enter with appropriate reverence required physical preparation. Priests washed their hands and feet to remind themselves to perform their sacrifices with integrity (Exod 30:19). To reinforce that, their intercessory work was essential for the wellbeing of their people; they donned a breastplate of twelve stones representing each of Israel's tribes. And to impress on their minds that their work on behalf of their people was a life or death matter, they wore bells to indicate whether their sacrifice had been accepted or whether God's holiness had killed them in the process (Exod 28:33–35).

There are many opinions about what should happen in the prelude. Some traditions prescribe entering the sanctuary in absolute silence.[14] Others advocate for music but opine that it should be quiet. One musician went so far as to say, "The last four minutes of prelude time are always quiet music so that a hush tends to descend on the church."[15] My opinion is that the music should mostly reflect the joy of the Songs of Ascent. Surely worshipers streaming into Jerusalem for Passover from parts far and wide did not arrive morbidly. These songs are joyful! Intentionally crafted worship services will have preludes that knit together the theme for the service as well as reflect the mood of the season or the congregation that Sunday. Sometimes

---

14. There are indeed points in a worship service, particularly in its earlier movements, when times of silence are pastorally helpful. Henri Nouwen writes (*Way of the Heart*, 63):

> Finally, I would like to stress the importance of silence in the ways a minister organizes his [or her] own life and that of others. In a society in which entertainment and distraction are such important preoccupations, ministers are also tempted to join the ranks of those who consider it their primary task to keep other people busy. It is easy to perceive the young and the elderly as people who need to be kept off the streets or on the streets. And ministers frequently find themselves in fierce competition with people and institutions who offer something more exciting than they do.
>
> But our task is the opposite of distraction. Our task is to help people concentrate on the real but often hidden event of God's active presence in our lives. Hence, the question that must guide all organizing activity in a parish is not how to keep people busy, but how to keep them from being so busy that they no longer hear the voice of God that speaks in silence.

15. Kettering, *Steps Toward a Singing Church*, 277.

the piece may overwhelm the congregation with power that plasters the worshiper to the pew and forces a silent awe at the otherness of God. At other times, it may be jovial and inspire joyful reunions in the pew. In other words, worship planners must be as dependent upon the Spirit's guidance as the preacher is when choosing their musical texts and moods to lead the worshiper into the presence of God, holding faithfully to the gospel while being mindful of the congregation's humanity.

Passing the Peace

For centuries, Christians have engaged in what is called the "passing of the peace" or sometimes just called "the peace." In some traditions, it was practiced during the celebration of the Lord's Supper, either before or after the prayer of consecration. The idea is to communicate in a visible, audible way that the church is united. Some traditions carried it out by kissing (men to men and women to women). Others practiced the following exchange: "May the peace of Christ be with you," to which the response was, "And with your spirit."[16] In doing so, we communicate that we are a family meeting in unity to worship our Father.

Many churches place this event after the prelude and announcements. During it, we move toward each other, shake hands, embrace, and even give "holy kisses." It looks and feels familial. Family greetings are very physical events, replete with backslapping, laughter, bright eyes, broad grins, warm embraces, tears and expressions of deep concern. This is a suitable expression of our unity as a family gathered to worship at the invitation of our Father.

At First Presbyterian Church in Augusta, Georgia, as well as at Second Presbyterian in Memphis, Tennessee, where I pastor now, I have regularly met with our minority members to ask how we can more sensitively accommodate them in our worship and ministries. Each time we meet, someone volunteers that passing the peace was what convinced him or her to join our church. The comment goes something like this: "Someone got up out of his seat and walked back several rows to me, grabbed my hand, looked me in the eye, asked my name, and told me how glad he was I was here. It's one thing for the pastor to say up front, 'Welcome to our church!' but it was an entirely different thing for someone to personalize that to me."

---

16. McClintock and Strong, *Cyclopedia*, 5.112–13.

The Introit

Introit comes from a Latin word meaning "to enter" and describes the ceremonial entrance of the choir and/or pastor into the sanctuary. Ultimately the pastor arrives at the chancel, picturing our entry into the presence of God. Like their biblical forefathers, the congregation is processing into the presence of God behind the leadership of the choir and ministers (1 Chr 15:25–28). As we enter into his presence, God calls us to worship or engages us in a responsive salutation. The effect is to confer on us grace, mercy, and peace. It is God's way of saying, "I am commanding you to worship me but I must first convey grace on you because you are not capable to do or believe anything I am about to prescribe, so I am giving you what you need." Our response is the same as saying, "Yes, Lord, we are not capable of following you. Please give us your grace that we might live in dependence upon you." Or as Augustine prayed (*Confessions*, 10.35), "Lord, command what you will, but give what you command!"

Invocation

The word *invocation* comes from *invocare* and means to "appeal to" or "cry out to." In this prayer, we cry out to God to come and help us worship in an acceptable way.[17] It is most appropriate to lift our hands heavenward when we invoke God's help. This should not make us uncomfortable for several reasons. For one, it is a biblical posture for prayer. The psalmists regularly call on God's people to lift their hands heavenward in prayer (cf. Pss 28:2; 63:4; 134:2; 141:2).[18] I suppose someone could say that such a posture was only a product of Middle Eastern culture and need not be applied elsewhere. However, Paul commanded "all men everywhere to lift up holy hands in prayer" (1 Tim 2:8), including Greeks as well as Jews. This posture is not bound to any culture, but is a universal symbol of our dependence upon God, and has always been practiced in the Christian church.[19]

John Calvin said that the great challenge in prayer is to humble the heart before God. Our hearts are naturally cold to him, and we are slow to acknowledge our great need of him in every way. Therefore, Calvin said that one way we train our hearts to depend on God is by forcing them to follow the actions of our body. As we lift our hands to God in prayer, people

---

17. On the content and attributes of an invocation, see Old, *Leading in Prayer*, 11–17. My focus in this essay is on the prayer's physical expression.
18. Psalm 119:48 forms the basis for our lifting our hands at the benediction.
19. Hastings, *Encyclopedia*, 10.183 and 201.

remember we are "far removed from God unless they raise their thoughts on high" (*Institutes* 3.20.5). Calvin concludes:

> Hence the rite of lifting up the hands, to which we have previously referred—one common to all ages and peoples, and still in force. But how rarely is there one who, in raising up his hands, is not aware of his own apathy, since his heart stays on the ground?[20]

In this posture, we are reaching out as children to a father in utter dependence. What father, especially a perfectly gracious one, can ever resist such a gesture? At some point in our development as human beings, we grow too sophisticated to reach up for our parents to hold us. Little children do it all the time; older children have to be in some kind of crisis before they reach out to their parents for help. Worship is then a weekly return to the childlikeness, which Jesus said must characterize us in order to enter the kingdom of heaven (Luke 18:17). Believers have for all times lifted their hands in prayer as a sign of such childlike dependence. [21] And Presbyterians were raising them in Geneva long before the charismatics in the 1900s! We pray corporately with uplifted hands so that no one is professing to be holier than anyone else. We do so with heads uplifted and eyes closed, so that only God is the focus in our mind's eye. In so doing, our physical actions reinforce our intellectual convictions and stir our affections for our Savior.

"Amen!"

At the conclusion of every prayer in the worship service, the leader should prompt the congregation to respond verbally with an "Amen!" In Hebrew, *amen* literally means "firm." In Scripture, it means "truthful" or "so be it" and is sometimes used to describe the character of God, as in Isaiah 65:16 where he is called "the God of amen." Likewise, Jesus is called "the *Amen, the faithful* and *true* witness" (Rev 3:14).

Responding to the faithfulness of God, an OT worshiper would accept oaths by saying, "Amen" (Num 5:22; Deut 27:15, 17: Neh 5:13; 8:6; 1 Chr 16:36; Ps 106:48). He would also agree with the prayers of the priest by saying, "Amen." That practice continued through synagogue worship and into the NT (Matt 6:13; Rom 9:5; 11:36; 15:33; 16:27; 2 Cor 13:13). Paul said it was important to pray in a known tongue so that the congregation

---

20. Calvin, *Institutes*, 3.20.16; see also his commentary on Pss 28:2 and 134:2 (*Commentary on the Psalms*, 1.466 and 3.168).

21. McClintock and Strong, *Cyclopedia*, 4.57–58.

could say "Amen" at the end (1 Cor 14:16). It has also continued in the church throughout history. Only in the last century has the practice diminished. In his time, the church father Jerome said at the conclusion of public prayer the corporate "Amen" of the people sounded like the "fall of water or the noise of thunder."[22]

We must involve ourselves thoroughly in the worship of God. Each of us is a priest before God; therefore, we must not be passive. We should make each prayer our own by saying "Amen" out loud. Rifqa Bary writes that learning that Christians have the privilege of participating intimately with the Lord even in corporate prayer by saying "Amen" was the first step to her conversion from Islam. In Sri Lanka, she recited prayers in Arabic she did not understand from her earliest childhood. It was not until she saw a wall hanging in a Christian friend's home with "Amen" elegantly embroidered on it and learned what the word meant that she realized there is a heavenly Father who delights to converse with us.[23] Making this full-throated corporal response will remind us that the one to whom we pray is the "Amen, the faithful and true witness" who answers our prayers.

Kneeling and Standing for Prayer

In discussing the invocation, I broached the subject of posture in prayer. While I could mention many ways Rob Rayburn has positively influenced me, his pastoral example in this matter has made a profound impact on my worship as well as that of those I have led.

The most common postures for prayer in the Bible are kneeling and standing (e.g., Pss 28:2; 95:6; 134:2; Acts 9:40; 20:36). There are a few places in Scripture where worshipers go from kneeling to standing or vice versa. The one posture we rarely observe in Scripture for prayer is sitting. There are only three occasions where individuals sat to pray: when Moses was tired, when Elijah sat under the broom tree and prayed to die (1 Kgs 19:14), and when Jonah sat under a fig tree and grumbled against God. These are hardly ideal patterns to imitate! On the contrary, kneeling so naturally and universally communicates a spirit of reverence and humility that it was actively encouraged during the Reformation. The 1559 *Book of Discipline* of the French Reformed Church, for example, specifically mentions a failure to kneel or uncover one's head for prayer as a gesture of disrespect that should be changed: "That great irreverence, which is found in divers persons who

---

22. McClintock and Strong, *Cyclopedia*, 1.94 and 8.1049–50, respectively.
23. Hill, "It is Good to Say Amen."

at public, and private prayers, do neither uncover their heads, nor bow their knees, shall be reformed."

Physical posture forces our minds to remember something spiritually important. Kneeling bends our bodies into a posture of humility, which will hopefully bend our souls as well. John Calvin said as much (*Institutes* 3.20.33): "As for bodily gestures customarily observed in praying, such as kneeling, and uncovering the head, they are exercises whereby we try to rise to a greater reverence for God." Elisabeth Elliot's brother, Thomas Howard, eloquently made a similar point when he reflected on his experience of walking into an evangelical church where worshipers knelt:

> It cannot be argued, then, that we must kneel. But it can indeed be argued that posture is immensely significant and that if we find shallowness to be a problem in worship services then it may be worth considering the matter. We sit for a thousand things—to eat, to chat, to work, to write notes, to rest. It may be that our bodies cry out for an attitude that will pluck us by the sleeve, as it were, and assist our inner-beings in the extremely difficult task of prayer.[24]

Kneeling is not a legalistic duty; for some it is physically impossible. The Bible simply commends it as something generally helpful in shaping our attitudes in prayer.

But what attitudes do we want our souls to have as a result? They are humility and gratitude.[25] Calvin said that on the one hand, the Christian is to recognize by his kneeling his unworthiness before God and express his respect for his majesty. On the other hand, he kneels as an act of deep gratitude to the God of his salvation (*Institutes* 4.10.30).[26] From Philippians 2:10, Calvin would argue that kneeling "designates true and godly worship" (*Institutes* 3.5.8). In Geneva, worshipers knelt for the first half of the service (he began each service with confession of sin) and stood for most of the rest.[27] In other words, they knelt in humble repentance for their sins as well as grateful anticipation of the assurance of pardoning grace. Then, when they heard that assurance, they stood as those released of great burdens. They also stood as an act of respect for the great King who spoke his will to them from the Word. Rising to our feet in the worship service is a biblically appropriate response to the declaration of our forgiveness.

24. Howard, *Evangelical is Not Enough*, 44.

25. See Calvin's commentary on Acts 9:40 and 20:36 (*Commentary on the Psalms*, 3.35–35).

26. Cf. Calvin's commentary on Ps 95:6 (*Commentary on the Psalms*, 3.34–35).

27. Nichols, *Corporate Worship*, 40–44.

Our new life in Christ is often pictured as a resurrection, which in Greek is translated literally "to stand again" (Rom 6:5; 1 Cor 15:58). Malachi said that God would rise with healing in his wings to forgive his people (Mal 4:2). Remember, Jesus' first instruction to Saul after he converted him was (Acts 9:6), "Get up!"

Rising upon receiving forgiveness has been a historical practice as well. John Bunyan imagines Christian rising after his burden is loosed at the cross in Pilgrim's Progress. Martin Luther rose to his feet on the *scala sancta* after being finally convinced that the just will live by his faith. And Charles Wesley says in his beloved hymn, "My chains fell off, my heart was free. I rose, went forth, and followed thee." Therefore, when the minister invites you, rise to your feet to hear God's assurance of pardoning grace and imagine your burden of sin rolling from your back into Christ's sepulcher, never to be borne by you again. It is this that moved Rutherford to say: "There is no law-music in heaven. There, all their song is, 'Worthy is the lamb.'"[28]

We remain standing for intercessory prayer for several reasons. For one, it reminds us that we may come confidently to our heavenly Father (Heb 4:16). Samuel Miller prescribed standing for prayer because it is the most appropriate joyful posture for those who have been relieved of their sins.[29] Standing also communicates respect. That is still a gesture in our culture. The press rise when the President enters the room. Courtrooms rise for judges. And we are supposed to rise when the elderly or a woman enters our presence. We rise therefore in joyful respect for our Father.

The Liturgical Robe

Though dismissed in the seventies and eighties as antiquarian or pompous, the liturgical robe is being reintroduced in many churches, especially by new, young leaders of churches. The basic reason is the same as that for the reintroduction of many historical practices in worship—they are rediscovering the historic rationale for them. Many postmodern people are weary of the absence of historic rootedness, so they are eager for historic and biblical bases for their practices.

The historic rationale for the liturgical robe is threefold, each discerned from the function of priestly garments described in texts like Exodus 28. First, a robe obscures the man. A robe (typically black or white) prevents one from being distracted by a minister's wardrobe. Without a robe, the minister's suit or tie or shirt are open to critique as being too flashy or

---

28. Tweedie, *Select Biographies*, 2.259.
29. Miller, *Thoughts on Public Prayer*, 93–103.

substandard or attractive. Any of these is distracting to the worshiper and too focused on the man as opposed to his role (Exod 28:41).

Secondly, a robe reveals the minister's primary role—to speak the Word of God to his people. A robe covers everything but his head so as to point to the mouth by which he preaches and prays for the sake of God's children (Num 22:38; Isa 51:16; Rom 10:14).

Thirdly, the liturgical robe honors the office rather than the man. God commanded that Aaron and his assisting priests be given special garments for their "dignity and honor" (Exod 28:2–40). The dignity and honor was attached to their function, not their persons. People would have delighted to give them these signs of dignity and honor because the priests brought God's blessings to them. The Aaronic garments were highly decorated, accenting his functions as an intercessor (Exod 28:6–39) and a prophet (Exod 28:15). Typically, the only adornments on the plain Geneva robe may be red roping or doctoral chevrons to represent academic theological degrees. The adornments are not to draw attention to the accomplishments of the man, but rather demonstrate the priority given to excellence in teaching God's Word.[30]

Purpose of the Lord's Supper

While we have been good as evangelical Presbyterians to tell the world what we do not believe about the sacraments, we have not always been clear about what we actually *do* believe. For instance, we all know clearly that baptism does not save a child, but what can we say God does do through baptism for the child and his or her parents? And while we have been clear that the elements of the Lord's Supper are not the actual body and blood of Christ, what can we say about the Lord's strategy in giving us a supper which focuses on his body? From the Scriptures, John Calvin summarizes three purposes for the Lord's Supper:

> Our Lord, therefore, instituted the Supper, first, in order to sign and seal in our consciences the promises contained in his gospel concerning our being made partakers of his body and blood, and to give us certainty and assurance that therein lies our true

---

30. If a liturgical robe is such a good idea, then why do some pastors not wear them in the evening service? Let me suggest that this has a pastoral function in keeping us from becoming legalistic. We must be careful to distinguish between good ideas and biblical mandates. Further, we must use wisdom to determine what is appropriate relative to certain situations. Our evening services in the churches I have pastored have been by design a less formal family service. Just as I do not wear a suit to eat with my family in the evening, a robe could be overbearing for our evening service.

spiritual nourishment, and that having such an earnest, we may entertain a right reliance on salvation. Secondly, in order to exercise us in recognising his great goodness toward us, and thus lead us to laud and magnify him more fully. Thirdly, in order to exhort us to all holiness and innocence, inasmuch as we are members of Jesus Christ; and specially to exhort us to union and brotherly charity, as we are expressly commanded.[31]

The first purpose of the Supper is to provide assurance of salvation.[32] The specific source of our encouragement is the body and blood of Christ (1 Cor 11:29-30). Of course, we know that we are saved by putting our trust in what Christ accomplished, but the Lord's Supper is more than a mere remembrance. Celebrating the Lord's Supper helps our faith connect to the benefits Christ accomplished in his body both in his life and death (1 Cor 11:26). In other words, because he was perfectly obedient and we are joined to him, we become more and more obedient as we nurture that spiritual connection to him.

Secondly, as we are connected more and more to the life of Christ, which is in heaven, we become better worshipers. That is, the one who beholds God face to face helps us more and more to see him (Col 3:1-4).

Finally, the measure of our increased obedience will be our growing love and service toward our brothers and sisters in Christ. The Lord's Supper helps us increasingly to see and love Christ. If that is true, then by definition our love for his brothers will grow as well (1 Cor 11:17-22).

It is for these reasons that Calvin and the Puritans taught that, as the early church celebrated the Lord's Supper every week, so should the churches of the Reformation.[33] However, they never pushed that legalistically, and to his regret, Calvin never was able to practice it in Geneva.[34] Regardless of how frequent our church's celebration, we should prepare carefully for the Supper and do everything in our power to celebrate when it is available.

The Lord's Supper is much more than a ceremony. Real transformative grace is conveyed to us as we celebrate.[35] It is not the elements that

---

31. Calvin, "Short Treatise," 167.

32. On these themes, see Old's discussion of my dissertation in *Holy Communion*, 633-51.

33. Cf. Kistler, *Puritans on the Lord's Supper*, 40 and 77. John Owen prescribed weekly communion (*Works*, 15.512). Generally, the Puritans celebrated monthly, following Calvin's compromise with the magistrates. Baptists and Independents tended to celebrate weekly or monthly; see Davies, *Worship of the English Puritans*, 136.

34. Cf. Calvin, "Articles," 49, and *Institutes* 4.17.44-46.

35. "A sacrament is an holy ordinance instituted by Christ, wherein, by sensible signs, Christ, and the benefits of the new covenant, are represented, sealed, *and applied*

bring grace to us but the Holy Spirit, who uses an objective sacrament to carry out his sanctifying work in us. If you consistently feed by faith on Jesus through the Lord's Supper, more will happen in your life than you will ever be able to account for.

Baptism

The Westminster Shorter Catechism assembles all of the biblical information on baptism in one succinct statement: "Baptism is a sacrament, wherein the washing with water in the name of the Father, and of the Son, and of the Holy Ghost, doth signify and seal our ingrafting into Christ, and partaking of the benefits of the covenant of grace, and our engagement to the Lord's" (*WSC* 94).

Let's think about each of those statements briefly. "Washing with water" symbolizes the work of the Holy Spirit, who is always said in Scripture to "come down" or to be "poured out" in order to carry out his work of cleansing from sin and empowering for a new life (Joel 2:28; Luke 3:22; Acts 2:1–4; 22:16; 1 Cor 6:11; Col 2:11–12; Heb 9:14). Of course, water is a more appropriate sign than the bloody rite of circumcision, since the blood of the Last Lamb has been shed once and for all (Heb 10:10; 1 Pet 1:18). Next, the Catechism explains that this application of water "doth signify and seal." That language comes from Romans 4:11, which describes the spiritual significance of Abraham's circumcision. Circumcision was the OT foreshadowing of the sacrament of baptism. Therefore, the spiritual principles regarding circumcision are applicable to baptism (Col 2:11–12). In this passage from Romans, the point is that a sacrament is first a symbol of a spiritual reality. Thus, Augustine called sacraments "visible words."[36]

However, sacraments are not empty symbols. Because the Holy Spirit is real and brings the presence of Christ into every worship service, he uses sacraments to seal to our consciences the reality of the promises being made. Though God's verbal promises should be sufficient, he accommodates to our weakness by adding a seal like that of a king's signet ring, whose impression in hot wax would certify an official document. The Spirit, likewise, convinces our minds that God is trustworthy. Through baptism, the Spirit seals that confidence to parents, but as these children are reared in the fear and admonition of the Lord and reminded of the significance of their baptisms, this event will become a seal to their consciences as well.

---

to believers." (*WSC* 92, emphasis added)

36. *Homilies on the Gospel of John* 80.3 (*NPNF*1 7.344); *Reply to Faustus* 19.16 (*NPNF*1 4.244).

What specifically, then, is being signified and sealed? The Catechism mentions that three facts of grace are being confirmed. First, we are assured of our "ingrafting into Christ" upon reception of him by faith (Gen 15:6; Gal 3:9; Eph 2:8–9). Ingrafting is an allusion to John 15 in which Christ declares our absolute need for him in all things, as a branch is dependent upon a vine. Jesus says, "Without me, you can do nothing" (v. 5). Thus, to parents, God says, "Without me you cannot be godly parents to your children." And through the parents, he will say to the children, "Without me you are as helpless as your parents to live for me."

Secondly, baptism symbolizes and seals covenantally (Gen 15:1–6; 17:1–8; Gal 3:8–9); that is, he has committed himself to saving a people for himself (Acts 17:1–26). He has also chosen to do so primarily by causing his grace to run through lines of generations (Isa 59:21; Acts 2:38–39). That explains why we observe throughout Scripture the "household" or representative principle (Gen 14:14–16; 17:23; Exod 12:3–4; 1 Cor 7:14). That principle relates to God's preference for visiting salvation on those who are under the authority of the head of the home (Gen 17:10–14, 23; Exod 12:43–48; Deut 10:16; Col 2:13; Heb 11:7). Therefore, it only makes sense that when God draws the head of a household to Christ that he would put his covenant sign on the whole household. That explains why the majority of baptisms in the NT are household baptisms (Acts 10:48; 16:15; 16:33; 18:8; 1 Cor 1:16). God's gracious ideal is that children never remember a day without trusting Christ.

Think of those in Scripture who trusted God for salvation from their earliest days: David trusted God from his mother's breast (Ps 22:9), Jeremiah was set apart as a prophet in his mother's womb (Jer 1:5), John the Baptist leapt in his mother's womb at the announcement of Christ (Luke 1:41), and Timothy knew the Scriptures from infancy through his godly mother and grandmother (2 Tim 1:5; 3:15). Thus John Calvin said that Timothy "sucked godliness along with his milk."[37] Therefore, in baptism, the church family and the parents are promising before God that they will faithfully point the children to Christ all the days of their lives—our "partaking of the benefits of the covenant of grace."

Finally, God reminds us in baptism that we have "an engagement to be the Lord's." Christ's Great Commission to the church was to go into all the world and make disciples, "baptizing them in the name of the Father, Son, and the Holy Spirit" (Matt 28:19–20). Therefore, we baptize children as disciples. That does not mean that we are declaring that they

---

37. See Calvin's commentary on 2 Timothy 1:5 (*Commentaries on the Epistles to Timothy*, 187).

are regenerate. Only the Holy Spirit can regenerate; not the ritual act of baptism. However, God puts his loving mark of privilege and responsibility on children as members of the Christian household, and effectively says, "You will be the recipients of immense spiritual blessings because of your parents and your church. Salvation and her benefits will be daily within your reach. Therefore, you must grab hold of them in faith and live in grateful response to them."[38] It is the responsibility of the church family and the parents to reinforce that gracious but awesome message to the children. What a kindness from our Father that he should accommodate himself to our physical natures and give us such an objective symbol in order to seal to our consciences that his promises to us are as real as the sight and feel of the water with which we baptize.[39]

Benediction

The benediction has always been a component of biblical worship. In fact, it marked the climax of the OT service as the high priest would raise his hands after the final sacrifice and pronounce the Aaronic blessing: "May the Lord bless you and keep you: The Lord make his face to shine upon you and be gracious to you: The Lord turn his countenance toward you and give you his peace" (Num 6:24–26; cf. Lev 9:22–23; 2 Chr 30:27).[40] Someone has called it the "liturgical equivalent of the rainbow" because the priest's lifting his hands and pronouncing blessing indicated to the worshiper that the sacrifice had been accepted.[41] That same benediction remained a traditional close to the service throughout synagogue worship. However, like so many other biblical practices, it declined in importance during the Middle Ages and was deliberately restored in Protestant liturgies.[42]

Martin Luther led the way in restoring the blessing to the close of the Reformed worship service.[43] Because he recognized the redemptive-historical significance of the blessing as well as the *inclusio* formed by Luke's beginning and ending his gospel with a priestly blessing, Luther argued that Jesus used the Aaronic benediction when he blessed his disciples

---

38. Old, *Worship That is Reformed*, 27.

39. On the benefit of the "seal" to the conscience, see Ferguson, *Baptism in the Early Church*, 485–86.

40. Old, *Leading in Prayer*, 349–53.

41. Kleinig, "Providence and Worship," 122.

42. Old, *Leading in Prayer*, 349; see also his *Patristic Roots*, 334–37.

43. Old, *Leading in Prayer*, 349–53.

(Luke 24:50–53).[44] Regardless of the accuracy of that conclusion, his fellow Reformers agreed that the benediction was a theological necessity in a worship service, because it conveys the idea that the covenant continues from generation to generation by means of the redemptive presence of God. Week after week, year after year, decade after decade, generation after generation, the people of God are to hear all of the promises and precepts imparted to them during the worship service by the presence of God through Christ, who marks them as the heirs of all of God's covenantal blessings (Gal 3:14; Eph 1:3).

Therefore, the benediction is the stitch that connects God's people every week to the tapestry of faithfulness God is weaving. In addition to the Aaronic blessing, God uses numerous benedictions in Scripture to convey the idea of his redemptive presence (e.g. 2 Cor 13:14; John 14:27; Eph 6:23; Phil 4:7; 1 Thess 5:28; Heb 13:20–21), an idea which is intended to bring peace to the soul of the worshiper. It is appropriate then that every benediction include a pronouncement of peace so that the service begins with the personal passing of the peace, one to another, and ends with God's personal bestowal of peace from heaven to earth.

Because the benediction was the exclusive prerogative of the Aaronic priesthood, only ministers of the Word have traditionally pronounced it. That is why it is traditionally the first act of a newly ordained minister to pronounce the benediction on God's people. That tradition remained during the Reformation, even with its strong emphasis on the priesthood of all believers.[45] The Reformers taught that the universal priesthood of believers referred primarily to everyone's ready access to God in prayer. At the same time, descending from the OT priesthood was an order of ministers entrusted with the particular duties of preaching and prayer by which the people of God were to be blessed (Eph 4:11). To put it another way, while every Christian has a shepherding responsibility toward his fellow Christian, God has especially loved his people by giving them official shepherds—called ministers and elders—who are responsible to watch over their souls (Acts 20:28). Therefore, the one particularly charged to minister the Word of God to the people is the one who appropriately pronounces God's blessing on them, which is to encourage their hearts that God will give them all the grace necessary to live out the privileges and responsibilities of the people of God.

As with other key elements of the worship service, posture is important too. As it is appropriate for the minister to raise his hands symbolically

---

44. Cf. Kapic, "Receiving Christ's Priestly Benediction."
45. Old, *Leading in Prayer*, 349–53.

calling down God's blessing on the people, it is appropriate for the people to lift up their heads and stretch forth their hands to receive it (Pss 28:2; 63:4; 134:2; 141:2; 1 Tim 2:8).

Conclusion

The Psalmist enjoins, "Come let us worship and bow down. Let us kneel before the Lord our Maker" (Ps 95:6). When the Holy Spirit inspired David to write those words, it defies logic to think he intended us to obey that command entirely in our minds. By taking on flesh, our Savior proved he is "for the body," and by worshiping him holistically, we demonstrate the "body is for the Lord" (1 Cor 6:13). The physical, intellectual, and emotional habits we form in worship cut grooves deep in our soul and ready us for eternity.[46] I have heard my dear friend Rob pray before worship services, "Holy Father, help us in this service, for we feel most ourselves when we worship you." Even so, let us give ourselves completely in every worship service, that the Lord may expedite his sanctifying process of conforming us to the image of the last Adam, his Incarnate Son Jesus Christ.

---

46. On this subject, see also Smith, *You Are What You Love*.

11

"And So I Will Go Unto the King"

Prayer and the Book of Esther[1]

Introduction

THE BOOK OF ESTHER tells a gripping story, full of drama and written with brilliant literary artistry. Theologically, the book is probably best known for Mordecai's words to Esther in 4:14: "For if you keep silent at this time, relief and deliverance will rise for the Jews from another place, but you and your father's house will perish. And who knows whether you have not come to the kingdom for such a time as this?" While these words are often popularly cited in Christian circles as a kind of pious *carpe diem*, they are crucial for the message of the book in demonstrating Mordecai's firm conviction that God's people will be delivered from their enemies. Given his certainty, one surmises a divine deliverance, although this is not explicitly stated. Indeed, this gap draws attention to Esther's most famous theological "problem," namely, the apparent absence of God and of all religious ceremony from the book, except for fasting. The Lord is never mentioned in the text, and what is more, anything that would directly point to the presence of God has been intentionally avoided in the Hebrew version of the story.[2] The book lacks any direct reference to temples, sacrifices, priests, prophets,

---

1. I am grateful for comments on an earlier version of this paper by the Rev. Wayne Larson and the Rev. Drs. C. John Collins, W. Brian Aucker, and Mark Ross. Any shortcomings that remain are my own responsibility.

2. There are two separate ancient Greek versions of the book of Esther that differ considerably from the traditional Hebrew version (the Masoretic Text), namely, the Septuagint (which contains the famous "Additions to Esther," included in the Apocrypha), and the "Alpha Text," both of which consistently add references to God. The relationship between these three versions is too complex to discuss here; for an overview, see Levenson, *Esther*, 27–34. This essay will focus on the story as found in the Masoretic Text. Similar "religious" additions are also made in the Aramaic Targums; see Ego, "Retelling the Story of Esther," 77–78.

divine revelation, and the like—even going to great lengths to avoid overtly "religious" language. It has often been pointed out, for example, that the Jews' fasting in chapter 4 fails to mention prayer, even though this usually accompanies a fast in the OT.[3] This suggests that the omission of God from the book of Esther is deliberate and represents an intentional literary strategy: By purposefully avoiding any direct references to the divine, the book actually provokes the reader to think even more about God. Just as being asked *not* to think of a white bear triggers thoughts about one (known in psychology as the "white bear problem" or "ironic process theory"), so also the reader of Esther cannot help but think about the role of God in the story, precisely due to his conspicuous absence.[4]

The book clearly has the practical purpose of explaining the addition of the festival of Purim as a recurring observance to the OT liturgical calendar,[5] but other more "theological" themes can also be discerned in spite of the striking absence of God. One primary theological motif is that of divine providence: Most readers have rightly interpreted the book's complex chain of remarkable "coincidences" as a sign of God's providential guiding of affairs, particularly in a world in which he appears to be absent.[6] Another distinct (though obviously related) motif is that of the preservation of God's people, a theme made especially poignant in light of the Holocaust: Hitler's program to exterminate the Jews invariably calls to mind Haman, "the enemy of the Jews" who "sought to destroy all the Jews . . . throughout the whole kingdom of Ahasuerus" (3:6). Additionally, the book seeks to reshape how God's people ought to think about their exiled state. As Levenson perceptively notes, the book of Esther represents a stratum of Second Temple Judaism "that has come to terms with diaspora," and the narrative "can be read as the story of the transformation of the *exile* into the *Diaspora*."[7] In other words, the book seeks to help God's people look beyond their circumstances to see the potential opportunities and advantages of being in a

---

3. Levenson, *Esther*, 17; see also Goswell, "Keeping God Out," 100; Fox, *Character and Ideology*, 240.

4. In reality, Esther is not the only portion of the OT that depicts an apparent absence of God; for an exposition of this theme in Exodus 1–2 and elsewhere in the Hebrew Bible, see Cowan, *Theology in Exodus*, 1–24.

5. See Esth 8:17; 9:17–32. Given that "fasting" is the only ritual activity explicitly mentioned in the book (4:16), it is worth noting that Purim is then grouped with the corporate "fasts and lamenting" of the Jews in 9:31.

6. See, e.g., Bush, *Ruth, Esther*, 323. Fox claims that these "coincidences" can be viewed as natural occurrences, thus obviating divine causality, but his argument is forced (*Character and Ideology*, 235–47). See the responses by Levenson (*Esther*, 19–21), Bush (*Ruth, Esther*, 325–6), and Cohen ("*Hu Ha-goral*," 124).

7. Levenson, *Esther*, 15; see also Bush, *Ruth, Esther*, 312–14.

dispersed state, as opposed to being geographically centered in Jerusalem as a socio-political body, with all of the limitations resulting from that. It is striking, after all, that the post-exilic historical books of Ezra and Nehemiah are squarely centered in Judea and pursue separation as a primary tactic in Jew-gentile relations (Ezra 4:2–3; 6:21; 9:1–2; 10:11; Neh 2:20; 9:2; 10:28; 13:3). In contrast, in the diaspora setting of Esther one can observe gentiles "declaring themselves to be Jews" in the aftermath of the book's events (Esth 8:17; cf. 9:27).[8] Levenson attempts to summarize the book's multifaceted message as follows:

> In a world in which arrogant and fickle regimes seek a control of events that they have not been granted, and in which the differentness of the Jews provokes murderous hostility, the Jews can, through their own wisdom and courage and with lucky happenstances ordained by a sovereign and favoring providence, defeat their would-be murderers, secure their position, rise to eminence, and even benefit Gentile kings in the process.[9]

An unexpected angle on the book is suggested by the Jewish liturgical tradition. The regular synagogue liturgy, known as the *Amidah*, has as its core a series of prayers known as the Eighteen Benedictions.[10] The Third Benediction, known as the "Sanctification of the Name" (*Qedushat Hashem*), is quite brief:

> You are holy, and your name is holy
> And each day, holy ones praise you.
> Blessed are you, O Lord, the holy God.

However, during the "Days of Awe" (Rosh Hashanah and Yom Kippur) there is a variation at this point in the liturgy, consisting of an additional set of petitions known simply by their introductory Hebrew phrase *Uvekhen* ("And so"):[11]

> And so [*uvekhen*] set your fear, O Lord our God, upon all your handiwork, and your terror upon all that you created. Let all beings see you, and all creatures bow down before you; and let

---

8. For exposition of this theme, see Rogland, "When the Church has Gone to the Dogs," 114–15.

9. Levenson, *Esther*, 21–22.

10. Some forms of the prayers display evidence of having been in existence in the first century AD; see Instone-Brewer, "Eighteen Benedictions."

11. There are variations in different traditions of the *Amidah* (Ashkenazi, Sephardic, etc.), with some versions containing more than three "additions." For a detailed study, see Liebreich, "Insertions in the Third Benediction."

them be formed as one union to do your will wholeheartedly. As we know, O Lord our God, that the dominion lies before you, strength is in your hand, power in your right hand, and your name is awesome over all that you created.

And so [*uvekhen*] grant glory, O Lord, to your people, a song of praise to those who fear you, and hope to those who seek you, and an opening of the mouth to those who wait for you, joy to all who inhabit the world, your land, and a sprouting of a horn to those who profess the unity of your name.

And so [*uvekhen*] let the righteous see and rejoice, and let the upright exult, and the faithful ones shout with a ringing cry, and may unrighteousness shut its mouth, and may all wickedness come to an end like smoke, for the reign of presumptuousness will pass away from the earth.

In addition, the Rosh Hashanah and Yom Kippur liturgies also include a famous *piyyut* or liturgical poem known as "Unetanneh Tokef" ("And let us declare the power"), which is introduced with the same Hebrew phrase *uvekhen*: "And so [*uvekhen*] let our consecration [of your name] ascend to you, for you, O our God, are king!"

In English translation, the Hebrew phrase translated "and so" may seem fairly minor, but it is in fact distinctive, at least in terms of its usage in the Hebrew Bible, only occurring in Ecclesiastes 8:10 and Esther 4:16.[12] In the latter passage, Mordecai challenges Esther to intercede with the king, and Esther responds by asking for a community-wide three-day fast, in which she and her handmaidens will participate. Then she adds, "And so [*uvekhen*] I will go to the king, though it is against the law, and if I perish, I perish." Several representatives of the Jewish tradition have seen a basic analogy between Esther's intercession with the Persian king in the fifth century BC and the intercession of God's people with the King of Kings in succeeding ages. Commenting on the *uvekhen* additions, for example, the *Encyclopedia of Jewish Prayer* states, "Just as Esther prayed and fasted for three days before approaching Ahasuerus to save the Jewish people, so we, too, approach the King on the Day of Judgment, asking God to accept repentance."[13] This connection has been made at least since the fourteenth century, being attested in Rabbi David Abudarham's commentary on the synagogue liturgy.[14] Similarly, Reuven Kimelman argues that the phrase

---

12. According to Holmstedt and Screnock, *uvekhen* means "thereupon" or "in such circumstances" (*Esther*, 158).

13. Nulman, *Encyclopedia*, 335–36, esp. 335.

14. Abudarham, *Sefer Abudarham*, 81. The work was first published in Lisbon in 1489, but I am citing the 1784 Prague edition.

uvekhen introducing "Unetanneh Tokef" evokes 4:16: "Esther's entrance in trepidation to the quarters of the king of Persia casts its ominous shadow over our entrance into the presence of the King of kings, the Holy One."[15] In other words, representatives of the Jewish liturgical tradition have understood the phrase *uvekhen* from these solemn prayers as drawing upon Esther 4:16, thus suggesting the book's relevance to the practice of prayer. This is especially striking, for as noted above, the book of Esther itself evidently has intentionally avoided mentioning prayer, even when it would have been natural to do so!

All of this raises an interesting question: Can a book that never mentions God teach lessons on prayer? Or is it the case that the Jewish tradition has made too much out of this short Hebrew phrase *uvekhen* ("and so")? This essay will argue that the book of Esther indeed has a great deal to say on the subject of prayer. While this may appear to be an unlikely thesis, given the apparent omission both of God and of prayer from the book of Esther, I believe that a careful literary, exegetical, and theological analysis of the text bears it out.

Analyzing Esther: Setting, Plot Development, Character

> When a book, any sort of book, reaches a certain intensity of artistic performance, it becomes literature. That intensity may be a matter of style, situation, character, emotional tone, or idea, or half a dozen other things. It may also be a perfection of control over the movement of a story similar to the control a great pitcher has over the ball.
>
> —Raymond Chandler[16]

To analyze biblical narrative accurately requires an appreciation of its literary and aesthetic qualities. As V. Philips Long has demonstrated, the artistic impulses of the OT historical writers do not stand in opposition either to their historiographical intentions or to their theological concerns.[17] In-

---

15. Kimelman, "*U-N'taneh Tokef* as a Midrashic Poem," 120. It is noteworthy that two of only three biblical attestations of the Hebrew noun *tokef* ("power") are found in Esther (Esth 9:29; 10:2; Dan 11:17).

16. From a letter written by Chandler to Earle Stanley Gardner, dated January 29, 1946 (*Letters*, 69).

17. Long, *Art of Biblical History*. That said, it must be acknowledged that much contemporary critical scholarship on Esther denies the historicity of the events narrated and maintains that the book's genre is more akin to "historical fiction." Evangelical scholarship, in contrast, by and large affirms the book's historiographical intent. For

deed, an appreciation of the literary features of OT narrative is essential for discerning its theological message and historical claims. While all of the features of the book of Esther are deserving of consideration, this essay will focus particularly on the factors of setting, plot development, and characterization.[18] By paying attention to these features and their interaction in Esther, it emerges that one of its central themes is that of intercession with God—or in other words, prayer.

A. Description of the Narrative Setting

Ostensibly, the book of Esther takes place chiefly in the palace of the Persian king, Ahasuerus, typically identified as Xerxes. Part of the book's fascination results from the drama, political intrigue, and plotting one might expect in a court setting. On a closer inspection, however, many qualities of the Persian court appear oddly reminiscent of the Lord's sanctuary. Consider the following features:[19]

1. *The structure of the Persian royal court reflects that of the temple and tabernacle.* The palace of Ahasuerus, like the temple complex, contained an inner court as well as an outer court.[20] Moreover, the term *birah*, used for the "fortress" or "citadel" of Susa,[21] is used to refer to the temple in 1 Chronicles 29:1 and 19, and often in the Mishnah and Talmud.[22]

2. *The Persian court's furnishings are evocative of those of the temple and tabernacle.* Several of the items mentioned at the feasts of chapter 1 are similar to the accoutrements of the Lord's sanctuary. Esther 1:6 mentions blue, purple, and flaxen linens, all of which have strong cultic

---

an overview of the discussion, see Laniak, "Esther," 176–82, and Provan et al., *Biblical History of Israel*, 294–97.

18. Cf. Laniak, "Esther," 170–74, who discusses additional elements such as point of view, patterning devices, intertextuality, and genre.

19. For a more detailed discussion, see my study, "Cult of Esther."

20. On the inner court, see Esth 4:11; 5:1; 1 Kgs 6:36; 7:12; Ezek 8:3, 16; 10:3; 40:19, 23, 27–28, 32, 44; 42:3; 43:5; 44:17, 21, 27; 45:19; 46:1. On the outer court, see Esth 6:4; Ezek 10:5; 40:17, 20, 31, 34, 37; 42:1, 3, 7–9, 14; 44:19; 46:20–21; cf. 2 Chr 4:9.

21. Esth 1:2, 5; 2:3, 6, 8; 3:15; 8:14; 9:6, 11–12.

22. E.g., *m. Pesaḥ.* 3:8: "And thus, whoever has gone out of Jerusalem and is reminded that he still has holy meat, if he has passed Mount Scopus, he burns it where he is at, but if not, he turns around and burns it before the sanctum [*habirah*] with wood from the [temple] pile." For additional references in rabbinic literature, see Grossman (*Esther*, 22–23), Koller (*Esther*, 99–100), and Rogland ("Cult of Esther").

associations.[23] Likewise, the reference to hangings upon "columns of marble" reflect the curtains of the sanctuary.[24]

3. *The king's guards are given a title that is used of temple guardians.* In the OT, royal guards are consistently designated *ratsim* (literally, "runners").[25] In the book of Esther, however, the Persian king's guards are called "guardians of the threshold" (*shomre hasaf*: 2:21; 6:2), a term used exclusively of temple guards elsewhere in the OT.[26] The term used for the royal guards in Megillat Esther is thus evocative of cultic functionaries.[27]

4. *The casting of pur is reminiscent of the high priestly use of the Urim and Thummim.* The narrator explains *pur* to be "lots" (Esth 3:7), which were used as a means of obtaining divine revelation (e.g. Jonah 1:7) and were understood as being under the Lord's control (Prov 16:33). The casting of lots occurs a number of times in connection with priestly duties,[28] and indeed, both in the OT and in other ancient Near Eastern cultures, the consulting of lots was widely viewed as a sacred matter,[29] often mediated through a priest. Thus Haman's casting of *pur* should be understood as an attempt at divination, that is, as an attempt to consult his gods.[30] The *Urim* and *Thummim* belonged to the particular

---

23. Note also Mordecai's garments of blue, purple, and flax in 8:15. Blue and purple linen was used in hangings of the tabernacle/temple and in the priestly garb (e.g., Exod 26:1, 31, 36; 27:16; 28:5–6, 8, 15, 28, 31, 33). Most instances of flaxen material occur in sacred settings (1 Chr 15:27; 2 Chr 2:14 [v. 13 in the Hebrew text]; 3:14; 5:12).

24. For "columns" used in the tabernacle's hangings, see Exod 26:32, 37; 27:10–12, 14–17; 35:11, 17; 36:36, 38; 38:10–12, 14–15, 17, 19, 28; 39:40. See further Grossman, *Esther*, 23–24, and Paton, *Critical and Exegetical Commentary*, 139. The noun *ritspah* ("pavement") also occurs only with the temple (2 Chr 7:3; Ezek 40:17–18; 42:3), though it is not frequently attested. See Rogland, "Cult of Esther."

25. See 1 Sam 22:17; 2 Sam 15:1; 1 Kgs 1:5; 14:22, 27–28 (cf. 2 Chr 12:10–11); 2 Kgs 10:25; 11:4, 6, 11, 13, 19.

26. See 2 Kgs 12:10 [v. 11 in the Hebrew text]; 22:4; 23:4; 25:18; 1 Chr 9:19; 2 Chr 34:9; Jer 35:4; 52:24.

27. The potential danger of approaching the king in the inner court unbidden (4:11) further implies its sanctity. On the role of the temple guards in protecting the holiness of the Lord's house, see, e.g., Sweeney, *Form and Intertextuality*, 133. This parallels the sanctity of Mount Sinai when the Lord descended upon it, which likewise carried with it the threat of death (Exod 19:12). (I am indebted to my colleague Mark Ross for this observation.)

28. Lev 16:8–10; 1 Chr 24:5, 7, 31; 25:8–9; 26:13–14; Neh 10:35.

29. See Hallo, "First Purim," 20.

30. Cohen argues that Haman's casting *pur* expressed his ability to deal with the Jews "by chance alone" ("*Hu Ha-goral*," 124), but the religious connotations of the act are too strong. See, inter alia, Fox, *Character and Ideology*, 242–43; see also Goswell,

purview of the high priest, being contained in his breastplate and used in a sacred setting, and appear to have served as an analogous means of revelation.[31]

Such features would not be lost on the ancient Jewish reader, familiar with the worship rites and institutions of the OT, both from Scripture and from repeated experience. The convergence of these various characteristics of the Persian court is strongly evocative of the divine sanctuary and furnishings with priestly and Levitical attendants. We can conclude that the book displays a recurring interest in the Israelite cult, though it is expressed subtly in keeping with the author's understated literary strategy. What is important to observe with regard to the story's setting is that there is a certain blurring of distinction between the Persian royal court and a sacred temple. The effect this has on the book's message will be explored below.

B. Plot Development

In addition to an author's use of descriptive language to establish the narrative setting, a good story also requires an engaging plot. The book of Esther does not disappoint in this regard, being full of drama, tension, and surprising twists, all coming to a satisfying *dénouement*. Literary analysis of the book's plot has tended to focus upon two recurring devices in particular, namely, the role of coincidences and reversals. As argued above, the book presents such a complex series of "coincidental occurrences" that the only reasonable conclusion is that the hand of divine providence has been guiding events all along. The book also features several sudden reversals in the plot, known as "peripety."[32] Thus, for example, the reward that Haman expected for himself is bestowed upon his nemesis Mordecai (chapter 5), and the stake that Haman prepared for executing Mordecai becomes the instrument of his own destruction (chapter 7). This thematic element is explicitly articulated in 9:1: "On the very day when the enemies of the Jews hoped to gain the mastery over them, *the reverse occurred*: the Jews gained mastery over those who hated them" (emphasis added).

These recurring motifs are indeed important for discerning the book's theological emphases. At the same time, it is vital not to miss a thematic element that is less dramatic, and therefore more easily overlooked—namely,

---

"Keeping God Out," 100–101.
31. For details, see Van Dam, *Urim and Thummim*.
32. Laniak, "Esther," 184–85; Bush, *Ruth, Esther*, 323–26.

the simple motif of being in the king's presence. The text takes pains to note when and how people enter (or exit) the presence of the king:

1. The book opens with a royal celebration, concluding with Ahasuerus presiding over a weeklong feast. At the culmination of this feast, the king orders Vashti "to be brought before him," but she refuses (Esth 1:11–12). It is this refusal to come into the king's presence that provides the catalyst for the subsequent events in the book.

2. Esther and the other virgins are required to undergo an extended ritual of preparation before "going in" or "being brought" to the king (Esth 2:12–17).[33] The ridiculously long duration of the process is undoubtedly a parody of Persian court etiquette,[34] but it serves to highlight the great significance of entering the king's presence.

3. Despite having been selected as queen, Esther expresses her concerns to Mordecai that she "has not been called to come in to the king" for thirty days (Esth 4:11). The reason for this is left unexplained, but the fact remains that she has not been in the king's presence for a considerable period of time and is therefore uncertain of the reception she will receive.[35] As she contemplates Mordecai's urging, she is aware of the danger of entering the inner court unbidden, making her appearance before the king in chapter 5 a moment of high narrative tension. For this reason, then, one is not surprised that Esther requests a corporate three-day fast in preparation for it, since the biblically literate reader assumes that the Jews are praying for a favorable reception.

4. Even after the revelation of Haman's wicked plot in chapter 7, Esther continues to seek out the king's presence. Although the tension is considerably lessened in view of her favorable reception in chapter 5, Esther once more enters the king's presence unbidden in 8:4, where a change of time and setting from chapter 7 must be assumed.[36]

5. The text likewise notes when Mordecai and Haman enter and leave the king's presence. Haman is summoned in from the outer court to meet with the king in 6:5, and Mordecai comes before the king in 8:1,

---

33. On the ritual character of the process, see Rogland, "Cult of Esther."
34. See Wells, "Esther," 38.
35. The narrative has already indicated that Esther is a "highly favored" figure by the supportive reception she receives from Hegai (2:9) and, obviously, in her selection by Ahasuerus as his new queen whom he loved "more than all the other women" (2:17). Nevertheless, in chapter 5 the stakes are life and death.
36. Cf. Levenson, *Esther*, 107.

presumably through Esther's mediation. In the same way, the text notes when Mordecai leaves the king's presence in 8:15.

Thus, the theme of "coming before the king" is a recurring one in the book of Esther, but unlike the striking coincidences and reversals that permeate the book, it is easily overlooked. What purpose would the author have in repeatedly utilizing this motif? It must be borne in mind that people did not visit the royal court to admire its grandeur and opulence, as visitors came to Versailles simply for the privilege of watching Louis XIV awaken in the morning. In the book of Esther, people seek the king's presence in order to present petitions of various kinds. Haman visits the royal court in chapter 6 to ask for Mordecai's execution (v. 4). From her initial visit to the court in chapter 5, the king assumes that Esther is coming with a request, for the first words out of his mouth in verse 3 are "What is it, Queen Esther? What is your request? It shall be given you, even to the half of my kingdom." Ahasuerus repeats this question after the next day's feast (7:2) and again after the first day of Jewish pre-emptive attacks (9:12). At her second feast, Esther reveals her "request" (*she'elah*) and "entreaty" (*baqqashah*) for the life of her people (7:3), and she approaches the king again in chapter 8 and "seeks favor" with him (*vattithannen-lo*) to overturn Haman's decree.[37] This motif is certainly not unique to Esther,[38] but it forms an important element of the book's plot structure: Supplicants seek access to the king's presence because he has the power to grant their petitions.

C. Characterization

In addition to a story's setting and plot development, compelling characters are another important component of good literature: Readers enjoy stories containing well-developed characters who gain our sympathy (or our dislike) as they travel the arc of a storyline. In this respect, however, biblical storytelling conventions differ considerably from modern ones, as most of the characters in OT or NT narratives tend to be "flat." That is, in general there is very little point-of-view narration or discernible character development displayed over the course of a biblical storyline. Given the concise

---

37. At first, Esther's entreaty in chapter 8 may seem superfluous in light of Haman's execution in chapter 7, but Levenson (*Esther*, 107) observes that "Ahasuerus has granted her things for which she has not asked," namely Haman's estate and a promotion for Mordecai (Esth 8:1–2). What the king has neglected or forgotten to deal with is the actual decree for the Jews' destruction.

38. Elsewhere in the OT we see people approaching the king with petitions: 2 Sam 14:4–8; 1 Kgs 1:15–16; 3:16–28; 2 Kgs 8:3–6; cf. 2 Kgs 6:26–29.

nature of storytelling in the Bible, this should not surprise us, since most narratives are too short to allow for character development in any significant way. Nevertheless, it is important to be cognizant of biblical literary conventions, lest one go too far in attempting to fill in perceived "gaps" in the story.[39] In OT or NT historical narrative, the significance of many characters is often tied to their official roles (king, prophet, and so on) or to what they represent in a specific episode or literary context. As Hans Frei observes, it is in the "intersection of character and particular event-laden circumstance" that the participants of a story can become recognizable narrative "types."[40] With regard to the narrative shape of the book of Esther, for example, Aaron Koller argues that "Mordecai and Esther are the Jews personified," and Jon Levenson similarly argues that Esther and Mordecai "are representative of the Jewish people collectively" and are a "personification of national hopes." Indeed, Levenson goes so far as to call them "allegorizations of Israel's national destiny."[41] Most modern scholars would be extremely hesitant to apply the concept of "allegory" to the book of Esther. Nevertheless, the work of Frei and others has led to a growing appreciation of the importance of typology for biblical interpretation, which is conceptually distinct from allegory, though related in certain respects, and scholars are increasingly seeing its application not only to OT narratives in general, but even to the book of Esther in particular.[42] Although all of the characters in the book of Esther contribute to the plot, for the purposes of this essay I will focus chiefly on the roles of Ahasuerus and Esther.

What is implicit in the earlier discussion of the book's priestly and cultic imagery and of the blurring of distinction between the Persian royal court and a divine sanctuary is that King Ahasuerus, in a sense, comes to stand in the role of God.[43] For some readers, this may seem strange or unnatural, but a number of factors lead to this conclusion. The Lord himself is commonly described as a king who reigns (Exod 15:18; Pss 10:16; 29:10; 93:1; Jer 10:10), with the temple as his throne (Pss 11:4; 93:2, 5; Isa 6:1). The

---

39. This tendency is particularly noticeable in the numerous additions, brief as well as expansive, in the Targumic version of Esther that seek to fill in these "gaps."

40. Frei, *Eclipse of Biblical Narrative*, 15.

41. Koller, *Esther*, 57 (cf. also 103); Levenson, *Esther*, 16.

42. For an overview, see Treier, "Typology." For studies of Esther that are open to typological perspectives, see note 46, and for arguments against such an approach, see especially Turner, "Finding Christ in a Godless Text." In pre-Enlightenment exegesis, as might be expected, allegorical interpretations of Esther are not hard to come by; see Vrudny's "Medieval Fascination" and "Medieval Treatment."

43. For an extensive development of this theme, see chapters 4–6 in Lewis, "Narrative Analogy," 116–255.

Lord's house can be envisioned both as a temple and as a palace; indeed, the Hebrew word *hekhal* can be used to refer to either structure, and both usages are well attested in the OT.[44] Moreover, it was not unheard of in the Ancient Near East or even in the OT itself for kings to be described in deific terms. All things considered, then, it is not far-fetched to view Ahasuerus—whose "house" also resembles both a palace and a temple—as being presented as godlike on some level.

This may be difficult for some to accept at first blush when confronted with the narrative of Esther, for after all, in the text, Ahasuerus is at best depicted as a rash and inept buffoon. Some commentators have noticed the implicit comparisons with God, but have rightly discerned that they contain an element of parody or satire.[45] While it may be that Ahasuerus, as a virtually omnipotent king, is being compared to God, he comes off very badly in that comparison. Likening Ahasuerus to YHWH actually serves to highlight the king's faults rather than to exalt him to a deified status; the analogy between the king and the Lord functions chiefly through the elements of *dissimilarity* or *disparity* between them. As a parallel, one can think of the way that certain NT parables compare God to a corrupt judge or an unhelpful neighbor (Luke 11:5-8; 18:1-8), which ultimately serve as a kind of argument from the lesser to the greater (see Luke 11:13 and 18:7). In a similar way, the fact that the king is depicted in godlike terms does not serve to deify Ahasuerus, but rather to exalt the true power and majesty of YHWH, the King of Kings.

What about the book's title character? Without a doubt, the salient feature of Esther's narrative arc is her unlikely ascent from orphaned Jewish exile to Queen of Persia. If King Ahasuerus is depicted in divine terms, what are the implications for Queen Esther as his bride? As noted above, some have suggested that Esther is a representation or personification of God's people. In that light, we observe that in a number of places the OT utilizes a marital analogy for the relationship between God and his covenant people, who are depicted with feminine and bridal imagery. While this imagery can be used negatively as a grounds for condemnation (Hos 2:2), it can be used positively as well (Hos 2:16, 19-20). Historically, the Christian tradition has embraced this imagery and viewed Esther as a representative of God's people, understood theologically as the church. This understanding is found at least as early as Jerome and in Christian commentary and art from the early and late medieval period, but it can also be observed in Reformation

---

44. I would suggest that this term was eschewed in favor of *birah* in the book of Esther due to its overwhelming associations with the Lord's house.

45. Koller, *Esther*, 100-1; Wells, "Esther," 17; cf. Angel, "*Hadassa Hi Esther*," 86-87.

and post-Reformation sources such as the work of Jonathan Edwards.[46] Undoubtedly, at times this has been the result of a fragmented reading strategy focused upon isolated textual details, leading to an arbitrary allegorizing of the story. The solution to such a pitfall, however, is not to overcorrect by avoiding typology altogether.[47] One can derive a sound narrative typology from an exegetical analysis of the book's literary features when read in light of well-established OT themes. When one does so, the book itself invites the reader to view Queen Esther not merely as an individual, but as a representative type of the people of God.

Conclusion: Divine Intercession in the Book of Esther

The literary factors of setting, plot development, and characterization converge to depict Esther (the bride) coming into the presence of the king (the divine bridegroom) to intercede for the life of her people, ultimately "finding favor in his eyes" and being granted her petitions. Though it required repeated attempts, her intercession was successful, and the bride, along with Mordecai (now restored from his earlier state of humiliation in chapter 4), was able to obtain the king's signet ring, signifying full acceptance and tremendous power/influence. To see the parallels between Esther's approach to Ahasuerus with praying to the Lord, as in the Jewish liturgical tradition, is completely defensible from an exegetical perspective sensitive to the literary and theological nature of OT narrative.

---

46. Jerome, *Letters* 53.8 (*NPNF2* 6.101); Edwards, "Notes on Esther," 60–61. More recently a number of scholars have argued that Esther is a messianic type, rather than a representative of her people. See Wells, "Esther," 11, 16–17; Tkacz, "Esther as a Type of Christ" and "Esther, Jesus, and Psalm 22"; Wechsler, "Shadow and Fulfillment," 280–83; see the additional literature mentioned by Lewis, "Narrative Analogy," 261. This view is based chiefly on Esther's willingness to die on behalf of her people (Esth 4:16). However, this overlooks the danger to which Mordecai also exposes himself for the sake of his people, and it seems to me that the biblical image of YHWH and his bride is too powerful to ignore. Both Mordecai and Esther represent the covenant people, but they do so in different ways, and I would argue that Mordecai's narrative arc, from a place of honor (2:21–23) to humiliation (4:1–2) to exaltation (6:10; 8:15; 10:2–3), embodies a more robust messianic typological pattern than Esther's. By the end of the story, Mordecai is depicted in both priestly and royal garb (on the former, see 8:15 and the second point of section A of this essay; on the latter, see 6:8–11), and is described as a "double" (*mishneh*) of King Ahasuerus, with his deeds being recorded in the royal chronicles, just like the kings of the OT. For further exploration of the typology of Mordecai, see Link and Emerson, "Searching for the Second Adam," 132–37.

47. As, e.g., Tomasino, *Esther*, 114–15, and Turner, "Finding Christ in a Godless Text."

Does this understanding of the book of Esther contribute in any way to a biblical theology of prayer? If by that question we are asking whether Esther teaches us something unique about prayer not taught elsewhere in Scripture, then perhaps the answer is negative. However, if the question is asking whether the book of Esther can in some way enrich our understanding or practice of prayer, then we can give a strongly affirmative answer. Part of the enjoyment of reading narratives is that they teach in a different fashion than more didactic texts, and they can exert a very different kind of emotional impact upon us.[48] While the book of Esther may not teach us some new "secret" about prayer, it can certainly shape the way we go about it.

In a sermon on Psalm 16:8, the late-nineteenth- and early-twentieth-century Scottish preacher Alexander Whyte of Edinburgh stressed the importance of "setting the Lord" before oneself when preparing to pray. According to Whyte, if one were to have asked David how he composed such beautiful psalms and prayers,

> David would have said, "Begin every prayer of yours by setting the Lord before you. . . . All I do," he would have said to you, "is just to set the Lord before me as often as I begin again to sing and to pray. I begin; and, ere ever I am aware, already my prayer is answered, and my psalm is accepted."[49]

Whyte goes on to construct an argument from the lesser to the greater:

> Now, if David could set Jehovah always before him in his prayers and in his psalms,—Jehovah, Whom no man could see and live,—how much more should we set Jesus Christ before us? Jesus Christ, Who, being the Son of God, became the Son of Man for this very purpose. And, so we shall! For, what state of life is there?—what need? what distress? what perplexity? what sorrow? what sin? what dominion and what disease of sin? what possible condition can we ever be in on earth?—in which we cannot set Jesus Christ before us in prayer and in faith, and for help, and for assurance, and for victory? Who are you? and what are you? *and what is your request and your petition?* Open your New Testament, take it with you to your knees, and set Jesus Christ out of it before you.[50]

---

48. See Doriani, *Putting the Truth to Work*, 90–91, on the importance of appreciating biblical imagery and the use of symbols for interpretation.

49. Whyte, *Lord, Teach Us to Pray*, 90–91.

50. Whyte, *Lord, Teach Us to Pray*, 96–97 (emphasis added).

Much like the *Uvekhen* additions of the Jewish liturgical tradition, Whyte has effortlessly, and fittingly, re-appropriated the book of Esther to the practice of prayer. The king's words to Esther ("And what is your request and your petition?") also apply to the Christian believer speaking to Jesus Christ. After all, Jesus Christ is the "king of kings and lord of lords" (Rev 17:14; 19:16) who far exceeds King Ahasuerus in power, glory, and grace. What is more, every Christian, as part of the ecclesial body of Christ (1 Cor 12:27), is also a member of the bride of Christ (Eph 5:22–33). As such, he or she has access through Christ's work to the "throne of grace" in order to find "timely help" (Heb 4:14–16). The believer has every reason to expect that his or her petitions will be heard favorably (Luke 11:8–13), even when they may not be answered as desired or expected.

Perhaps one of the reasons why Christians make so little of prayer is because they fail to see what a privileged thing it is to be allowed to present our petitions to the Lord in the first place. It may be that we have forgotten this when we approach the Lord, who indeed is seated on a "throne" of grace. It is in that regard that a study of the book of Esther provides a helpful corrective: The narrative's powerful imagery gives the reader a greater appreciation of the divine king's greatness, the ease of access granted to his people by means of prayer, and the certainty one can have of his willingness to hear and answer. In this way, Esther helps us to "set the Lord before us" when we pray.

The book's narrative reminds us not only of the privilege of entering into the Divine King's presence, but also of the responsibilities that it entails. It is no small thing to come into the Lord's presence. While we need not fear being arbitrarily struck down when we make our approach, the narrative reminds us that prayer requires preparation. The spontaneous "arrow prayers" of Nehemiah are well and good (Neh 2:4), but more often it requires intentional discipline to cultivate the practice of humble prayer. The virgins' anointing in 2:12–17 and the Jews' fasting in 4:16 as preparation even to enter the king's presence is an eloquent testimony to this reality. Again, one of the reasons that prayer may be so challenging is because it is often attempted with little spiritual preparation beforehand.

It is a pleasure to offer this essay in honor of the Rev. Dr. Robert S. Rayburn, himself a great devotee of Alexander Whyte, who taught and modeled a life of prayer throughout his ministry.

12

That Your Generations May Know
Epistemology and Covenant Succession

A Father's Introduction

I FIRST HEARD ROB RAYBURN speak in 1984. Shortly after that, my wife and I and two young boys joined Faith Presbyterian Church. We were very young in our faith and received the teaching of the church with great enthusiasm, including Rob's teaching on what the Bible says about our children. Being young parents, we were thrilled to have such instruction, encouragement, and hope set before us. The teaching on covenant succession was clear and deeply imbedded in the Bible; therefore, I thought in my naiveté that this was the teaching of all Reformed and Presbyterian churches. I assumed that all conservative Reformed churches found this teaching as wonderful as it was presented to us. I was surprised later to learn that this assumption was mistaken.

One Sunday morning in the early years of my pastorate I preached a sermon from Genesis 17 where the Lord promises to be our God and the God of our children. My message was one that extolled the doctrine of covenant succession. Upon leaving the church I was met by a parishioner, a Christian college professor who told me he had some advice for me. He told me that I had better tone down teaching on this particular subject. The reason he gave was that there was no way all my children (I have four sons and two daughters) would walk faithfully with the Lord, because I had too many, and that when they turn away from the Lord, I would have to "eat my hat."

That incident, about twenty-four years ago, was one of the earliest of many encounters with members of Reformed and Presbyterian churches skeptical of the doctrine of covenant succession. By the grace of God, all six of my children are walking with the Lord, and I have not yet had to "eat my hat"! Indeed, I have the unique privilege of co-authoring this essay with my firstborn son, now also an ordained minister of the gospel. While it is fitting that a chapter written in Rob's honor would be written by a father and son, given his important work on the subject of covenant succession, it is not mere sentimentality that leads us to do so. We believe that it attests to the deep biblical truth of this doctrine and to the glorious graciousness of our covenant Lord, who promises to be our God and the God of our children.

Covenant Succession

Rather than repeat the biblical arguments for the doctrine of covenant succession, which have already been presented elsewhere,[1] we want to address some of the reasons why it continues to be objectionable to the contemporary evangelical mind. Of course, one straightforward factor is a simple lack of familiarity with the doctrine.[2] More significantly, covenant succession does not play well with modern sensibilities laden with the pervasive individualism and voluntarism of American evangelical culture. The Great Awakening and the resultant revivalism played a key role in the modern eclipse of the doctrine of covenant succession, as has been well documented by Lewis Bevins Schenck.[3] Yet historical factors alone do not fully explain the resistance to it in Presbyterian circles, to say nothing of American evangelicalism as a whole. If the revivalism of American Christianity was the spark that set fire to this important biblical doctrine, Kantian epistemology is the fuel that keeps the fire raging. Often overlooked, a paradigmatic shift in the modern mindset concerning knowledge has occurred, and the doctrine of covenant succession will not be understood, let alone embraced and recovered, until we fundamentally reassess what it means to know.

What is Knowledge?

What *does* it mean to know? Or in the context of covenant children, what does it mean to know God?[4] What does it mean to have faith? Is knowledge

---

1. See especially Rayburn's influential "Presbyterian Doctrines," as well as Wikner, *To You and Your Children*.

2. Cf., Rayburn, "Presbyterian Doctrines," 2–3. Recently, when a teaching elder in our presbytery approached our own congregation regarding "concerns" that we were propagating the doctrine of covenant succession, he admitted that he had never heard of it before, and neither had any of the several other teaching elders he initially approached to explain it to him.

3. Schenck, *Presbyterian Doctrine of Children in the Covenant*.

4. Interestingly, Frame concludes that "'knowledge of God' essentially refers to

or faith limited to, or primarily expressed in discursive thought and articulated information? Kant asserted that "the understanding cannot intuit anything."[5] In other words, knowledge is exclusively discursive, which is the opposite of intuitive.[6] The modern conception of knowledge associates knowing with work. As Joseph Pieper summarizes Kant's epistemology in his book *Leisure: The Basis of Culture*: "Man's knowledge is realized in the act of comparing, examining, relating, distinguishing, abstracting, deducing, demonstrating—all of which are forms of active intellectual effort. Knowledge, man's spiritual, intellectual knowledge . . . is activity, exclusively activity."[7]

However, Pieper argues that this is precisely the problem. He maintains that we do not understand what knowledge is, what it means to know something, and how we go about knowing. For Pieper, leisure is foundational for knowledge, as implied by the fact that the etymological roots for the English word "school," namely Greek *skolē* and Latin *schola*, refer to leisure. This in itself suggests that Kant's epistemology is on the wrong track.

Pieper notes a couple of common shortcomings with the modern view of knowledge. One such shortcoming is that knowledge is always active, outward, and busy. This stands in contrast to the ancients and medievals who spoke of different kinds of knowledge, which could include "an element of pure, receptive contemplation, or as Heraclitus says, of 'listening to the essence of things.'"[8] During the Middle Ages, a distinction was made between two types of knowledge, namely, *ratio* and *intellectus*: "Ratio is the power of discursive logical thought, of searching and of examination, of abstraction, of definition and drawing conclusions. Intellectus, on the other hand, is the name for the understanding in so far as it is the capacity of *simplex intuitus*, of that simple vision to which truth offers itself like a landscape to the eye."[9] Pre-moderns understood the process of knowing as belonging to both the *ratio* and to the *intellectus* and believed that the contemplative vision of the *intellectus*, which is passive or receptive in nature, was indispensable to knowledge. Indeed, the *intellectus* was prized as knowledge gained by non-activity, in a purely receptive vision.

---

a person's friendship (or enmity) with God" (*Doctrine of the Knowledge of God*, 48).

5. Kant, *Critique of Pure Reason*, 91.

6. Cf. Pieper, *Leisure*, 32.

7. Pieper, *Leisure*, 32. Josef Pieper (1904–1997) was a specialist in the thought of Thomas Aquinas who taught philosophical anthropology at the University of Münster for many years. His writings were highly acclaimed, and many were translated into English—including his work on "leisure," which featured an introduction by T. S. Eliot.

8. Pieper, *Leisure*, 33.

9. Pieper, *Leisure*, 33–34.

In contrast, for modern minds, the only desirable kind of knowledge is *ratio*. Knowledge is viewed as activity; it consists of what we have determined and discovered for ourselves. Knowledge (and therefore truth) is not found in what we *receive*, but in what we *do*. For the modern mind, then, knowledge is only found in our ceaseless subjecting, dissecting, and working; it is, as it were, "Sabbathless."

A second shortcoming (closely related to the first) concerning the modern conception of knowledge is that it requires effort and labor—even suffering. According to Kant, "the law is that reason acquires its possessions through work."[10] Pieper comments,

> If you want to know something, then you must work; in philosophy "the law is that reason acquires its possessions through work" that is the claim on man. But there is another, a subtler claim, not perhaps immediately visible, in the statement, the claim made by man: if to know is to work, then knowledge is the fruit of our own unaided effort and activity; then knowledge includes nothing which is not due to the effort of man, and there is nothing *gratuitous* about it, nothing "inspired", nothing "given" about it.[11]

The significance of such a perspective is that "man seems to mistrust everything that is effortless; he can only enjoy, with a good conscience, what he has acquired with toil and trouble; he refuses to have anything as a gift."[12] This conception of knowledge is antithetical to Christian truth because it posits a world that is giftless, graceless, and therefore necessarily without a giver.

If knowledge is only attained through our work, then it only includes what is due to the effort of man, and there is nothing gratuitous about it. This conception of knowledge necessarily brings with it an implicit suspicion and hostility toward what has come before, that is, the body of knowledge that has preceded us. Therefore, discovery is valued over tradition because discovery is ours; it is something that we have done. Tradition is viewed with suspicion because, of course, it is simply what has been given to us. Modern man thus values discovery and discards heritage. Today we value finding ourselves or making something of ourselves, rather than finding value in a heritage that we receive.

This epistemology has disastrous consequences theologically. The idea that knowledge can only be obtained from work implies that knowing God

---

10. Quoted in Pieper, *Leisure*, 32.
11. Pieper, *Leisure*, 36.
12. Pieper, *Leisure*, 42.

and belonging to his covenant is up to the individual. Furthermore, the *assurance* that someone does know God is grounded in how hard he or she works at knowing God. According to Kantian epistemology, effortless intuition (the contemplation and reception of the promises of God to generation after generation) is viewed with suspicion at best, and as worthless or false at worst. In a similar way, the modern mind has difficulty viewing the covenant promises of God as valuable or as true, because it has done nothing to discover them. According to this modern conception of knowledge, the heritage of God's people cannot be a prized possession precisely because such a status is given, and no labor has been put into achieving it.

Not only has this approach to knowing helped to erode what remains of the doctrine of covenant succession, it is distinctly opposed to the epistemology of Scripture. In his book *Knowledge by Ritual*, Dru Johnson has argued that the Bible's presumption is "that rituals bring participants to know something about the world that they could not have known otherwise."[13] He thus argues that "Israelite rituals function as a means to an epistemological end" and that this should "force modern readers to rethink their basic conceptual scheme of knowledge in order to reconcile the body's primary role in biblical accounts of knowing."[14]

Knowledge-by-ritual is, according to Johnson, a key feature of biblical knowing. In Genesis 15, for example, Abraham's doubt is answered by a covenant-making rite: When Abraham asks for confirmation of God's as-yet unfulfilled promises, God does not respond by inviting Abraham to a lecture series, but by instituting a known ritual. Johnson also draws attention to the OT's explicit assertions that festivals be celebrated for epistemological reasons. Thus, for example, Leviticus 23:43 states that Israel should keep the Feast of Booths "that your generations may know that I made the people of Israel dwell in booths." Johnson points out that, according to Deuteronomy 31:13, the Feast of Booths was instituted for "Israel's children who have not known" the revelation of God's salvation and Torah, so that they might learn to fear and obey him. In light of this, he poses some pertinent questions:

> This example alone broaches a fundamental question about the fact-knowing view of epistemology: If Israel were meant to know facts—consecration by God, sanctification, and that Israel once lived in booths—then why perform the prescribed actions of Sabbath rest or booth-living? If these are mere facts to be known, why cannot they verbally pass along the facts?[15]

---

13. Johnson, *Knowledge by Ritual*, xvi.
14. Johnson, *Knowledge by Ritual*, xvii and xix.
15. Johnson, *Knowledge by Ritual*, 12.

Apparently, merely "telling the story" was insufficient to communicate what God wanted Israel to know: "There is some way in which Israel needs to discern that information beyond mere recognition, *some insight to be gained only by performing the festivals and Sabbaths*."[16]

After God's people were delivered from Egypt, their life became thoroughly dominated by ritual. In her book *Mudhouse Sabbath*, Lauren Winners notes an expression so curious at the ratification of the Mosaic covenant that it became the topic of an ancient rabbinic Midrash.[17] In Exodus 24:7 we read, "Then he took the Book of the Covenant and read it in the hearing of the people. And they said, 'All that the Lord has spoken we will do, and we will be obedient.'" The Midrash observes that the literal phrase is "we will do and we will hear" (*na'aseh venishme'a*), which on the surface makes no sense: How can a person perform God's commandment before they hear it? But the counterintuitive lesson, the Midrash insists, is precisely that one must carry out God's commands and eventually, by so doing, one will come to "hear," that is, to understand and believe. Scriptural epistemology would indicate that rituals were intended to enable Israel to know; the skilled repetition of a given practice is the best way to ensure that a doubter's faith will return.

The covenant promises of God include his claim on our children: "I will be your God and the God of your children after you." Belonging to the covenant requires no effort on our children's part to obtain. And yet it is common today for parents to mistrust such a gift, to view with suspicion such promises and claims. For many, the promises only become "real" or "valuable" when their children have exerted themselves in some way. Christian parents often speak and act as though it is only when their children have had an experience defined by discursive thought that they can have confidence that their children belong to God. This is perfectly in line with Kantian epistemology: the covenant of God is only valued when individuals have labored to "make it their own."

As a result, many children in Reformed churches grow up with a certain measure of uncertainty or even guilt about being a covenant child.[18] It may be due in part to the fact that they do not have a dramatic conversion story, but more often than not they are simply under the impression that what they have is not valuable because they did no work and were not active in their belonging to God's people—they simply received the

---

16. Johnson, *Knowledge by Ritual*, 12 (emphasis added).

17. Winner, *Mudhouse Sabbath*, x.

18. See the observations on this phenomenon by Rayburn, "Emphasis on the Christian Family." Our own experience confirms this many times over.

inheritance. The metanarrative of knowledge in the church as well as in our culture implies that if you didn't exert mental effort, then what you have must not be worth very much!

Turning from theoretical epistemology to liturgical practice, Johnson observes: "Any attempt at a sacramental theology that regards the authority of Scripture must reckon with this principle: *we practice rites to know.*"[19] Interestingly, the major theological and even liturgical exception in the Reformed tradition to the kind of "earned knowledge" described above is found in the sacrament of baptism. Churches that practice paedobaptism do not require "advanced knowledge" or discursive abilities in order for the infant to come to the font. In the sacrament of baptism, we encounter a conception of knowledge opposed to Kant: Baptism is a claim made by God on the children of God's people; it is a gift received, not achieved. In stark contrast, when it comes to the participation of baptized church members in the Eucharist, we find the dominating influence of Kantian epistemology, for in many churches, access to the Eucharist must be gained through mental activity. That is, a child[20] must embrace certain theological ideas, and these must then be articulated through a "credible" profession of faith. Rather than participation in a ritual leading to knowledge, in many places the church requires "knowledge" that earns participation to the ritual. It seems then that in the Eucharist one can only enjoy, with a good conscience, that which one has acquired with toil and trouble. From such a perspective, one cannot truly experience the Eucharist as a gift.[21]

This type of inconsistency in the sacraments can be found in the Reformer John Calvin. In the case of baptism, Calvin insists that the sacrament is owed to infants of believers (*Institutes* 4.16.5): "Yet if they are participants in the thing signified, why shall they be debarred from the sign?" Calvin believed that as children of Abraham were heirs of the covenant, so too the children of Christians are heirs of the covenant (*Institutes* 4.16.7): "The Lord Jesus . . . tenderly embraces the infants offered to him, chiding the disciples for trying to deny them access to him, because they were leading away from him those to whom the Kingdom of Heaven belonged." Calvin is adamant that infants out to be brought to Christ, and that they should receive the

---

19. Johnson, *Knowledge by Ritual*, 268.

20. It must be remembered that the discussion here relates specifically to baptized covenant children; the case of adult converts to Christianity is obviously different.

21. In a recent conversation with a few other ministers, one recalled being a part of a church in which a mentally handicapped child was never granted access to the table, because she could not articulate "the answers." One of the other ministers on hearing the full story simply said, "And that would have been the one thing she *could* have understood."

sacrament of baptism (*Institutes* 4.16.7): "If it is right for infants to be brought to Christ, why not also to be received into baptism, the symbol of our *communion* and *fellowship* with Christ?" For Calvin, this access is not granted to them because of anything they have accomplished or earned, but rather "are baptized into *future* repentance and faith, and even though these have not yet been formed in them, the *seed* of both lies hidden within them by the secret working of the Spirit."[22]

However, in his discussion of whether children should be admitted to Christ's body and blood at the table, Calvin abruptly changes course (*Institutes* 4.16.30): "If only those who know how to distinguish rightly the holiness of Christ's body are able to participate worthily, why should we offer poison instead of life-giving food to our tender children?" This is remarkably unexpected considering what we saw above.[23] If infants of the covenant are baptized into *future* repentance and faith, the seed of both being put there by the secret working of the Spirit, why should a child not participate in Eucharist as nourishment for *future* faith that "rightly distinguishes the holiness of Christ's body?"

While this inconsistency may feel strained to some who seek to maintain a great difference in the two sacraments,[24] the inconsistency is palpable when understood within Calvin's robust doctrine of election. Calvin insists that baptism is a covenantal sign, not a decretal sign. In other words, baptism is not a sign or guarantee of election. Likewise, Calvin also asserts that the Eucharist is a covenantal sign and seal, not a guarantee of election. Thus for Calvin, baptism and the Eucharist are not signs and seals for the elect only; baptism does not *make* any one elect, and neither does participation in the Eucharist. The sacraments are covenantal signs for the visible church that judge the non-elect participants, and seal the promises of God to the elect. Calvin argued for infant baptism based on the promises of God to his covenant people. Why then the prohibition of the Eucharist to children, given his doctrine of reprobation and election? If the Lord's Supper cannot and does not determine the elect, as Calvin maintains, then the Eucharist will be "poison" *only* to the non-elect and will spiritually nourish the elect.

22. *Institutes* 4.16.20 (emphasis added).

23. On the question of how infants, who don't know good or evil, are regenerated, Calvin writes (*Institutes* 4.16.17): "We reply that God's work, though beyond our understanding, is still not annulled. Now it is perfectly clear that those infants who are to be saved (as some are surely saved from that early age) are previously regenerated by the Lord . . . we can see clearly that the angel, when he declared this to Zechariah meant . . . that John would, while yet unborn, be filled with the Holy Spirit. Let us not attempt, then, to impose a law upon God to keep him from sanctifying whom he pleases."

24. For a critique of such a position, see Rayburn, "Minority Report," 507–8.

The inconsistency is almost too obvious. If the elect are the elect, why does Calvin not apply the same "seed" imagery and future hope that he has with infant baptism to participation in the Eucharist?

The effects of Kantian epistemology are particularly evident in the way that 1 Corinthians 11:27–29 is understood and applied to contemporary sacramental practice. These verses form the lynchpin of any argument—oftentimes the only exegetical argument—against the inclusion of the church's infants and very young children in the Eucharist,[25] and the "effort"-laden conception of knowledge is not difficult to discern in such discussions. Yet the modern understanding of Paul's words as excluding infants and very young children from the Lord's Supper is a far cry from their intent in the original context. Let us briefly consider how this is so.

To recover the context of Paul's eucharistic teaching, we begin by noting that the Supper appears to have originally been part of an actual meal eaten by the community in a private home. Sharing the symbolic bread and cup occurred as part of the common meal (vv. 20–21). Scholars debate whether it was at the beginning, middle, or end of the actual meal. In any case, those with greater resources, the well-to-do, were feasting on their own food and wine (imitating pagan festivals?) while others who were less wealthy had yet to arrive, or were simply not given anything and therefore went hungry. Paul sharply criticized the Corinthians' behavior at the Lord's Supper, and by using the word *synerchesthe* (vv. 17–18, 20, 33–34; 14:23, 26), he seems to be playing on a potential double meaning: When the Corinthians "come together," they are not "coming together."[26]

In these "house churches," much of the responsibility for seating and service and eating fell to the hosts. They were responsible for the protocol that would be followed. They were responsible for when the meal began and who sat in the triclinium versus the atrium. The problem for Paul was one of either timing, location, or both with regard to the manner in which the Lord's Supper was being carried out. The result of their sacramental observance was a split in the congregation between the "haves" and the "have-nots."[27]

In vv. 27–29, commentators have remarked that the pronouns used indicate limits of application. That is to say, Paul was not talking to everyone. The audience being addressed were those responsible for the divisions. (For

---

25. To be sure, other biblical passages are occasionally mentioned—sometimes vague references are made to the quasi-"catechetical" questions of the Passover directives (Exod 12:26; 13:14)—but 1 Corinthians 11:27–29 remains at the center of all such discussions. For two relatively recent examples, see Knight, "1 Corinthians 11:17–34," and Venema, *Children at the Lord's Table*, 101–25.

26. Hays, *1 Corinthians*, 194.

27. Hays, *1 Corinthians*, 196.

our purposes it is worth noting that adults typically create class divisions in a church, not children, least of all the youngest of children.) Not only does the context suggest such a limitation of addressee, the polemical nature of Paul's remarks suggests a particular sphere of application: congregations that are rife with different parties and guilty of infighting of the worst kind (e.g., 1:10–17; 3:1–9; 4:6–7, 18–21; 6:1–11; 8:9–13; 12:21–26). It would be exegetically irresponsible to ignore such clear contextual limitations and to treat Paul's words as if they are what he would have said to a healthier, more unified church body:

> As the context makes clear and as the commentators confirm, Paul's remarks are specifically directed against an impious and irreverent participation (a true manducatio indignorum). Much more would need to have been said before it could be concluded that Paul was speaking to the general question of who may come to the table, or to the question of children's participation, or that he intended to exclude them from the supper. We do not understand Acts 2:38 to deny baptism to little children, Rom. 10:13–14 to deny them salvation, or 2 Thess. 3:10 to deny them food.[28]

As Richard Hays points out, vv. 27–28 have often been "seriously misinterpreted" by being taken out of context in that "the call for self-examination in verse 28 has been heard as a call for intense introspection."[29] This should be obvious from the context: Paul declared in verse 17 that the eucharistic loaf indicated the unity of the body of Christ, and the specific problem mentioned in verse 18 was the provoking of divisions with a "contemptuous disregard for the needs of others in the community."[30] Thus, self-examination was not a summons for the Corinthians to make sure they could properly articulate or mentally understand what was taking place in the eucharistic elements; rather, it was "a straightforward call to consider how their actions at the supper are affecting brothers and sisters in the church, the body of Christ."[31]

In one of his memorable turns of phrase, C. S. Lewis observed, "The command, after all, was Take, eat; not Take, understand."[32] Yet many interpreters arrive at the opposite conclusion, taking "let a man examine himself" as a call for intellectual knowledge and understanding, which

---

28. Rayburn, "Minority Report," 510.
29. Hays, *1 Corinthians*, 200.
30. Hays, *1 Corinthians*, 200.
31. Hays, *1 Corinthians*, 200.
32. Lewis, *Letters to Malcolm*, 136.

according to Kantian categories involves concerted mental effort.[33] Access to the sacrament, then, is attained through study and preparation, with the intellectual labors of prospective participants witnessed by a few elders in a back room at the church.[34]

What we fear has been lost in the church's approach to the table is the notion that the Eucharist is a gift. The Eucharist is not primarily (if at all) our service to God; it is his gift to us, so that we might come to know him. There can be the temptation to think that we are "in" because we have labored to understand what is really happening, and perhaps more importantly (for some) what is *not* happening, in the sacramental elements! Kantian epistemology approaches the Eucharist as a problem to be solved, rather than as a gift to be received, when in reality, as Johnson argues, there may be some knowledge that can only be gained by participation in the ritual.

The biblical doctrine of covenant succession is grounded in God's character, his holiness, his righteousness, his promises, and his gifts. The hope of the Christian parent is not in his or her own faith, with its weak muscles and doubt-filled bones, but the faithfulness of God's Son and the faithful participation in the gifts he has given us. We would argue that the recovery of the doctrine of covenant succession must begin by recovering biblical epistemology. We must realize that our place and our children's place in the covenant has been given as a gracious gift from God our Father, and that the sacraments of the church have been given in order that our generations may come to know him. Hence it may be time to reconsider reflecting that truth liturgically by admitting to the table "those to whom belongs the kingdom of God."

---

33. To the argument that "in remembrance of me" requires intellectual abilities children do not possess, it should be remembered that it is the church collectively, not individuals, who do this in remembrance. The celebration of the Eucharist was not intended as a personal reminder but rather, as Paul explicitly says (v. 26), as an objective proclamation of the gospel in the context of gathered worship. Furthermore, there is in fact a great deal of exegetical debate whether the "remembrance" has a Godward direction (calling upon God to "remember" Christ's sacrifice) or a manward one. For discussion, see Fee, *First Epistle to the Corinthians*, 552–54.

34. Regarding a child's profession of faith, Poythress notes how often it is viewed with suspicion or is subjected to unreasonable standards of verification: "It is easy to put improper emphasis on intellectual and verbal apprehension of the truth. When we look at children, we naturally hope that their intellectual apprehension of God's truth will grow, and that their faith will come to maturity. We encourage such growth. Our hopes and our encouragement are quite proper. But if we equate intellectual maturity with the essence of faith, we change salvation from a free gift into the property of those with proper intellectual credentials. And then we contradict the gospel, which tells of God's mercy to the undeserving, mercy that utterly ignores all supposed human credentials and vaunted abilities (Rom 9:11–12; Tit 3:5–7)" ("Indifferentism and Rigorism," 18–19).

A Son's Afterword

Growing up in a pastor's home, and now being a pastor myself, has led me to wonder at the reason for the Levitical line of priests: What was the rationale for the sons of priests becoming priests, and the grandsons of priests becoming priests instead of selecting men of aptitude from each tribe to serve? Was there a knowledge of God's law and his people and his worship that could only be intuited through growing up in those particular homes? What was it like for the grandsons of priests to be thoroughly inundated in biblical ritual? What insight and compassion was gained from the next generations of priests as they sat around and listened to their grandfather and their father tell stories, laugh, read and sing?

I know what it was like to grow up in the home of a pastor. I remember the trivial theological conversations, as well as the heated sacramental quarrels. After late night meetings at the church, the way my father closed the front door often told me if things went well or poorly. I remember hearing my father weep after combative and divisive church meetings. I remember the countless droves of people in and out of our home. I remember disagreements ending in deep hugs and arguments concluding with laughter and cigars. I remember painful talks about the struggles of the sheep. Perhaps the most significant part of my formation as a minister has come from what I caught, rather than what I was taught.

My father has continued to teach and encourage families with what we believe to be the biblical understanding of children and the covenant. And despite all his personal failures and faults, all six of his children remain part of the covenant people of God because of the faithfulness of God's Son. Through that ongoing process, what I have seen and experienced is the importance of faithfully participating in another ritual: that of repentance and absolution, specifically *parental* repentance. My dad claims he could write volumes on how to parent poorly, yet the hope that we have found in the biblical doctrine of covenant succession is grounded on God's promise and our continually returning to him to repent of our parental arrogance and negligence. Confession of sin is a gift and God gives gifts for our good. We would simply implore the church to embrace his gifts, all his gifts, with thanks. As parents, we are to live before the face of God, and at the feet of our children.

13

Goudimel's Simple Setting of the Genevan Psalter

Claude Goudimel may be the finest Reformed composer that history mentions. The luster of such a claim diminishes when you consider how few Reformed composers of any importance there actually are for history to mention. It has to be admitted that on balance the Reformed movement has produced more orators, statesmen, and philosophers than musicians. Nevertheless, it is indicative of Goudimel's quality that for some time he was widely believed to be the teacher of none other than Palestrina. He was not, in fact, Palestrina's teacher. The claim has been discredited because it lacks good evidence, but not because Goudimel's music lacks style or technique. On the contrary, his music is so refined that the thought that he might have taught the greatest of all Renaissance composers was never implausible. Goudimel's music was at one time so admired that some music scholars in Catholic France felt the need to obscure or contradict his Calvinist conversion; even, it would seem, going so far as to suggest that his setting of the Genevan Psalms was for Roman Catholics.[1]

We can only wonder what such a skilled composer might also have achieved had he not been martyred, along with thousands of other French Calvinists, in the St. Bartholomew's Day massacre of the Huguenots. Nevertheless, he is one of the outstanding composers of his generation. Regrettably, today his music is almost never heard, with the important exception of a few of his Psalm settings that appear in hymnals. His finest compositions lie in obscurity, forgotten gems of the Reformation. It is a shame that his work is not more frequently heard. Anyone might be forgiven for thinking that the Lutherans, Anglicans and Roman Catholics have the monopoly on world-class composers.

---

1. Ellis, *Interpreting the Musical Past*, 184.

Goudimel set the Genevan Psalter several times in different styles, but the setting containing the simplest style had a profound influence on the development of congregational song. The importance of these simple settings for church music is ironic, since it was expressly stated in the preface of their principal edition that they were not supposed to be sung in church.[2] Singing in harmony, of course, was not done in Calvinist worship. So the stated purpose of Goudimel's harmonized psalter was for music making in the home. Today, in a time when music making around the table is vanishingly rare, one suspects Goudimel's psalm settings are not often sung in homes anymore. Yet they are indeed sung in churches all over the world, precisely the opposite of their original intent.

It is not in their current use, however, that Goudimel's psalm settings derive their chief importance. They are important mainly because of the extreme simplicity of their style and the influence of that style on later congregational song. Their impact on the Reformed church was not direct and immediate, but in a roundabout way via the German Lutherans.

Goudimel's setting of the Genevan tunes was not the first attempt at harmonizing them. It had been done previously by Loys Bourgeois, but when Bourgeois composed his settings, the Genevan Psalter was still incomplete. Goudimel's was the first setting of the completed Psalter, which is surely part of the explanation for its success.

The term "success" must be qualified. It did not receive multiple reprintings right away. A more immediately successful setting of the Psalter was by Claude Le Jeune, which quickly went through thirteen editions in the beginning of the seventeenth century.[3] However, Goudimel's setting received a more widespread distribution in a German version produced by Ambrosius Lobwasser in Leipzig in 1573. Although Goudimel is not named in the Lobwasser Psalter, his settings are essentially unchanged except for one important alteration. In Goudimel's version, the main melody is most often found in the tenor. But Lobwasser, following the unstoppable trend, moved the melody to the highest voice, the soprano. These days we take it for granted that the melody of a hymn should be heard in the soprano voice. Yet Goudimel's Psalms can take on a remarkably vital strength when the melody is restored to the tenor. A conscientious choir director might try giving the choir a hymn like "God Shall Arise" in Goudimel's harmonization with the melody in the tenor (see Example 1). Known as the battle hymn

---

2. "To the melody of the psalms we have, in this little volume, adapted three parts, not to induce you to sing them in Church, but that you may rejoice in God, particularly in your homes." The full quotation may be found in Strunk, *Source Readings*, 349.

3. Pidoux, "Polyphonic Settings," 71.

of the Huguenots, "God Shall Arise" especially benefits from the powerful sound of such a voicing.

Example 1: Psalm 68 "God Shall Arise"—Goudimel's Harmony with the Tune in the Tenor

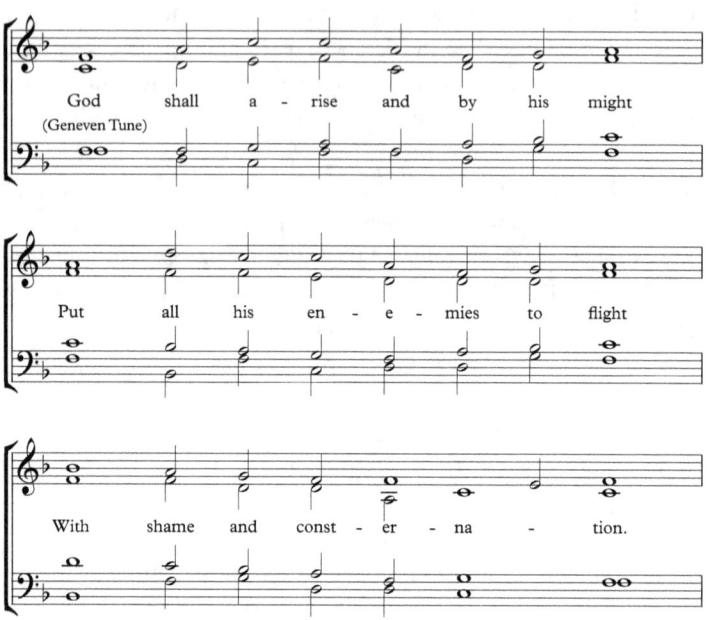

It was mostly through the Lobwasser Psalter that Goudimel's setting became internationally influential. Even the Lutheran church, which had a mature musical impulse from its inception, was changed by the appearance of Goudimel's work. It was not a matter of brilliance or intricacy. Rather, it was the simplicity of style that made such an impression. As Friedrich Blume has pointed out, "the historically important factor for Lutheran church music was not Lobwasser's texts, or the French melodies introduced with them, but the presentation in simple, four-voice, note-against-note cantional settings at such a relatively early time."[4] The "cantional setting" mentioned is now the trademark style of traditional congregational song: straightforward four-voice harmony, soprano, alto, tenor, and bass all singing the same words at the same time to the same rhythms, with the main melody in the soprano. And its universal prominence in hymnals owes a considerable debt to the success of the Goudimel/Lobwasser Psalter.

4. Blume, *Protestant Church Music*, 134.

In order to appreciate Goudimel's simple style, it will be useful to hear it against the backdrop of a more sophisticated style. Example 2 gives the opening of Goudimel's setting of Psalm 118, *Rendez à Dieu* with analytic annotations. It is composed in a style more elaborate than Example 1. The main tune may be found unaltered in the soprano part. It is a familiar melody that is still in use today, found in a variety of English hymnals with the title "Give Thanks Unto the Lord Jehovah."

Example 2: Goudimel, *Rendez à Dieu*

The style of Example 2 is characterized by the interaction of all the voices with the straightforward, unadorned, and unaltered presentation of the Genevan tune. In a motet like this one, the tune is called the *cantus firmus*, which means, "fixed melody." In this case, the soprano sings the *cantus firmus*. The three other voices accompany the melody with free and lively lines that seem to echo and converse with the *cantus firmus*. They often hint at imitating the main tune, especially at the beginning of phrases. Yet they rarely follow through on the promise, diverging instead in interesting and sometimes unexpected ways.

When the bass begins, it echoes the soprano, entering two beats after it. The three-note group C-A-G (marked *a* in Example 2) is copied from the main tune, but the word placement is slightly different. There are two syllables on the note A instead of one. The bass also ends this passage with a kind of imitation. On the words "*benin et clement*" (marked *c* in the example) the bass sings the notes C-A-D-C in tandem with the soprano and using the same intervals: down a third, up a fourth, down a step. Such echoes and parallels keep the bass closely connected to the main tune. A Huguenot singer, who would probably know the tune by heart from years of singing psalms in church, would then enjoy the subtle but constant interaction with it while maintaining his usual bass role as the foundation of harmony and controller of cadences.

The tenor voice imitates the melody more fully and directly. In the first phrase (labelled *X*), the tenor's melody copies the main tune with only slight alterations: the first syllable, "*Ren-*," is shortened from a whole-note to a half-note, and the second two notes (marked with an asterisk) are sung a step higher than the original (B-A instead of A-G). The tenor continues imitating the soprano in the second phrase, but only as far as the first two notes, G-E, on the words "*Car il*" (marked *b*). But these two notes are so striking and prominent that they are all that is needed to suggest the whole phrase. Notice also that the tenor's echo of the soprano comes sooner in the second phrase (labelled *Y*) than it does in the first phrase. In the first phrase (*X*), at "*Rendez*," the tenor repeats the soprano line a measure and a half after, but in the second phrase (*Y*), at "*car il*" the distance is half a beat. Having one ear trained on the melody, so to speak, the tenor would sense his drawing nearer in time to the *cantus firmus*.

At first, the alto partners with the soprano in both rhythm and text, but soon diverges by introducing a melismatic flourish with quarter-note and eighth-note rhythms. Appropriately, the alto sings these flourishes on the words "*Dieu*" (God) and "*gloire*" (glory). Something subtler happens in the second phrase. The alto imitates the *cantus firmus* in a more obscure way. She sings the soprano's tune upside down, or "inverted" (compare *Y* in the soprano and alto). There are some slight modifications, to be sure: the rhythm is shortened—whole-notes turned to half-notes—so that the alto arrives at the cadence simultaneously with the soprano, and the first note has been adjusted for the sake of harmony. But a practiced singer, a skilled amateur who was used to encountering such devices as inversion, and who was listening for them, would relish the gratification of spotting it here.

Psalter settings such as that of Example 2 were obviously never destined for congregational song. They are too complicated. They require a high degree of musicianship and practice to perform successfully. Nevertheless, Reformed churches that have shed their traditional scruples about choral singing in worship might find a place for settings like this one in their service where the choir usually sings. And ambitious families or groups of friends can enrich their lives by learning to sing settings like this one for fun in their living rooms.

Example 2 is sophisticated. Much simpler and more direct are the early four-part settings of the Genevan psalms that were destined to gain a footing in congregational song. There were a number of composers who made simple four-part settings, notably Claude Le Jeune and Loys Bourgeois, but Goudimel's settings were the simplest and most direct of all. Le Jeune's marvelous settings came after Goudimel's. They possess richer harmonies with freer and more interesting counterpoint, but they present more of a challenge to singers.

Bourgeois's settings came before Goudimel's. In fact, they were the first of their kind. In the heyday of Calvin's Geneva, Bourgeois was the principal music editor for the Psalter. He was very good at his work, although he sometimes annoyed the Genevan elders by his constant "tweaking" of the tunes. He was arrested once supposedly for the unauthorized altering of the psalm tunes. Let that be an example to music directors everywhere: A musician's "improvement" may be an elder's grounds for charges! Despite his frustrations, Bourgeois's work on the Psalter was that of an expert, and the tunes were much improved under his hand. Today his name is so closely associated with the Huguenot Psalter that some hymnals attach his name to anything Genevan. However, it is misleading to do so. He probably composed few if any of the tunes from scratch. If he did compose any, we cannot be sure which ones. Additionally, his harmonizations of the tunes are not usually the ones found in hymnals. Nevertheless, he deserves credit for being the first to add additional parts to the tunes. His work was groundbreaking, but the music was not widely distributed. Was it because the idea of singing the Psalms in parts was too controversial? Was it because the Psalter was still incomplete? Or was it that Bourgeois was not altogether appreciated? The story of his career comes to an obscure end. He left Geneva, and the last trace of him seems to be a record of his children being baptized into the Roman Catholic Church.

A comparison between Bourgeois's and Goudimel's setting of the same psalm will allow the details of Goudimel's style to come into focus. Example 3 gives their harmonizations of Psalm 1. Only the tenor and bass are shown. In both versions, the Genevan tune is found in the tenor. The bass is a particularly important part in music such as this because it exerts a controlling influence over the harmony. Therefore the choices composers make about their bass lines can reveal much about their style. Goudimel's bass line in Example 3 is similar to Bourgeois's, but the differences are revealing.

For the sake of comparison, Bourgeois's version has been transposed to be in the same key as Goudimel's, and the two versions are vertically aligned. Differences between them have been enclosed within a box and assigned letters *a* through *o*. The differences are of several kinds. First is Goudimel's avoidance of the interval of the sixth. An "interval" measures how many scale steps there are between two notes. Thus, an interval of a sixth means that two notes span six scale steps (e.g., A up to F). In five instances Bourgeois's bass forms the interval of a sixth with the tenor (at *c*, *e*, *f*, *n*, and *r*, each with a "6" placed under the staff). This is significant because a sixth is the most unstable of all the consonant intervals. Whenever there is a sixth above the bass, the harmony lacks firmness. It can sound changeable, transient, soft—not soft in volume but in character—but also quite lovely. In modern terms it creates an inverted chord, which means that the root of the chord is not played in the bass. (The root of a chord is the note that generates the chord and gives it its name: e.g., C is the root of a C chord.) When the root of a chord is given to the bass, the chord sounds solid and stable. But when something other than the root is given to the bass, the chord sounds rather supple. In Example 3, Bourgeois has chosen the supple chord five times. Goudimel never uses it. Indeed, in all his simple settings, it is rare to find the interval of a sixth formed between the bass and the melody.

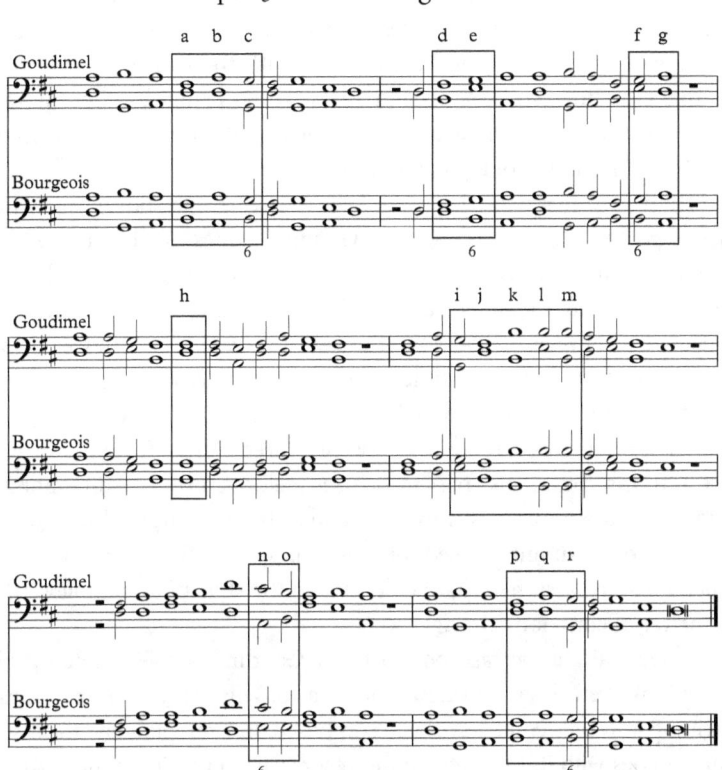

Example 3: Two Settings of Psalm 1

A second significant difference between the two bass lines is Goudimel's unabashed use of the tonic in places where Bourgeois avoids it. The tonic is the first note in a scale, and it defines the key. In Example 3, the tonic is the note D. Chords built on the tonic are the most stable and consonant of all: To be on the tonic is to be at rest. Therefore the tonic is ordinarily cast as the beginning and the end—the point of origin and of destination. For the same reason, composers will often avoid the tonic in the middle of a phrase. After all, the essence of a middle is that it is neither a beginning nor an end; a middle is not at rest. It is therefore significant that Goudimel used the tonic in the bass seven times, whereas Bourgeois avoided it (at *a*, *b*, *g*, *h*, *j*, *p*, and *q*). Only once does Bourgeois choose tonic where Goudimel does not (at *d*). In the first phrase, which is identical to the last phrase, five out of ten bass notes in Goudimel's version are the tonic. As a result, the phrase is unshakably grounded and sturdy, if perhaps a little plodding. By contrast, Bourgeois' phrase is subtler, gentler, restrained, but less assertive.

Both composers begin each phrase with the tonic in the bass. They also end the first and last phrases that way. But they avoid closing on the tonic at the end of interior phrases. This is natural. A composer generally doesn't want to arrive home, so to speak, until the end. It seems redundant that Goudimel ends the second phrase with the tonic, rather than take Bourgeois's route and use the dominant one (A). But it may be perceived as extending the stability of the beginning.

The two differences that have been described are bound up with a third important difference. Because Goudimel does not use the interval of a sixth with the bass, and because he uses the tonic so often, his bass line is jumpy and disjointed. Bourgeois's bass line is smoother and more connected. As a measure of "smoothness," Bourgeois's bass moves by step twenty-three times, but Goudimel's does so only thirteen times. As a measure of "jumpiness," Goudimel's bass moves by a skip or leap thirty-four times, but Bourgeois does so only twenty-three times. To put it in more musical terms, Bourgeois's bass prioritizes melodic form and direction, but Goudimel's bass prioritizes sturdiness and stability. Goudimel was not unskilled in counterpoint. Indeed, he was a master, as Example 2 illustrates. Rather, it can be assumed that he developed the style of his simple settings as a matter of conscious choice.

I have drawn a contrast above between Goudimel's style and Bourgeois's. We can look even closer into Goudimel's way of setting the Genevan tunes by imagining how they could have been composed. In Example 4 and the discussion that goes with it, I will attempt to reconstruct a portion of his setting of Psalm 42: "Ainsi qu'on oit le cerf bruire." I do not insist or even suggest that these are the steps by which the composer really did create the music. (How could such a thing be known?) But attempting to view the music from the creative standpoint can reveal something of its essential logic.

Imagine starting with the melody for Psalm 42. Example 4a gives the beginning of the given melody, called the *cantus firmus* (c.f.). I have placed the melody in the tenor voice as Goudimel usually did. This tune is found in many hymnals with various texts, often "Comfort, comfort ye my people."

In Example 4b, a soprano line has been added. It is the simplest of soprano lines, merely a parallel line a sixth higher. I said earlier that Goudimel avoided the interval of a sixth with the bass because it was unstable. But there is no instability when it comes to sixths in the upper parts, as long as the bass provides stable support. In fact, singing in parallel sixths and thirds is quite lovely and natural. Who hasn't at times been either pleased or annoyed by the singer down the pew who "harmonizes" a tune by singing along a third or sixth higher? Singing thirds and sixths is easiest way to learn to sing in harmony. It's child's play, and no real skill or training is necessary. However, just like the singer down the pew, some of the notes don't seem to work. If you sing or play Example 4b, you may notice that three of the notes sound a little odd. These have been marked with a question mark. We will deal with them presently.

Next, we add a sturdy bass. The bass line should adhere to the following three restrictions: 1) the first and last notes of both phrases must be the first degree of the scale (in this case, the C); 2) the bass should create no dissonance; 3) the bass should not be placed a sixth below an upper voice (in modern terms: no inverted chords). Those three basic restrictions limit the possibilities rather severely. Example 4c gives the result. Adding the bass has created four problems. They are marked with an "x." Three of the errors occur where previously there had been a question mark. In those cases the problem is that, since the bass begins and ends each phrase on C (following rule 1), it is forced to create a sixth with the soprano, breaking rule 3. The simple solution is to change the soprano note. Compare Examples 4c and 4d to see the corrections.

There remains one error in Example 4c, the third "x." This error is also a matter of a sixth between the bass and soprano, but it may not be clear why the bass has to have the note it does. The process of elimination will show why. Example 4e provides alternative bass notes for that spot. Let us take them in order. Can the bass move to D? No. That would create parallel octaves between bass and soprano, something strictly avoided in this style. Can the bass move to B? No. That creates a dissonant diminished fifth. Can the bass move to A? No. That creates a sixth, the interval we are trying to avoid. It also creates a fourth with the soprano, another unstable interval. Can the bass move to G? No. That creates a dissonant seventh. So the bass should move to F, and we must change the soprano note.

Example 4d corrects the four errors. It also adds an alto voice. The alto voice simply completes each triad, finding an appropriate note to tuck in between the soprano and tenor. It sacrifices melodic interest for a supporting role. (Alas! Poor altos. Such has always been the case.) Example 4d is indeed Goudimel's setting. To summarize the basic idea: Tenors sing the melody. Sopranos "harmonize" by singing the melody a sixth higher, adjusting notes wherever necessary. Basses bounce along, always landing on the roots of chords. Altos fill in what's missing. It would not be difficult to teach families to sing this way. And with very little training, it is not difficult to learn how to create your own similar harmonizations. In other words, this is music for the kitchen table—it is not high art.

Example 4. Beginning of Psalm 42 Reconstructed

I have so far emphasized the difference between Goudimel's simple psalm settings and other repertoire. I have drawn a contrast between them and his more sophisticated motets. I have also drawn a contrast between them and Loys Bourgeois's similar settings. I will conclude by pointing out the similarity between Goudimel's simple psalms and the popular secular songs of the French court, the Parisian *chansons*. The comparison is not arbitrary. Goudimel worked and published among the *chansoniers* of the day, and the style of his the psalm settings is very similar to that of the Parisian songs that were so popular during that time. Example 5 gives a famous instance. It is the beginning of a *chanson* by Claudin de Sermisy, *Tant que vivray*.

Example 5: Claudin de Sermisy, *Tant que vivray*

Like the psalm settings, it is in four parts, all singing the same straightforward rhythms. The tenor and soprano carry the melodic interest, a sturdy bass sings mostly roots of chords, and the alto fills in what is missing. To modern ears, it could easily be mistaken for a classic hymn, especially if it is sung at a properly sanctimonious cathedral tempo instead of a prancing parlor tempo. Try singing either the tenor or soprano lines using the words of "For all the Saints." It is not hard to pretend that it was made for the hymnal, rather than for the bawdy French court. But that is the point: What we now hear as the "hymn style" used to have more in common with secular songs than any kind of ecclesiastical music.

What is more, the words for *Tant que vivray* were by Clement Marot. Calvinists know Marot as the chief poet for the Genevan Psalter. But of course Marot was first the favorite poet of the French courts. His experiments with metrical psalmody that were destined to change the course of hymnody were not at Calvin's instigation. As perfectly as metrical psalmody suited the new liturgy, it owed its genesis to trends in vogue with the poets and *chansoniers* of the Parisian court. Calvin did not at first commission Marot to write metrical psalms. Rather, he appropriated those metrical psalms that Marot had already composed, probably without Marot knowing it. Only later was there a collaboration. There is more than a hint of shrewdness in all this. Could the French court be won over through the Calvinist songs? The events of history proved that this was not the case.

Bibliography

Abudarham, David. *Sefer Abudarham*. Prague: N.p., 1784.
Achtemeier, Paul J. *1 Peter*. Hermeneia: A Critical & Historical Commentary on the Bible. Minneapolis: Fortress, 1996.
Aland, Kurt, et al. *Novum Testamentum Graece*. 27th ed. Stuttgart: German Bible Society, 1993.
Alexander, Charles M., ed. *Alexander's Hymns No. 3*. New York: Revell, 1915.
Alexander, James W. *Forty Years' Familiar Letters of James W. Alexander, D.D., Constituting, with Notes, a Memoir of His Life*. Edited by John Hall. 2 vols. New York: Scribner, 1870.
Allison, Gregg R. "Toward a Theology of Human Embodiment." *Southern Baptist Journal of Theology* 13 (2009) 4–17.
Anderson, Lynn. "Why I've Stayed." *Leadership* 7 (1986) 76–82. http://www.christianitytoday.com/pastors/1986/summer/86l3076.html.
Anderson, Matthew Lee. *Earthen Vessels: Why Our Bodies Matter to Our Faith*. Bloomington, MN: Bethany, 2011.
Anderson, R. Dean, Jr. "An Examination of the Liturgy of the Westminster Assembly as Formulated in the *Directory for the Publick Worship of God*." *Ordained Servant* 3 (1994) 27–34. https://www.opc.org/OS/html/V3/2a.html.
Angel, Hayyim. "*Hadassa Hi Esther*: Issues of Peshat and Derash in the Book of Esther." *Tradition* 34 (2000) 79–97.
Assis, Elie. "Zechariah 8 and Its Allusions to Jeremiah 30–33 and Deutero-Isaiah." *Journal of Hebrew Scriptures* 11 (2011) 2–21. http://www.jhsonline.org/Articles/article_148.pdf.
Barclay, John M. G. "Mirror-Reading a Polemical Letter: Galatians as a Test Case." *Journal for the Study of the New Testament* 31 (1987) 73–93.
Bauckham, Richard. *Jesus and the God of Israel: God Crucified and Other Studies on the New Testament's Christology of Divine Identity*. Grand Rapids, MI: Eerdmans, 2008.
Bauman-Martin, Betsy. "Speaking Jewish: Postcolonial Aliens and Strangers in 1 Peter." In *Reading First Peter with New Eyes: Methodological Reassessments of the Letter of First Peter*, edited by Robert I. Webb and Betsy Bauman-Martin, 144–78. Edinburgh: T. & T. Clark, 2007.
Bavinck, Herman. *Het Doctorenambt*. Kampen: Zalsman, 1899.
Baxter, Richard. *The Reformed Pastor*. Reprint, Edinburgh: Banner of Truth: 1989.

Beale, G. K., and D. A. Carson, eds. *Commentary on the New Testament Use of the Old Testament*. Grand Rapids: Baker, 2007.

Beecher, Henry Ward, ed. *Plymouth Collection of Hymns and Tunes for the Use of Christian Congregations*. New York: Barnes, 1855.

Berkley, Timothy. *From a Broken Covenant to Circumcision of the Heart: Pauline Intertextual Exegesis in Romans 2:17-29*. SBL Dissertation Series 175. Atlanta: SBL, 2000.

Birch, Bruce C. "Divine Character and the Formation of Moral Community in the Book of Exodus." In *The Bible in Ethics*, edited by John W. Rogerson et al., 119-35. Sheffield: Sheffield Academic, 1995.

Blomberg, Craig. *1 Corinthians*. NIV Application Commentary. Grand Rapids: Zondervan, 1994.

Blume, Friedrich. *Protestant Church Music*. New York: Norton, 1974.

Boatner, Edward, and Willa A. Townsend, eds. *Spirituals Triumphant: Old and New*. Nashville: Sunday School Publications Board, 1927.

Boice, James Montgomery. *The Christ of Christmas*. Chicago: Moody, 1983.

Boston, Thomas. *Tractatus Stigmologicus, Hebræo-biblicus: Quo Accentuum Hebraeorum Doctrina Traditur, Variusque Eorum In Explanenda S. Scriptura Usus Exponitur*. N.p.: Besseling, 1750.

Boyer, Horace Clarence. *How Sweet the Sound: The Golden Age of Gospel*. Washington, DC: Elliott & Clark, 1995.

Boyer, Horace Clarence, ed. *Lift Every Voice and Sing II: An African American Hymnal*. New York: Church Hymnal Corporation, 1993.

Bright, John. "The Book of Jeremiah: Its Structure, Its Problems, and Their Significance for the Interpreter." *Interpretation* 9 (1955) 259-78.

———. "An Exercise in Hermeneutics: Jeremiah 31:31-34." *Interpretation* 20 (1966) 188-210.

Brown, Francis, et al. *A Hebrew and English Lexicon of the Old Testament*. Oxford: Clarendon, 1907.

Brown, John. *The Necessity and Advantage of Earnest Prayer for the Lord's Special Direction in the Choice of Pastors: With an Appendix of Free Thoughts Concerning the Transportation of Ministers*. Edinburgh: Paterson, 1783.

Burns, Bob, et al. *Resilient Ministry. What Pastors Told Us about Surviving and Thriving*. Downers Grove: InterVarsity, 2013.

Bush, Frederic W. *Ruth, Esther*. Word Biblical Commentary 9. Dallas: Word, 1996.

Calhoun, David B. *Princeton Seminary: The Majestic Testimony 1869-1929*. Edinburgh: Banner of Truth, 1996.

Calvin, John. "Articles Concerning the Organization of the Church and of Worship at Geneva." In *Theological Treatises*, translated and edited by J. K. S. Reid, 47-55. Library of Christian Classics. Philadelphia: Westminster, 1954.

———. *Commentary on the Acts of the Apostles*. Translated by Christopher Fetherstone. 2 vols. Reprint, Grand Rapids: Baker, 2003.

———. *Commentary on the Book of Psalms*. Translated by James Anderson. 3 vols. Reprint, Grand Rapids: Baker, 2003.

———. *Commentaries on the Epistles to Timothy, Titus, and Philemon*. Translated by William Pringle. Reprint, Grand Rapids: Baker, 2003.

———. *Institutes of the Christian Religion*. Translated by Ford Lewis Battles and edited by John T. McNeil. Library of Christian Classics 21. Philadelphia: Westminster, 1960.

———. *Sermons on the Acts of the Apostles, Chapters 1–7*. Translated by Rob Roy McGregor. Edinburgh: Banner of Truth, 2008.

———. "Short Treatise on the Lord's Supper." In *Tracts Containing Treatises on the Sacraments: Volume 2*, translated and edited by Henry Beveridge, 163–98. Edinburgh: Calvin Translation Society, 1849.

———. *Tracts and Letters*. Edited by Jules Bonnet et al. 7 vols. Edinburgh: Banner of Truth, 2009.

———. *Tracts and Treatises on the Reformation of the Church*. Translated and edited by Henry Beveridge. 3 vols. Reprint, Grand Rapids: Eerdmans, 1958.

Carpenter, Delores, ed. *The African American Heritage Hymnal*. Chicago: GIA, 2001.

Chandler, Raymond. *Selected Letters of Raymond Chandler*. Edited by Frank MacShane. New York: Columbia University Press, 1981.

Chapell, Bryan. "Insights from the Westminster Standards for Today's Preachers." *Presbyterion: Covenant Seminary Review* 31 (2005) 1–17.

Chevallier, Max-Alain. "Israël et l'Eglise selon la premiére Epître de Pierre." In *Paganisme, Judaism, Christianisme: Influences et affrontements dans le monde antique, Mélanges offerts à Marcel Simon*, edited by André Benoit et al., 117–30. Paris: Boccard, 1978.

Cohen, Abraham D. "'*Hu Ha-goral*': The Religious Significance of Esther." *Judaism* 23 (1974) 87–94.

Cole, Keith. *Robert Harkness: The Bendigo Hymnwriter*. Bendigo, Victoria: Cole, 1988.

Collins, Billy. *The Art of Drowning*. Pittsburg: University of Pittsburg Press, 1995.

Collins, C. John. "Abiding in the Vine: True Branches Have no Choice but to Stay Connected to Christ." *Christianity Today* 60:2 (March 2016) 46–49.

———. "Echoes of Aristotle in Romans 2:14–15: Or, Maybe Abimelech Was Not So Bad After All." *Journal of Markets and Morality* 13 (2010) 123–73.

———. "Ephesians 5:18: What Does *plērousthe en pneumati* Mean?" *Presbyterion* 33 (2007) 12–30.

———. "The Eucharist as Christian Sacrifice: How Patristic Authors Can Help Us Read the Bible." *Westminster Theological Journal* 66 (2004) 1–23.

———. *Isaiah*. Biblical Theology for Christian Proclamation Series. Nashville: Broadman and Holman, forthcoming.

———. *Reading Genesis Well: Navigating History, Science, Poetry, and Truth in Genesis 1–11*. Grand Rapids: Zondervan, forthcoming 2018.

———. "Theology of the Old Testament." In *The ESV Study Bible*, edited by Wayne Grudem, 29–31. Wheaton: Crossway, 2008.

———. "What the Reader Wants and the Translator Can Give: 1 John as a Test Case." In *All for Jesus*, edited by Robert A. Peterson and Sean M. Lucas, 333–59. Fearn: Christian Focus, 2006.

Cooper, John W. *Body, Soul, and Life Everlasting: Biblical Anthropology and the Monism-Dualism Debate*. Grand Rapids: Eerdmans, 1989.

Cowan, Donald. *Theology in Exodus: Biblical Theology in the Form of a Commentary*. Louisville: Westminster John Knox, 1994.

Danker, Frederick W., et al., eds. *A Greek-English Lexicon of the New Testament and Other Early Christian Literature*. 3rd ed. Chicago: University of Chicago Press, 2000.

Darden, Robert. *People Get Ready! A New History of Black Gospel Music*. New York: Continuum, 2006.

Davids, Peter H. *The First Epistle of Peter*. New International Commentary on the New Testament. Grand Rapids: Eerdmans, 1990.

Davies, Horton. *The Worship of the English Puritans*. Reprint, Morgan, PA: Soli Deo Gloria, 1997.

Dett, R. Nathaniel. "The Emancipation of Negro Music." *The Southern Workman* 47 (1918) 172–76.

Dett, R. Nathaniel, ed. *Religious Folk-Songs of the Negro: As Sung at Hampton Institute*. Hampton, VA: Hampton Institute, 1927.

Doriani, Daniel M. *Putting the Truth to Work. The Theory and Practice of Biblical Application*. Phillipsburg, NJ: Presbyterian and Reformed, 2001.

Dryden, J. de Waal. *Theology and Ethics in 1 Peter*. Wissenschaftliche Untersuchungen zum Neuen Testament 209. Tübingen: Mohr, 2006.

Edwards, Jonathan. *Apocalyptic Writings*. Edited by Stephen J. Stein. The Works of Jonathan Edwards 5. New Haven: Yale University Press, 1977.

———. *A History of the Work of Redemption*. Edited by John F. Wilson. The Works of Jonathan Edwards 9. New Haven: Yale University Press, 1989.

———. "Notes on Esther." In *Notes on Scripture*, edited by Stephen J. Stein, 60–63. The Works of Jonathan Edwards 15. New Haven: Yale University Press, 1998.

Ego, Beate. "Retelling the Story of Esther in Targum Sheni in Light of Septuagint Traditions—Main Outlines." In *The Targums in the Light of Traditions of the Second Temple Period*, edited by Thierry Legrand and Jan Joosten, 72–83. Supplements to the Journal for the Study of Judaism 167. Leiden: Brill, 2014.

Eire, Carlos M. N. *War Against the Idols: The Reformation of Worship from Erasmus to Calvin*. Cambridge: University of Cambridge Press, 1986.

Elliott, John H. *1 Peter: A New Translation with Introduction and Commentary*. Anchor Bible 37b. New York: Doubleday, 2001.

———. *Home for the Homeless: A Sociological Exegesis of 1 Peter, Its Situation and Strategy*. Philadelphia: Fortress, 1981.

Ellis, Katherine. *Interpreting the Musical Past: Early Music in Nineteenth-Century France*. Oxford: Oxford University Press, 2005.

Excell, E. O., ed. *Make His Praise Glorious*. Chicago: Excell, 1900.

Fairbairn, Patrick. *The Interpretation of Prophecy*. Reprint, Edinburgh: Banner of Truth, 1964.

Fee, Gordon D. *The First Epistle to the Corinthians*. New International Commentary on the New Testament. Grand Rapids: Eerdmans, 1987.

Feldmeier, Reinhold. *Die Christen als Fremde*. Wissenschaftliche Untersuchungen zum Neuen Testament 64. Tübingen: Mohr, 1992.

Ferguson, Everett. *Baptism in the Early Church: History, Theology and Liturgy in the First Five Centuries*. Grand Rapids: Eerdmans, 2009.

Ferguson, Sinclair. "Foreword." In *The Work of the Pastor*, by William Still, 7–10. Rev. ed. Fearn: Christian Focus, 2010.

Fox, Michael V. *Character and Ideology in the Book of Esther*. 2nd ed. Grand Rapids: Eerdmans, 2001.

Frame, John. *The Doctrine of the Knowledge of God*. Phillipsburg, NJ: Presbyterian and Reformed, 1987.

Frei, Hans. *The Eclipse of Biblical Narrative: A Study in Eighteenth and Nineteenth Century Hermeneutics*. New Haven: Yale University Press, 1974.

Gentry, Peter, and Stephen Wellum. *Kingdom Through Covenant: A Biblical-Theological Understanding of the Covenants*. Wheaton: Crossway, 2012.

Gladwell, Malcolm. *Outliers: The Story of Success*. New York: Back Bay, 2011.

Godfrey, W. Robert. "The Westminster Larger Catechism." In *To Glorify and Enjoy God: A Commemoration of the 350th Anniversary of the Westminster Assembly*, edited by John L. Carson and David W. Hall, 127–42. Edinburgh: Banner of Truth, 1994.

Gordon, Bruce. *Calvin*. New Haven: Yale University Press, 2009.

Goswell, Gregory R. "Keeping God Out of the Book of Esther." *Evangelical Quarterly* 82 (2010) 99–110.

Green, Gene L. *Jude & 2 Peter*. Baker Exegetical Commentary on the New Testament. Grand Rapids: Baker Academic, 2008.

Greenberg, Moshe. *Ezekiel 21–37: A New Translation with Introduction and Commentary*. Anchor Bible. New York: Doubleday, 1997.

Grossman, Jonathan. *Esther: The Outer Narrative and the Hidden Reading*. Siphrut: Literature and Theology of the Hebrew Scriptures 6. Winona Lake: Eisenbrauns, 2011.

Hallo, William. "The First Purim." *Biblical Archaeologist* 46 (1983) 19–26.

Harris, Michael W. "Conflict and Resolution in the Life of Thomas Andrew Dorsey." In *We'll Understand It Better By and By*, edited by Bernice Johnson Reagon, 165–82. Washington, DC: Smithsonian, 1992.

———. *The Rise of the Gospel Blues: The Music of Thomas Andrew Dorsey in the Urban Church*. New York: Oxford University Press, 1992.

Hastings, James, ed. *Encyclopedia of Religion and Ethics*. 13 vols. New York: Scribner, 1908–1926.

Hays, Richard. *1 Corinthians*. Louisville: Westminster John Knox, 1997.

Heilbut, Tony. *The Gospel Sound: Good News and Bad Times*. New York: Simon and Schuster, 1971.

Henderson, Robert W. *The Teaching Office in the Reformed Tradition: A History of the Doctoral Ministry*. Philadelphia: Westminster, 1962.

Hill, Megan. "It is Good to Say Amen." http://byfaithonline.com/it-is-good-to-say-amen/.

Hiršs, Ilmars. *Ein Volk aus Juden und Heiden: Der Ekklesiologische Beitrag des Ersten Petrusbriefes zum christlich-jüdischen Gespräch*. Institutum Judaicum Delitzschianum Münsteraner Judaistische Studien 15. Münster: LIT, 2003.

Hodge, Charles. *Systematic Theology*. 3 vols. Reprint, Grand Rapids: Eerdmans, 1979.

Holmstedt, Robert D., and John Screnock. *Esther: A Handbook on the Hebrew Text*. Baylor Handbook on the Hebrew Bible. Waco: Baylor University Press, 2015.

Horne, Chevis. *Forty Years in the Same Pulpit: What Makes for Long Pastorates*. Macon, GA: Smyth and Helwys, 1995.

Horrell, David G. *Becoming Christian: Essays on 1 Peter and the Making of Christian Identity*. Library of New Testament Studies 394. London: T. & T. Clark, 2013.

Howard, Thomas. *Evangelical is Not Enough: Worship of God in Liturgy and Sacrament*. San Francisco: Ignatius, 1984.

Instone-Brewer, David. "The Eighteen Benedictions and the *Minim* Before 70 CE." *Journal of Theological Studies* 54 (2003) 25–44.
Jobes, Karen H. *1 Peter*. Baker Exegetical Commentary on the New Testament. Grand Rapids: Baker Academic, 2005.
Johnson, Dru. *Knowledge by Ritual: A Biblical Prolegomenon to Sacramental Theology*. Journal of Theological Interpretation Supplement 13. Winona Lake: Eisenbrauns, 2016.
Jones, Peter. *The Gnostic Empire Strikes Back: An Old Heresy for a New Age*. Phillipsburg, NJ: Presbyterian and Reformed, 1992.
Joseph, Abson Prédestin. *A Narratological Reading of 1 Peter*. Library of New Testament Studies 440. London: T. & T. Clark, 2012.
Joyce, George. "The Pope." In *The Catholic Encyclopedia, Vol. 12*, edited by Charles G. Herberman et al., 260–75. New York: Robert Appleton Company, 1911.
Kant, Immanuel. *Critique of Pure Reason*. Translated by J. M. D. Meiklejohn. New York: American Home Library, 1902.
Kapic, Kelly M. "Receiving Christ's Priestly Benediction: A Biblical, Historical, and Theological Exploration of Luke 24:50–53." *Westminster Theological Journal* 67 (2005) 247–60.
Keil, Carl F. *Jeremiah*. Edinburgh: T. & T. Clark, 1874.
Keller, Tim. "Preaching to the Heart." http://resources.thegospelcoalition.org/library/preaching-to-the-heart.
Kettering, Donald D. *Steps Toward a Singing Church*. Philadelphia: Westminster, 1948.
Kimelman, Reuven. "*U-N'taneh Tokef* as a Midrashic Poem." In *The Experience of Jewish Liturgy: Studies Dedicated to Menahem Schmelzer*, edited by Deborah Blank Reed, 115–46. The Brill Reference Library of Judaism 31. Leiden: Brill, 2011.
Kistler, Don, ed. *The Puritans on the Lord's Supper*. Morgan, PA: Soli Deo Gloria, 1997.
Kleinig, Vernon. "Providence and Worship: The Aaronic Blessing: Numbers 6:22–27." *Lutheran Theological Journal* 19 (1985) 120–24.
Knight, George W., III. "1 Corinthians 11:17–34: The Lord's Supper: Abuses, Words of Institution and Warnings and the Inferences and Deductions With Respect to Paedocommunion." In *Children and the Lord's Supper*, edited by Guy Waters and Ligon Duncan, 75–95. Fearn: Christian Focus, 2011.
———. "Two Offices (Elders/Bishops and Deacons) and Two Orders of Elders (Preaching/Teaching Elders and Ruling Elders): A New Testament Study." *Presbyterion* 11 (1985) 1–12.
Koller, Aaron. *Esther in Ancient Jewish Thought*. Cambridge: Cambridge University Press, 2014.
Kuchumov, V. A. "Eldership in Russia: Some Consequences of the Petrine Reforms." *Russian Studies in History* 52 (2013) 38–65.
Laniak, Timothy S. "Esther." In *Ezra, Nehemiah, Esther*, by Leslie C. Allen and Timothy S. Laniak, 165–269. New International Biblical Commentary 9. Peabody: Hendrickson, 2003.
Law, William. *A Serious Call to a Devout and Holy Life*. London: Methuen, 1899.
Levenson, Jon D. *Esther*. Old Testament Library. Louisville: Westminster John Knox, 1997.
Lewis, C. S. *Letters to Malcolm: Chiefly on Prayer*. London: Geoffrey Bles, 1964.
———. "Preface." In *George Macdonald: An Anthology*, edited by C. S. Lewis, xxii–xxxix. New York: HarperCollins, 2001.

Lewis, Stephen. "Narrative Analogy and the Theological Message of Esther: Israel's Conflicted Relationship with an Angry Sovereign." PhD diss., Westminster Theological Seminary, 2018.
Liebreich, Leon J. "The Insertions in the Third Benediction of the Holy Day 'Amidoth." *Hebrew Union College Annual* 35 (1964) 79–101.
Lieu, Judith M. *Christian Identity in the Jewish and Graeco-Roman World*. Oxford: Oxford University Press, 2004.
———. *Neither Jew Nor Greek: Constructing Early Christian Identity*. T. & T. Clark Cornerstones. 2nd ed. London: T. & T. Clark, 2015.
Link, Peter, and Matthew Emerson. "Searching for the Second Adam: Typological Connections between Adam, Joseph, Mordecai, and Daniel." *Southern Baptist Journal of Theology* 21.1 (2017) 123–44.
Lloyd-Jones, D. M. *Knowing the Times: Addresses Delivered on Various Occasions 1942–1977*. Edinburgh: Banner of Truth, 1989.
Locatell, Christian. "Jeremiah 31:34, New Covenant Membership, and Baptism." *Scriptura* 114 (2015) 1–14.
Lohse, Eduard. *Die Texte aus Qumran*. Munich: Kösel, 1964.
Long, Edwin M. *Illustrated History of Hymns and their Authors*. Philadelphia: Landis, 1882.
Long, Thomas G. *Accompany Them With Singing: The Christian Funeral*. Atlanta: Westminster John Knox, 2009.
Long, V. Philips. *The Art of Biblical History*. Foundations of Contemporary Interpretation 5. Grand Rapids: Zondervan, 1994.
Lowman, Moses. *Paraphrase and Notes on the Revelation of St. John*. 2nd ed. London: Noon, 1745.
Luther, Martin. *The Christian in Society II*. Edited by Walther I. Brandt. Luther's Works 45. Philadelphia: Muhlenberg, 1962.
———. "The Pagan Servitude of the Church." In *Martin Luther: Selections from His Writings*, edited by John Dillenberger, 249–362. Garden City, NY: Doubleday, 1961.
———. *Works of Martin Luther*. 6 vols. Reprint, Grand Rapids: Baker, 1982.
Lyall, Frank. "Introduction." In *The Work of the Pastor*, by William Still, 13–16. Rev. ed. Fearn: Christian Focus, 2010.
Machen, J. Gresham. "Christianity and Culture." *The Princeton Theological Review* 11 (1913) 1–15.
Marovich, Robert M. *A City Called Heaven: Chicago and the Birth of Gospel Music*. Champaign, IL: University of Illinois Press, 2015.
Marsden, George M. *Jonathan Edwards: A Life*. New Haven: Yale University Press, 2003.
Marsh, J. B. T. *The Jubilee Singers and Their Songs: Supplement by F. J. Loudin*. Reprint, Mineola, NY: Dover, 2003.
Mbuvi, Andrew M. *Temple, Exile, and Identity in 1 Peter*. Library of New Testament Studies 345. London: T. & T. Clark, 2007.
McClintock, John, and James Strong, eds. *Cyclopedia of Biblical, Theological, and Ecclesiastical Literature*. 12 vols. New York: Harper, 1867–1887.
McNeil, John T. "John Calvin: Doctor Ecclesiae." In *The Heritage of John Calvin: Heritage Hall Lectures 1960–1970*, edited by John H. Bratt, 9–22. Grand Rapids: Eerdmans, 1973.

Metzger, Bruce. *A Textual Commentary on the Greek New Testament*. 2nd ed. New York: United Bible Societies, 1994.
Michaels, J. Ramsey. *1 Peter*. Word Biblical Commentary 49. Waco: Word, 1988.
Miller, Samuel. *Thoughts on Public Prayer*. Philadelphia: Presbyterian Board of Publications, 1849.
Mirsky, Aharon. *Sefer Debarim* [Deuteronomy]. Daʻat Miqraʼ. Jerusalem: Mossad Harav Kook, 2001.
Mitchell, A. F., and J. Struthers, eds. *The Minutes of the Sessions of the Westminster Assembly of Divines*. Edinburgh: Blackwood, 1874.
Moon, Joshua N. *Hosea*. Apollos Old Testament Commentary. London: InterVarsity, forthcoming.

———. *Jeremiah's New Covenant: An Augustinian Reading*. Journal of Theological Interpretation Supplements 3. Winona Lake: Eisenbrauns, 2011.

Moskovitz, Y. Z. *Sefer Yehezqel* [Ezekiel]. Daʻat Miqraʼ. Jerusalem: Mossad Harav Kook, 1985.
Murray, Iain. "The Directory for Public Worship." In *To Glorify and Enjoy God: A Commemoration of the 350th Anniversary of the Westminster Assembly*, edited by John L. Carson and David W. Hall, 169–91. Edinburgh: Banner of Truth, 1994.
Murray, John. *The Collected Writings of John Murray*. 4 vols. Edinburgh: Banner of Truth, 1977–1982.
Nichols, James Hastings. *Corporate Worship in the Reformed Tradition*. Reprint, Eugene, OR: Wipf and Stock, 2014.
Nicoletti, Steven. "Infant Baptism in the First-Century Presupposition Pool." *Tyndale Bulletin* 66 (2015) 271–92.
Nouwen, Henri. *The Way of the Heart*. San Francisco: Harper & Row, 1981.
Nulman, Macy, ed. *The Encyclopedia of Jewish Prayer. Ashkenazic and Sephardic Rites*. London: Aronson, 1996.
Old, Hughes Oliphant. *Holy Communion in the Piety of the Reformed Church*. Powder Springs, GA: Tolle Lege, 2013.

———. *Leading in Prayer*. Grand Rapids: Eerdmans, 1995.

———. *The Patristic Roots of Reformed Worship*. Zurich: Theologischer Verlag, 1970.

———. *Worship that is Reformed According to Scripture*. Atlanta: Westminster John Knox, 1984.

Owen, John. *The Works of John Owen*. Edited by William H. Goold. 16 vols. Reprint, Edinburgh: Banner of Truth, 1965–1968.
Packer, J. I. *Knowing God*. Downers Grove: InterVarsity, 1973.
Paton, Lewis Bayles. *A Critical and Exegetical Commentary on the Book of Esther*. International Critical Commentary. New York: Scribner, 1908.
Pelikan, Jaroslav. *The Christian Tradition: A History of the Development of Doctrine, Vol. 1: The Emergence of the Catholic Tradition (100–600)*. 5 vols. Chicago: University of Chicago Press, 1971.
Peterson, Eugene H. *Under the Unpredictable Plant*. Grand Rapids: Eerdmans, 1992.
Pidoux, Pierre. "Polyphonic Settings of the Genevan Psalter: Are They Church Music?" In *Cantors at the Crossroads: Essays on Church Music in Honor of Walter E. Buszin*, edited by Johannes Riedel, 65–74. St. Louis: Concordia, 1967.
Pieper, Josef. *Leisure: The Basis of Culture*. Translated by Alexander Dru with an introduction by T. S. Eliot. London: Faber & Faber, 1952.

Poythress, Vern. "Indifferentism and Rigorism in the Church: With Implications for Baptizing Small Children." *Westminster Theological Journal* 59 (1997) 13–29.

Prasad, Jacob. *Foundations of the Christian Way of Life According to 1 Peter 1, 13–25: An Exegetico-Theological Study.* Analecta Biblica 146. Rome: Editrice Pontificio Istituto Biblico, 2000.

Provan, Iain, et al. *A Biblical History of Israel.* Louisville: Westminster John Knox, 2003.

Rabin, Chaim. *The Zadokite Documents.* Oxford: Clarendon, 1958.

Rayburn, Robert G. *O Come, Let us Worship: Corporate Worship in the Evangelical Church.* Grand Rapids: Baker, 1980.

Rayburn, Robert S. "Colossians, No. 15: Colossians 4:2–6." http://www.faithtacoma.org/colossians/2012-12-16-pm.

———. "The Contrast Between the Old and New Covenants in the New Testament." PhD diss., University of Aberdeen, 1978.

———. "An Emphasis on the Christian Family, Part 1." http://www.faithtacoma.org/characteristicsoffaith/an-emphasis-on-the-christian-family-part-1.

———. "Hebrews." In *Evangelical Commentary on the Bible*, edited by W. A. Elwell, 1124–49. Grand Rapids: Baker, 1989.

———. "The Liturgical Authority of the Old Testament." http://www.bible-researcher.com/rayburn1.html.

———. "Ministry by the Generation." *The 1996 Covenant Seminary Preaching Lectures.* https://www.covenantseminary.edu/resources/preaching-lectures-1996/.

———. "Minority Report of the Ad-Interim Committee to study the Question of Paedocommunion." In *PCA Digest Position Papers 1973–1993 Part V*, edited by Paul R. Gilchrist, 503–15. Atlanta: Presbyterian Church in America, 1993.

———. "Miscellany." http://www.faithtacoma.org/proverbs/2012-03-11-pm.

———. "Mystery." http://www.faithtacoma.org/luke/2013-09-29-am.

———. "The Presbyterian Doctrines of Covenant Children, Covenant Nurture and Covenant Succession." *Presbyterion: Covenant Seminary Review* 22 (1996) 76–112.

———. "Retirement." http://www.faithtacoma.org/work/2006-06-04-pm.

———. "Studies in the Book of Kings: 2 Kings 12:1–21." http://www.faithtacoma.org/kings/2011-04-17-pm.

Reagon, Bernice Johnson, ed. *We'll Understand It Better By and By: Pioneering African American Gospel Composers.* Washington, DC: Smithsonian, 1992.

Rendtorff, Rolf. "What is New in the New Covenant?" In *Canon and Theology: Overtures to an Old Testament Theology*, translated by Margaret Kohl, 196–206. Minneapolis: Fortress, 1993.

Renehen, Robert. "On the Greek Origins Incorporeality and Immateriality." *Greek, Roman and Byzantine Studies* 21 (1980) 105–38.

Richardson, Christopher. *Pioneer and Perfecter of Faith: Jesus' Faith as the Climax of Israel's History in the Epistle to the Hebrews.* Wissenschaftliche Untersuchungen zum Neuen Testament II 338. Tübingen: Mohr, 2012.

Richardson, Joe M. *Christian Reconstruction: The American Missionary Association and Southern Blacks, 1861–1890.* Athens, GA: University of Georgia Press, 1986.

Richardson, Paul. *Israel in the Apostolic Church.* Society for New Testament Studies Monograph Series 10. Cambridge: Cambridge University Press, 1969.

Rogland, Max. *Alleged Non-Past Uses of* Qatal *in Classical Hebrew.* Assen, Netherlands: Van Gorcum, 2003.

———. "The Cult of Esther: Temple and Priestly Imagery in Megillat Esther." *Journal for the Study of the Old Testament* (forthcoming).

———. "When the Church has Gone to the Dogs." In *Celebration! 180 Years of God's Providential Care*, edited by R. J. Gore, 107–17. Greenville, SC: Erskine Theological Seminary Press, 2018.

Ruth, Thermon T., and Linda Saylor-Marchant. *From the Church to the Apollo Theater*. Brooklyn: Ruth, 1995.

Rutherford, Samuel. *The Letters of Samuel Rutherford: With a Sketch of His Life and Biographical Notes of his Correspondents by Andrew Bonar*. Reprint, Edinburgh: Banner of Truth, 1984.

Ryken, Phillip, et al., eds. *Give Praise to God: A Vision for Reforming Worship Celebrating the Legacy of James Montgomery Boice*. Phillipsburg, NJ: Presbyterian and Reformed, 2003.

Sankey, Ira D. *My Life and the Story of the Gospel Hymns: And of Sacred Songs and Solos*. New York: Harper, 1907.

Sargent, Benjamin. *Written to Serve: The Use of Scripture in 1 Peter*. Library of New Testament Studies 547. London: T. & T. Clark, 2015.

Schaff, Philip, ed. *The Nicene and Post-Nicene Fathers, Series 1*. 14 vols. Reprint, Peabody: Hendrickson, 1994.

Schaff, Philip, ed. *The Nicene and Post-Nicene Fathers, Series 2*. 14 vols. Reprint, Peabody: Hendrickson, 1994.

Schenck, Lewis Bevins. *The Presbyterian Doctrine of Children in the Covenant: An Historical Study of the Significance of Infant Baptism in the Presbyterian Church in America*. Reprint, Eugene, OR: Wipf and Stock, 2001.

Scholer, David M. "Forward: An Introduction to Philo Judaeus of Alexandria." In *The Works of Philo*, translated by C. D. Yonge, xi–xviii. Updated edition. Peabody: Hendrickson, 1993.

Seifrid, Mark. "Romans." In *Commentary on the New Testament Use of the Old Testament*, edited by G. K. Beale and D. A. Carson, 607–94. Grand Rapids: Baker, 2007.

Selwyn, Edward G. *The First Epistle of St. Peter: The Greek Text with Introduction, Notes, and Essays*. 2nd ed. Reprint, Grand Rapids: Baker, 1952.

Seward, Theodore F., ed. *Jubilee Songs as Sung by the Jubilee Singers of Fisk University*. New York: Biglow and Main, 1872.

Sibley, Jim R. "You Talkin' to Me? 1 Peter 2:4–10 and a Theology of Israel." *Southwestern Journal of Theology* 59 (2016) 59–75.

Smith, James K. A. *You Are What You Love: The Spiritual Power of Habit*. Grand Rapids: Brazos, 2016.

Steeves, Cynthia Dawn. "The Origin of Gospel Piano: People, Events, and Circumstances that Contributed to the Development of the Style." DMA diss., University of Washington, 1987.

Stein, Stephen J. "Editor's Introduction." In *Apocalyptic Writings*, edited by Stephen J. Stein, 1–93. The Works of Jonathan Edwards 5. New Haven: Yale University Press, 1977.

Stevenson, Robert Louis. *Essays*. New York: Scribner, 1918.

Storms, Sam, and Justin Taylor, eds. *For the Fame of God's Name: Essays in Honor of John Piper*. Wheaton: Crossway, 2010.

Stout, Harry S., ed. *The Jonathan Edwards Encyclopedia*. Grand Rapids: Eerdmans, 2017.

Strunk, Oliver. *Source Readings in Music History*. New York: Norton, 1950.
Stuart, Kenneth. *Alexander Moody Stuart, D.D.: A Memoir, Partly Autobiographical*. London: Hodder and Stoughton, 1899.
Sweeney, Marvin. *Form and Intertextuality in Prophetic and Apocalyptic Literature*. Forshungen zum Alten Testament 25. Tübingen: Mohr, 2005.
Temple, William. *Readings in St John's Gospel*. Wilton, CT: Morehouse, 1939.
———. "Esther, Jesus, and Psalm 22." *Catholic Biblical Quarterly* 70.4 (2008) 709–28.
Tindley, Charles A., et al., eds. *Soul Echoes: A Collection of Songs for Religious Meetings*. Philadelphia: Soul Echoes, 1905, 1909.
Tkacz, Catherine Brown. "Esther as a Type of Christ and the Jewish Celebration of Purim." *Studia Patristica* 44 (2010) 183–87.
Tomasino, Anthony. *Esther*. Evangelical Exegetical Commentary. Bellingham, WA: Lexham, 2016.
Tov, Emanuel. *The Book of Baruch, Also Called 1 Baruch (Greek and Hebrew)*. Missoula: Scholars, 1975.
Townsend, Willa A., et al., eds. *Gospel Pearls*. Nashville: Sunday School Publications Board, 1921.
Trebilco, Paul R. *Jewish Communities in Asia Minor*. Society for New Testament Studies Monograph Series 69. Cambridge: Cambridge University Press, 1991.
Treier, Daniel J. "Typology." In *Dictionary for Theological Interpretation of the Bible*, edited by Kevin J. Vanhoozer, 823–27. Grand Rapids: Baker Academic, 2005.
Turner, Laurence A. "Finding Christ in a Godless Text: The Book of Esther and Christian Typology." In *No One Better: Essays in Honour of Dr. Norman H. Young*, edited by Kayle B. De Waal and Robert K. McIver, 5–21. New York: Peter Lang, 2016.
Turner, Steve. *Amazing Grace: The Story of America's Most Beloved Song*. New York: HarperCollins, 2002.
Tweedie, W. K., ed. *Select Biographies*. 2 vols. Edinburgh: Wodrow Society, 1845–1847.
Van Dam, Cornelis. *The Urim and Thummim: A Means of Revelation in Ancient Israel*. Winona Lake: Eisenbrauns, 1997.
VanderKam, James C. *The Book of Jubilees*. Sheffield: Sheffield Academic, 2001.
Van Dixhoorn, Chad, ed. *The Minutes and Papers of the Westminster Assembly 1643–1653*. 5 vols. Oxford: Oxford University Press, 2012.
Venema, Cornelis P. *Children at the Lord's Table: Assessing the Case for Paedocommunion*. Grand Rapids: Reformation Heritage, 2009.
Vrudny, Kimberly. "Medieval Fascination with the Queen: Esther as the Queen of Heaven and Host of the Messianic Banquet." *ARTS: The Arts in Religious and Theological Studies* 11 (1999) 36–43.
———. "Medieval Treatment of the Queen: The Austrian Manuscripts and the Quest for Esther." *ARTS: The Arts in Religious and Theological Studies* 8 (1995) 14–21.
Wallis, Wilber. "Irony in Jeremiah's Prophecy of a New Covenant." *Journal of the Evangelical Theological Society* 12 (1969) 107–10.
———. "The Pauline Conception of the Old Covenant." *Presbyterion* 4 (1978) 71–83.
Walton, John. *Ancient Near Eastern Thought and the Old Testament*. Grand Rapids: Baker, 2006.
Warfield, B. B. *The Westminster Assembly and Its Work*. Oxford: Oxford University Press, 1931.
Watson, J. R., and Emma Hornby, eds. *The Canterbury Dictionary of Hymnology*. https://hymnology.hymnsam.co.uk/.

———. "John Wesley Work (II)." http://www.hymnology.co.uk/j/john-wesley-work-(ii).

Wechsler, Michael G. "Shadow and Fulfillment in the Book of Esther." *Biblioteca Sacra* 154 (1997) 275–84.

Welden, Dale B. "The Impact of the Long-Term Pastorate." DMin diss., Covenant Theological Seminary, 2001.

Wells, David F. *No Place for Truth*. Grand Rapids: Eerdmans, 1993.

Wells, Samuel. "Esther." In *Esther & Daniel*, by Samuel Wells and George Sumner, 1–91. Brazos Theological Commentary on the Bible. Grand Rapids: Brazos, 2013.

Wellum, Stephen. "Baptism and the Relation Between the Covenants." In *Believer's Baptism: Sign of the New Covenant in Christ*, edited by Thomas Schreiner and Shawn Wright, 97–162. Nashville: Broadman and Holman, 2006.

White, J. G. *The Churches and Chapels of Old London: With A Short Account of Those Who Have Ministered in Them*. London: Gray, 1901.

Whyte, Alexander. *Characters and Characteristics of William Law*. London: Hodder and Stoughton, 1893.

———. *Lord, Teach Us to Pray*. Reprint, Grand Rapids: Baker, 1976.

Wikner, Benjamin K., ed. *To You and Your Children: Examining the Biblical Doctrine of Covenant Succession*. Moscow, ID: Canon, 2005.

Williams, Michael. "A New and More Glorious Covenant." *Presbyterion* 28 (2002) 77–103.

Winner, Lauren. *Mudhouse Sabbath: An Invitation to a Life of Spiritual Discipline*. Brewster, MA: Paraclete, 2003.

Work, Jerome Frederick, and John Wesley Work Jr., eds. *Folk Songs of the American Negro*. Nashville: Work Bros & Hart, 1907.

———. *New Jubilee Songs as Sung by Fisk Jubilee Singers*. Nashville: Fisk University, 1901.

Work, John Wesley, Jr. *The Folk Song of the American Negro*. Nashville: Fisk University, 1915.

Wright, Christopher. *Knowing Jesus through the Old Testament*. Downers Grove: InterVarsity, 1992.

———.*The Message of Jeremiah*. Bible Speaks Today. Downers Grove: InterVarsity, 2014.

Wright, N. T. *The Climax of the Covenant*. Minneapolis: Fortress, 1992.

———. *The New Testament and the People of God*. Minneapolis: Fortress, 1992.

———. "Romans 9–11 and the 'New Perspective.'" In *Between Gospel and Election: Explorations in the Interpretation of Romans 9–11*, edited by Florian Wilk and J. Ross Wagner, 37–54. Wissenschaftliche Untersuchungen zum Neuen Testament 257. Tübingen: Mohr, 2010.

Zakai, Avihu. *Jonathan Edwards's Philosophy of History*. Princeton: Princeton University Press, 2003.

Zolten, Jerry. *Great God A'Mighty! The Dixie Hummingbirds: Celebrating the Rise of Soul Gospel Music*. New York: Oxford University Press, 2003.

www.ingramcontent.com/pod-product-compliance
Lightning Source LLC
Chambersburg PA
CBHW052340230426
43664CB00041B/2502